Make Money While You Sleep

How to Turn Your Knowledge into Online
Courses That Make You Money 24hrs a Day

Lucy Griffiths

HODDER &
STOUGHTON

First published in Great Britain in 2021 by Hodder & Stoughton
An Hachette UK company

1

Copyright © Lucy Griffiths 2021

The right of Lucy Griffiths to be identified as the Author of the Work has been
asserted by her in accordance with the Copyright, Designs and Patents Act 1988.

A CIP catalogue record for this title is available from the British Library

Trade Paperback ISBN 978 1 529 38189 4
eBook ISBN 978 1 529 38190 0

Typeset in Celeste by Hewer Text UK Ltd, Edinburgh
Printed and bound in Great Britain by Clays Ltd, Elcograf S.p.A.

Diagram on page 93 based on the theory created by
psychologists Andy Ryan and Dawn Markova.

Hodder & Stoughton policy is to use papers that are natural, renewable
and recyclable products and made from wood grown in sustainable
forests. The logging and manufacturing processes are expected to
conform to the environmental regulations of the country of origin.

Hodder & Stoughton Ltd
Carmelite House
50 Victoria Embankment
London EC4Y 0DZ
www.hodder.co.uk

To my darling little boy Ben, who was the catalyst
to escape my old way of working and find a new
way of living. I love you very much, thank you for
being funny, beautiful and brilliant YOU. ♡

And to Tim, my best friend and soulmate: I love you.
Thank you for being my biggest supporter and champion
on this crazy rollercoaster of entrepreneurship and life.

Contents

PART 1
The World of Digital Courses

CHAPTER 1

Introduction to the World of Digital Courses and Passive Income

Imagine if there was a way to harness your expertise and knowledge and sell it online. Where you can create income and set flexible hours that work for you and your family.

What if there was a way that you could work from wherever you wanted to in the world? What if you could earn money while you spent time with your family? What if you could choose how you work, and the hours you work?

What if you could make money while you sleep?

Selling your knowledge online by creating digital courses is one of the most lucrative income streams. This recurring revenue gives you the financial freedom and flexibility to work and live life *your* way.

Wherever you are in your life right now and whatever you're dealing with, I want to promise you . . .

Making money while you sleep is possible for you too.

It's not rocket science.

It's not magic.

At times it can be cluster-friggingly hard, but it is utterly possible.

The magic is about automating your processes and building an audience so you can get leads on repeat to sell your digital courses.

This book will show you how you can create a digital course and make money while you sleep.

This book is for you if:

- You want to share your knowledge and expertise online and create a digital course business to fit around your family and your life.
- You want to travel and have adventures and enjoy the freedom to work from anywhere in the world.
- You're on maternity leave and wondering how on earth you're going to juggle the 6am starts, the late-night phone calls, the long commute and your old way of working before you race to the nursery to spend a precious hour with your little one.
- Perhaps you're stalling on the conveyor belt of corporate life and you desperately want to press the eject button on hotdesking and escape the rat race.
- Or are you successfully running your business but you're so busy working IN the business that you have no time to work ON the business – let alone take a break?
- Maybe HR is knocking with an offer of redundancy but you're not sure whether to accept it – and if you did, what you'd do next.
- Or maybe you're approaching retirement age so you want a little boost to your income to help you do what you've always wanted to do but never had the time.
- Perhaps, like me, your health impacted your career options and you have struggled with the commutes and the daily grind. Having the flexibility to choose your hours means you can work when you feel good, then rest when you don't.
- Or maybe your face no longer fits in the 9–5?

If any of these describe your situation, fear not, the good news is that you can stick two fingers up to whatever society expects of you.

So, are you ready to work less and live more?

Building any business, including a course-based business that generates passive income, is hard work. It's hours of early mornings and late nights and checking and rechecking to get things done. But once you've done the slog, the good news is that it sells itself on repeat. And then your time is your own.

That's the beauty of selling digital courses; you get to choose how you spend your days – whether that's more time for your family, more travel, or fulfilling creative projects that may not pay the bills.

So, what on earth is a digital course?

Put simply, it's a series of videos and workbooks that teach us a new skill or experience. Just as you might pay for online learning through a college or university, these are pre-recorded videos that share expertise on various topics.

It is estimated that the online course industry will be worth $3.25 billion by 2025.* If you're a small-business owner, coach, consultant, nail technician, gardener, DIY enthusiast, baker or lone parent, you could turn what you know into a digital course. The beauty of courses is that you share your experience ONCE on video, and then you can sell this same digital product again and again through the wonders of automation.

We live in the most liberating of times where you can package your superpowers into a series of videos that you record using as little equipment as your iPhone, then sell them on repeat to thousands of customers across the world from your kitchen. Geography, education or background is no longer a barrier to your success. It doesn't matter if you're in your twenties or seventies, you can now take your years of learning and experience and turn that knowledge into a commodity that you sell over and over. You can create a course teaching people to

* www.forbes.com/sites/tjmccue/2018/07/31/e-learning-climbing-to-325-billion-by-2025-uf-canvas-absorb-schoology-moodle/?sh=38c22c283b39

use TikTok from the beach in Koh Samui, Thailand, or show others how to raise goats from your tiny smallholding in Scotland.

You don't have to be particularly tech-savvy; you don't have to know how to use HTML code or understand how automation works to create a system that sells. You just need to embrace the concept of passive income and start making a digital course that works for your life regardless of where you live in the world.

As a parent, I thought that I had to give up my career to fit work around childcare. Creating online courses enables you to pursue your passions, see your family and still make money. That's the beauty of consistent income; you get to choose your hours and create a life that works for you. You no longer have to clock into your 9–5-day job; you no longer have to be on the entrepreneurial treadmill of working crazy hours. You get to decide how you run your life and your business. You set the hours when you're at your laptop and the way you want to work. The business that you've worked so hard for no longer has to be a noose around your neck, chaining you to the desk. You are still writing emails and social media posts and planning launches, but you are working smarter and not harder.

This is the freedom that creating a course business gives you; the world is now your oyster and there is nothing to stop you pursuing that bucket list of dreams – whether that's driving round the world in a beaten-up Beetle or spending more time soaking up the (ahem, sunshine) in your back garden or caring for your kids or grandkids. It's your life, your rules.

However, just because it's called a passive income business, that doesn't mean you don't have to do anything. You do. In the beginning, there's an intense period of work before your idea runs itself (with your fantastic support team), and this book will guide you through the principles of building your digital course business.

Throughout the next fourteen chapters, I'm going to share the secrets of some of my friends and students, about how they carved out their digital niche and successfully sold online. People like Lea Turner, who took her experience on LinkedIn and turned it into a course. Or Rob who worked in the military for 20 years, and then, as his military life ended, wondered what he was going to do next. After completing a yoga course, he created a course teaching beginner's yoga and breathwork.

Or Kathleen from Auckland, New Zealand, who took her ballet studio online during the Covid-19 lockdown and created a series of 'Silver Swan Ballet' courses for women over 50, which is now selling globally. Or you might be inspired by 60-year-old Janet from Michigan, US, who was months away from retirement when she was made redundant after 29 years working in ICU in a hospital. She picked herself back up and built a course teaching us how to shop for our wardrobe.

All of these students have varying backgrounds, live in different countries and have myriad experiences, but they all have one thing in common: they've had the guts and gumption to create a digital course.

And now you're here today, reading this book. You've taken the massive leap of faith in believing that you can make money while you sleep, so now you have to implement the steps that I'm going to show you in these pages and learn how you too can sell digital courses over and over again.

If it's possible for them, it's possible for you too. You don't have to be a teacher or the smartest person in the room to create a course, you just need to know about one thing and share your learning and experience about it with others. And the irony is the more niche your idea, the more profitable you will be. People don't want to buy a 'generalist' course, they want something specific, so if you can show them a deep dive into one area, your system will be more successful.

If you feel you don't have enough knowledge in a specific area, often the reality is that you know much more than you think you do – and remember, you don't have to know *everything* for the course. Not so long ago, I spent £3,000 buying an online business course. There was so much content, and it was overwhelming. I then bought a second course about the same subject for £200, knowing it would take me about two hours to complete. Guess which programme I completed? That's right, the one that I knew would take me two hours to finish.

People desire tasty bite-sized snacks rather than the whole buffet. They want to learn from you and get the *'beginner's guide to . . .'* or *'the advanced guide to . . .'* but they don't need everything thrown into one course. In small chunks, microlearning is regarded as a much more effective way of teaching for online courses, and throughout this book I will teach you how to structure courses that are quick and tasty for your audience to consume.

The most successful courses are the ones that your students actually spend the time on and *complete*. And once they've actually done the work and seen the results, they will become your most prominent advocates and recommend your course to everyone.

Before that little nagging doubt pops into your head, yes, I'm going to talk through ways to successfully sell your course organically through social media, YouTube, how to do your own publicity and also how to use paid ads, e.g. on Facebook or Instagram. I'll show you the methods that I've used to sell thousands of courses and generate seven-figure revenues.

You might be someone who's already created a course, and perhaps you've sold a few, but it's now getting dusty on your laptop. I know it's heartbreaking when you pour all your energy and enthusiasm into something, and then it doesn't sell. I've been there, and I've also experienced those awkward moments when your family or friends ask: *'How's it going?'*

Wherever you are in your business idea, entrepreneurship is a rollercoaster of emotions. You may feel like you're throwing spaghetti at the wall of marketing and nothing is sticking. You may feel you're tired of trying so hard to make it work, and somehow your business is still only just limping by. So, if you want to take your side hustle from hobby status to the real deal, and if you'd like to stop feeling like a business failure in front of your friends and family, then you're in the right place.

By the time you've read this book, I want you to come away with a new direction and a plan to sell your knowledge and sell it on repeat. Marketing your courses on autopilot will help you get that consistent income that you crave, and will remove the feast-or-famine mentality that so many entrepreneurs face.

I'll talk through your stumbling blocks and personal limitations around creating a course, and I'll show you how you can sidestep your fears and successfully sell your digital courses even when you are scared of doing so.

It may be that you're in business but you're fearful of being visible and putting yourself out there online. And while your head says that you need to market your digital courses, your heart is telling you to hide. I hear you; I used to worry that I was too old, not pretty or intelligent enough to show up on social media and talk about myself. I know what it's like to feel vulnerable and exposed when you make yourself visible, but the reality is that if you want to sell your course successfully, you just have to put aside your fears and go for it.

I spent many years dreaming of being an entrepreneur before actually leaping into it. I remember my cousin saying to me when I was about 21, and editing a business magazine, *'What do you know about business?'* That comment stuck. For so long I didn't think I was worthy of dipping my toe in the entrepreneurial world.

What do you want to do?

Knowing what to create for a course is tricky! Perhaps you have a vision and a plan before you read this book, but maybe you're a little like me and you struggle to find your thing.

You may doubt yourself and your abilities. Sometimes the thing we are meant to do is dangling right in front of our noses, and it takes us a while to find it. My lack of self-belief was making me cling to a narrative that I wasn't good enough or talented enough to teach video-making and storytelling, even though I had years of experience as a journalist. So don't worry, I will help you to find and pursue your passion.

Perhaps you're secretly wishing that you could create a business but that little voice in your head is holding you back. Maybe you doubt your abilities and talents. Sometimes our fears about what others may say or think hold us back from actually pursuing the things that we want to do. In those cases, it's as though you need a 'permission slip' to follow your heart and go with your gut.

If you're going to create something that you sell over and over again, and talk about on repeat, you want to be certain that you're passionate about the topic. You may think that you should create a series of courses about property, because that's what makes money, but your heart wants to teach painting. Go with what your heart is telling you, because when you're working on this months later, your passion project will propel you through the blips and bumps on the journey.

You just have to find your 'thing' and ensure that you're operating in what the author Gay Hendricks calls your 'Zone of Genius'.*

So, remember, if you're going to spend hours working on your courses and selling them, you need to choose something that lights you up and excites you years later. Creating a course isn't just

---

* Gay Hendricks defined the term 'Zone of Genius' in his book *The Big Leap*.

'creating a course', it opens the doors to new possibilities and new adventures. Think about:

✓ What do you love to talk about?
✓ What excites you every day?

Whenever I doubt my ability to succeed, I always think of Richard Branson, who has created multiple billion-dollar businesses. He did this after failing at school and being written off for being dyslexic. Or Sara Blakely, the founder and inventor of Spanx, who knew little about hosiery but had an incredible idea to create stretchy undergarments to suck us into shape. Both these entrepreneurs had passion for their product and showed guts and gumption to go for it. They started out knowing little about business, but they were open to ideas, embraced new possibilities and hoovered up information and ideas as they went.

When I first started out, I created my 'inspiring' entrepreneurs list to keep me on track when I might wobble. And I followed them on social media. Their words inspired me enormously when I didn't think I was good enough or intelligent enough to package my knowledge online.

I want you to come away from this book feeling that you *can* turn your experience and know-how into a course that sells on autopilot. I'll show you that you can package your expertise and create recurring income, and you can take yourself off the hamster wheel of work and redesign your life and business.

It sounds so simple when I say all you need to do is create the course, build your sales page and find a steady flow of eyeballs to read about your course and buy it. The reality is you will have moments of frustration; yes, at times, building a course-based business is complex, complicated and bloody hard work, but that doesn't mean you can't make this a reality. And it certainly doesn't mean you can't create the kind of passive income that you dream of. Like every business, you need to dig deep, find your reserves of grit and gumption and keep going through the highs and the lows. You can turn what you know into an online course regardless of your age, background and education.

This book will take you step by step from idea generation to understanding your ideal customer, to selling your digital course or membership on repeat.

Passive income is about generating revenue on repeat. It's also known as recurring income, but whatever term you use, it's something that requires a hefty dose of drive, determination and hard work to get up and running.

Still questioning whether this book is for you and whether your skills can make you recurring income? Here are a few ideas to help you see how you too could make money while you sleep.

If you're a graphic designer, you could create a digital product such as a template pack teaching people how to design graphics to use on Pinterest. You could sell a collection of pretty Pinterest pin designs and use the social media site as your number one marketing tool. Once you've created the digital products and built sales pages to sell them, you just need to find a new audience to *keep* selling them on repeat. Using advertising can help drive traffic to your digital product.

If you're a fitness instructor or a cake-maker, you could create recurring revenue from a membership where people pay an amount per month to be part of your 'club' and learn from you and enjoy being part of your community.

For example, Carrie Green was lonely in the online world and wanted to create a community for female business owners to collaborate and learn. She set up the Female Entrepreneur Association and turned her Facebook group into a multimillion-pound company.

Anna Parker-Naples was an actor who wanted to spend more time with her family. After a traumatic pregnancy, she set up her online business to teach people how to use podcasting to grow their business. Now she has a multiple-six-figure membership.

Ebooks are another way to create recurring revenue. Serial entrepreneur Stefan James began selling books on Amazon and realised that if he sold them for $1 each, he could sell at scale. He started getting people to turn his audio recordings and ideas into books. Fast-forward 10 years and he has a multimillion-dollar company and over 1 million subscribers on YouTube.

Not sure what course to create? Let's get creative!

Brainstorm what you want to do

Now let's make a start and do some fun brainstorming to get ideas flowing as to what you may want to do! Allow yourself the freedom of time and space – do something that makes you feel inspired. I find it really helpful to give myself permission to be creative and allow my juices to flow. Going for a walk in the countryside, meditating or just playing Lego with my son helps me to unwind from the 'should-dos' and follow that intuitive voice within.

✓ Do whatever makes you feel most creative.
✓ Remember no idea is a bad idea – you don't know what it will trigger, so just write it down.
✓ Allow yourself to free-flow some ideas. I love to listen to inspiring music as I'm brainstorming, so play your favourite tracks.

1. What's your idea?
Write down your idea or ideas and just free-flow . . .

2. Brain dump

Have a huge brain dump to write down your ideas for the course. What does your potential customer need to learn? Write everything down. Don't censor yourself . . . One crazy idea may lead to another one that works perfectly for your audience.

Now let's take that idea and refine it. What is the transformation that you want your audience to have? The more specific the better . . .

Remember, there's no such thing as a bad idea . . . All ideas might lead you to something interesting, and where you want to focus your energy.

Check out Julia Cameron's *The Artist's Way* if you want to unleash your creativity further.

The good news is that there are multiple ways to make money using passive income and by building multiple income streams.

Finding your entrepreneurial way is about trial and error, but this book will help you to turn your idea into a course-based business that can be truly life-changing for you and your family.

Right here, right now as you're reading this book or driving to work you can mull over your possibilities and potential because the exciting thing is that you can generate wealth online through digital courses, and build a hugely successful business just by leveraging the power of the internet and the wonder of passive income. It just takes dreams, guts and grit.

So, are you ready to maximise your knowledge, create a digital course and make money while you sleep? I know you can do this!

If you'd like some additional support, check out www.make-moneywhileyousleepbook.com/bonus – you can print out your own permission slip, and you'll also find some additional training to help you create your course as you read through this book.

CHAPTER 2

Researching Your Course (and Pre-selling It!)

When I used to go off on backpacking adventures around the world, I loved diving into the experience and 'winging it'. I was the queen of following my gut and hoping for the best. And it invariably turned out well. I'd stumble across scrumptious meals from roadside cafes or befriend locals who'd show me the secret sights and best places to hang out in town. And most of the time, winging it worked – except when I encountered cockroach-infested hotels or got food poisoning from sampling live sea cucumber. Yes, that experience still haunts me; I picked up the rubbery-looking thing with my chopsticks, took a large bite and, as I munched, was somewhat horrified to discover that sea cucumber was not the vegetable I was expecting. It was alive and worming its way along my chopstick. The slimy, rubbery texture and rancid taste is the stuff of nightmares. I soon learned that doing some research meant that I could bypass the unsavoury dishes and focus on exploring the sights.

The point of me going off on a tangent about slimy creatures is because I want to stress that creating a course isn't about winging it. Otherwise you might find you end up re-recording elements, or having to change your sales strategy, pricing and messaging in your ads, for example.

Creating a course isn't about perfectionism, but you do need to plan, prepare and – crucially – deliver your audience's needs. And to do that means research, so that you know you're giving people what they want. Just winging it and rambling away about your chosen topic with a few meanders is NOT the best way to create a course that people want to buy.

I've seen courses created by people who have a big audience but they just didn't sell. Why? Because they didn't really ask their audience what they NEEDED and WANTED.

Creating a course is no different from other business initiatives. It is about taking people on a learning journey and solving a problem or a pain point. It's showing them how to use software or how to milk goats or grow a business. The course offering needs to align with you and who you are, and what your audience desires.

I often see people create courses without actually researching their ideal client or customer needs, and they aren't prepared to take the time to listen. And then they wonder why their course has flopped.

This chapter is perhaps the most important in this book, but it doesn't feel particularly sexy. I know for us winging it lovers, it's tempting to skip this section and rush on to the bit about outlining your course. But wait! Doing the research enables you to avoid making time-consuming and costly mistakes, so it's a good investment of your time to ask questions and test out your ideas, listen to feedback that might surprise you and get under the skin of your ideal clients. And in the process, you will also stand an excellent chance of being able to sell your course before you even create it.

So I'm here to stop you in your tracks and remind you of the sea cucumber.

The ability to find a customer, sell your product or service to that customer, and satisfy the customer so that he buys from you again should be the central focus of all entrepreneurial activity. The greater clarity you have with regard to your ideal customer, the more focused and effective your marketing efforts will be.

Brian Tracy*

Don't get caught up in the fantasy . . .

When you're first starting out, every business guru going tells you to create your 'ideal client'.

When I started up my business, I was encouraged by specific business coaches to fantasise about the perfect person who would buy from me – what kind of car they would drive, what type of holiday they would go on. I created a mini-fantasy in my head of the perfect person who wanted to buy my services, but the focus was on the material goods they aspired to own (or owned) rather than the problem they needed solving.

I remember spending hours agonising and stressing over this fictitious character, but the real truth is that your ideal client is the person willing to spend money with you, and creating an idea of this perfect person that is going to buy from you is complete and utter nonsense.

It's bad for your business.

There is good business sense in understanding who you want to talk to in your messaging and marketing, though.

Once you're off the starting blocks, it is essential to speak to the right person so that you can be very clear in your marketing and messaging about who you're talking to and what they do. But don't get hung up on the idea of your perfect person because this concept will shift as you start selling and understanding who your target audience *really* is, and switching off a chunk of the population from the start because you've decided they're too old, too young, too

* www.entrepreneur.com/article/75648

female or too male doesn't make good business sense.

You don't want to needlessly eliminate certain demographic groups. You're in business to sell to anyone who might need what you're offering. For example, my branding is pink and red; I initially thought I was talking to a specific age group of women, but actually I realised that I speak to men too. If you are specific with the pain point rather than the abstract demographic, it is easier to sell and adjust according to your customers' needs.

What's your customer's problem?

Understanding who your customer is, and what their problem is, is the key to your success.

Knowing the specific problem your clients are facing means you can connect with your audience and imagine them in everything that you do! The more information and understanding that you have of that problem, the easier it is to 'build your tribe' or your group of people who resonate with that issue and what you have to say, and therefore they will like you, follow you and eventually buy from you.

You want to get under that person's skin and understand what their pain point is and how you can best help them overcome this challenge. You want to create a story around this person (though remember not to be boxed in by outdated 'demographics'), imagine them, talk to them and identify with them.

The more this person becomes 'real', the easier it is to imagine them while creating a course and to talk to them in your marketing.

I began doing this 25 years ago while working in local radio. We were encouraged to see our female listener as a 'human' and get under her skin. What did she care about? What motivated her to get out of bed each morning and go to work? What issues mattered to her?

It drove our radio stories' content and ensured that we focused on family issues, health and local stories. We skipped the subjects that she didn't care about or tried to tell them in a way that would matter to her and might engage her.

And the same is true in creating an avatar or ideal client for your course. The avatar is the fictional story that helps us to understand our ideal customers more efficiently. You focus on ONE person and tell a story about them and who they are.

Ask yourself the following questions so you can create an image of your ideal customer who will buy your course. Spend some time on this; the more specific you can be, the better.

DESCRIBE YOUR AVATAR

1. What is your customer's pain point or problem?
2. What keeps your customer awake at night worrying?
3. What do they stay up at night worrying over? And how does this relate to your course topic?
4. What does your course idea solve for them?
5. Why do they need your course? What problem are you solving, or what desire are you creating within them?
6. What has happened to trigger them to start searching for a solution to that problem (that you're solving)?
7. How are they going to find you and the answer to the problem? For example, are they searching on Google, scrolling on social media, such as Instagram, or listening to a podcast.
8. How are you solving that problem better than your competitors?
9. What did they already try that didn't work before they came searching for an alternative solution in your course?
10. What are the benefits to them in buying your product?
11. What are their goals and values? What do they care about (e.g. the environment or if a product is Fairtrade)?

12. What would be their objections to buying your course?
13. Describe your average customer.
14. What does their typical day look like?
15. How much time do they spend online? What is their propensity to learn online?
16. How old are they? The more specific you can be, the better.
17. Are you creating a course for men or for women, or both?
18. Do they have children?
19. If they have children, do they live at home – will this be a barrier to them learning, and do you need to talk about this in your marketing?
20. What do they care about? What inspires them?
21. How does your ideal client earn money? Are they in business, and do you need to think about their payday in your marketing?
22. What's their annual income? Are you wanting to create something for six-figure entrepreneurs or for single parents budgeting the books?
23. What is the person's ethnicity and religion? Does this even matter for your course?
24. Are they the boss, or do they work for a boss?
25. What are their passions? What motivates them?
26. Does geography matter? Do you want to think globally, or is it a course for a specific country with certain legal/taxation implications?

How did you go? What did you learn? What do you need to know more about to sell your course successfully?

Doing the research isn't just about imagining your ideal client; it's also about talking to them and getting under the skin of their problem and pain point.

Do they need or want your course?

People don't buy a course for the sake of it; they buy a course because they are seeking answers to a problem and want help to solve it. So, spending time figuring out what the problem is and how you can best solve your customer's issue makes it easy to pre-sell to them! Ask yourself what things keep them awake at night, and what are their particular struggles?

It's imperative to establish if your customers need and want your course. So how do you know the difference between a need for something and a want or desire for it?

I think about my friend Ciaran, who lives in Bangkok but would travel back to Belfast to see his family. He had two flight options: Ryanair or British Airways. When he 'needed' to travel to see his mum, he would take the first flight out with Ryanair and, as he put it, would 'hold his nose' about the service, the overall experience and lack of breakfast. When it was a more leisurely journey, he would choose to travel with British Airways, and he *wanted* this experience. Air travel then moved from a need to a desire, and he was willing to pay twice as much for the experience.

With your course, how can you shift your customer's thinking so that they desire what you do rather than just 'need' it?

It's about showing the transition clearly, and ensuring your course is desirable – even if you're just talking about spreadsheets. When they desire something, they will go out of their way to get it and be willing to pay more for it.

Research enables you to gain invaluable knowledge about your audience – if you are solving a problem that they have, they will be hungry for the solution. They won't just need the course; they'll also want the answer.

So, when you're doing your research, be sure to listen to the subtle difference between your audience's 'needs' and 'wants'. Notice their enthusiasm levels and their engagement on your social media posts; take note of their passion for the concept. Are they excited, or do they say this would be very useful? Are they, albeit in a virtual sense, jumping up and down saying 'OMG, I want this now,' or are they saying, 'I'm sure it will be very helpful' (which is polite speak for: that sounds good for someone else, but it's not really for me).

In order to test to see if people NEED it, if they WANT it, and if they have the ability to pay for it, ask yourself three questions:

- Is there a need for the course?
- Is there an ability to pay for the course?
- Is there a willingness to pay for the course?

Ultimately, it's the willingness to pay that is most important when determining your course success.

I want you to create such a demand for your course that it's a must-have in your industry, and your potential customers are super excited to buy from you and are drooling at your offer.

Understanding who your audience is and what they NEED and WANT from you is critical when building and pre-selling a course.

How can you learn more about your ideal client?

I often see people create courses without actually researching their ideal client or customer needs, but the reality is that it matters to understand what people are willing to pay for the course. You want to ask people what they need through surveys and questionnaires.

Ideally, you want to use social media platforms to do this, especially if you have an established presence and an audience of people willing to engage with you. If you don't already have an audience, looking on Amazon at some of the review comments on books that your ideal client would be reading will help you to see the kind of language they use to talk about their pain points.

Your audience could be accessed through something like Instagram or LinkedIn, or you could use the power of Clubhouse or YouTube. You get to decide and test out where is best to connect with your audience and ask questions. Here are some suggestions. You don't have to use all these methods; use the ones that most resonate – AND think about where your ideal client hangs out according to your profile of them. If you want to talk to professionals, you could look at LinkedIn, and if you're going to speak to graduates, perhaps it's best to be active on TikTok.

INSTAGRAM STORIES

Before you start creating your course, you could post questions or polls on your Insta Stories. Ask your audience specific questions about your course idea as you begin to build it. Ensure that you use hashtags specific to your audience to reach people who will most resonate with this content and have these pain points.

Look at the accounts of people in your industry. What hashtags are they using? Begin to take note of these; I save a bunch in my phone compiled into groups with a maximum of 30 hashtags in each group.

When creating a course for *Psychologies Magazine*, we used Instagram Stories to ask people what their biggest challenges were when it came to finding a career they loved. The research helped us to validate our ideas and know we were on the right track with the course.

Norland Nanny and sleep consultant Claire Watkin created a sleep-training course for new mums. She used Instagram to research her ideal clients. She followed mummy bloggers on the site and forged relationships with them. From there, she was able to reach more mums to ask questions and build her audience.

I started following mummy influencers on Instagram and then one of them DM-ed me within 5 minutes of following her and invited me to speak to her group of mummies. I then did a follow-up video for her with trainings and was able to start building my audience and understanding their challenges and pain points.

FACEBOOK GROUPS

Facebook groups are an incredible resource for connecting with other like-minded people in your niche area and getting to know them. And in the process, you can ask questions and also build a potential client base.

Psychologist Justine Knott was creating a course helping people recently diagnosed with epilepsy. She combined her personal experience of epilepsy with her background as a psychologist to help people struggling with the ramifications of the diagnosis. Justine reached out to people in established epilepsy Facebook groups asking if they would mind completing a questionnaire. Before she knew it, she had a ton of responses and a gold mine of information to help her create and structure her course.

Initially it hadn't occurred to me to ask questions of my target population. Lucy suggested doing research with my ideal client group so I thought I would give it a go. I was trying to decide what needed to be part of my course on Living Well and Thriving with Epilepsy; I know what issues I myself had struggled with as a person with epilepsy, especially when I was first diagnosed. I knew my subject matter (mental health) back to front, having worked in this field for more than two decades. What I needed to know was what did the majority of epilepsy sufferers need in a course?

I had been a member of an Epilepsy Facebook group for years, and often posed questions about issues I was dealing with.

Groups on Facebook consist of people with specific needs and interests. They provide an important source of support and information for people. They are also a rich source of information for honing in on your ideal client and teasing out your course material. First I did a search within the group for posts about mental health, such as anxiety and depression. I noted down key themes and fashioned some of these ideas into a survey, using SurveyMonkey. I found this helped clarify my thoughts and brainstorm more ideas for my course. I joined more groups for people with epilepsy. In those groups where I was a new member, I first answered questions and made comments within the groups before I started the survey. As in our marketing, people need to know, like and trust you before they will respond with personal information.

I posted my survey in several groups. I was astonished by the response rate, obtaining more than 60 responses in one day. I included some open questions in my questionnaire that yielded important information that I had not thought to add into my course. This also gave me ideas for future courses. For example, in response to a question, 'What is your biggest struggle with epilepsy?' many said that they struggled most with not feeling understood or supported by family members. I could see that an additional short course for loved ones to educate them about epilepsy would be important. There were other learnings for me. I had known that depression and anxiety would be major areas of concern for this group, but survey responses highlighted the impact on their social relationships; loneliness and isolation. I have made this a priority in my course.

A positive by-product of doing this survey was that the process helped people feel listened to. Many responded to thank me for asking these questions; they felt heard and validated. They were keen to know about the course I was creating; 85 per cent of respondents provided their email, providing me with the start of my marketing list.

I learned that what we think we know may not be correct. We start with a hypothesis of what our ideal client needs, but we need to fine tune that by testing it out. In essence, researching our target market by asking them more questions helps us make sure we are on the right track. If our material is aligned with client needs, we have a worthwhile product that will be easily marketed and will, in effect, sell itself.

You can also take note of what people are ASKING in Facebook groups. By providing answers to questions you give value and people are very grateful, then they want to know more about you and what you do. From developing this relationship, you're able to then talk to them about your course and ask if they would be up for helping you map it out. Most people enjoy helping others, so they'll want to support you.

I also ask people questions when they join my Facebook group. I would take photos of the most pertinent and revealing answers, then save this data in a spreadsheet. These questions gave me ideas for content for many years, and it was one of the best ways to ensure that I had answered many people's questions in creating my Confident on Camera course.

YOUTUBE

YouTube is obviously about video, but it's also this vast pool of people who are commenting and engaging, but business owners often overlook it.

Look at the content and the successful content creators in your niche that are relevant to your course idea, then start following their channels and taking note of the most popular videos. You can click on 'most popular' videos for each channel on YouTube, and this gives you some significant clues to the video content that people are searching for.

Focusing on videos in your niche will show you what people need to know and what they are searching for. Think about the user experience . . . They're sitting at home and stuck with a problem, and 95 per cent of the world asks their friend Google for help.

Google *owns* YouTube, so YouTube videos rank highly on Google as a solution. If you're answering that problem, your video will show up higher. The questions that people are asking in the comments of those videos are gold dust! They give you content ideas and help you understand the problems you need to solve in your course. Make a note of these comments and screengrab them. They will help you to create the course content and also the marketing. You want to address their questions and problems in both of these.

Management consultant Jonathan Bradley had a highly successful training business pre-pandemic, but when the world went into lockdown, he realised that he needed to rethink his business model and create passive income.

He didn't have an audience when he started out, so he used YouTube as a way to validate his course idea and see the types of questions that people were asking about navigating corporate life in middle management.

Note: before that little voice in your head says, 'why would they buy my course if they can find the answers on YouTube?', please remember that many people can spend 24 hours trawling YouTube for solutions to the problems they have OR they can pay X amount and buy your course that is tailored to their needs. What is more valuable to your customer, the solution or their time?

I'll talk about audience-building on YouTube in a later chapter, but this is a gentle nudge not to overlook the power of using Google search and YouTube to research your content.

QUORA

Quora is a question-and-answer platform where people go to find solutions to their problems. Millions of people use the site to find information.

Selina Yankson is the mid-career mentor for professionals wondering, 'what next?!' Selina harnessed the power of Quora to identify the struggles that her ideal client was facing. By giving in-depth and really helpful responses on Quora, Selina generated millions of views on her content and a steady flow of clients.

LINKEDIN

Lea Turner has exploded her reach and reputation on LinkedIn in the past year. I'll share her story in more detail later, but take note how you can use LinkedIn or any social media platform to ask your clients what they really, really want.

Before I started building my first digital course, I had a look at what else was available in my niche; what price points, the volume of information covered, and the format in which it was presented. I wanted to know where I felt comfortable position-ing myself.

I also discussed with previous clients what parts of my train-ing they found most valuable, and what aspects of my service stood out most for them. They cited mostly how simple the advice was, and that it was easily actionable. That gave me a great place to start when laying out the content and format of what I went on to create.

I did also quiz people on what they DON'T like about online courses, so I could decide what I wanted to avoid. Mostly they told me that they're often boring and the videos go on too long – far more than is actually necessary – and people lose interest! I have hopefully avoided both of those things.

CLUBHOUSE

Krishna Patel from Skincare Makers Club used Clubhouse to talk to the skincare community and identify what their struggles and challenges were.

> *I started out on the app by joining rooms dedicated to skincare and beauty. By contributing to the discussions and helping others wanting to start up skincare brands, I grew a following on Clubhouse. During the panel discussions, I would say: 'If you would like my free guide, then DM me on Instagram.' Once they had sent me a message, I was able to connect with them and their needs more personally and that helped me map out future digital products too.*

From this, she was able to grow her following on both Clubhouse and Instagram and pre-sell her digital courses and templates. She had a steady flow of skincare business owners viewing her as an authority in her field and ultimately wanting to buy her digital products.

As you can see, there are a variety of ways that you can ask questions. You have to figure out where YOUR audience best resonates. You want to understand what they need rather than what you *think* they need. The answers will surprise you, liberate you from your preconceived ideas and assumptions, and enable you to connect with an audience of people who want to buy what you're creating. This allows you to sell your course before you've even started it!

Think about your customer and their problem that you're going to solve in the course. Your ability to identify a pain point that someone is willing to pay to solve is the cornerstone of your business. Identifying your customer's problem – and your solution – is key to the success of your course. Ask the following:

✓ How best can you connect with your audience to ask them questions?

✓ What questions should you ask your potential customer (and ideal client) to understand more about their struggles and challenges?

✓ What problem(s) do they need to solve?

✓ What are the specific solutions your customer is seeking in buying your course?

Interviewing your ideal client

Once you've identified your ideal clients, you should arrange three to six interviews or focus meetings with them. You want to talk to them so that you can build a relationship with them. So ask them if they wouldn't mind spending 15–20 minutes of their precious time helping you with some research.

Before you skip this section and think that you've done this or you already know what your clients need, I strongly recommend taking the time to do this. Asking these questions is extremely helpful on two levels:

1. *You can use the information for your marketing and sales copy.* The words and phrases they use can help you craft your sales pages and your course structure. While you may 'know' your ideal client, you don't always know about them and their needs with regard to your course.

2. *They might become potential clients.* Building connections with people who are struggling with a niche area of expertise is incredibly useful. Even if they don't become your client right now, they could become your biggest cheerleader, will advocate for your course and may buy from you in the future.

I have always used research as a way to pre-sell my courses and see if it's actually worth creating. Building a course is intense and stressful, so why make life difficult for yourself if you can't then sell the course after you've created it? Do yourself a favour and spend time doing the research. I promise you'll create a better course and you'll have an audience base to sell to.

Where can you meet your ideal client?

You need to find out where these people hang out. You could ask in Facebook groups (you may need to ask the owner of the group for permission to post about this), or you could ask your friends and family on Facebook if they know anyone who fits your target demographic. Or you could ask on Instagram Stories, through a post on LinkedIn or via a question on Quora or Reddit.

Write something along the lines of: 'I'm after your help. I'm looking for someone that has XXX problem and wants to get to YYY [result].' Show that your course is about the transformation they are going to undergo as they learn a new skill or overcome a problem. Ask people if you can interview them for 20 minutes on a Zoom chat.

If you are at a networking event or work event, you can use this as an opportunity to ask your ideal client questions and further understand their pain points. When you know they are your ideal client, you can then ask them if they would mind sparing 20 minutes of their time for a Zoom chat to help you with some research, or you could ask them to complete a survey.

Preparation for interviews

When it comes to the interviews, you want to make sure that you're prepared. Be on time and ensure that you understand how to use Zoom in advance.

You can record Zoom calls, so ensure that you have this set up automatically for the scheduled call so you don't forget. Try to ask open questions that don't 'lead' the interview. Allow them to talk; their words are gold dust. Before you start, think:

- What questions do you want to ask your ideal client?
- What is their pain point?
- What's the biggest challenge they're facing right now?
- How can you best solve their problem?

Here are a few questions that I used when I first created my Confident on Camera course four years ago:

✓ What is your biggest struggle with being on camera?
✓ What makes you worry about it?
✓ How does it impact your business?
✓ If you could snap your fingers and change one thing about being on video, what would it be?
✓ How would it feel to be free of that problem?
✓ How much would you be willing to spend to make that change?
✓ What results would you expect to get from working together?
✓ Is there anything about my offer that would discourage you from purchasing it?
✓ Is there anything about my offer that would encourage you to purchase it?
✓ How much time would you be willing to invest in getting results?

Don't forget to record each interview and save them!

Doing your research through surveys

Doing market research and surveying people is an excellent way to find out what people really need and want. You can then share this with people on social media, or if you have an established mailing list you could email your followers and ask them to complete the survey.

Please note: if you're asking your friends and family to complete the quiz and they are not your ideal client, you might not get the responses you want, so try to talk to someone who is struggling with the problem that you're aiming to solve.

When it comes to asking questions in surveys, the more open-ended the question, the better the outcome if you are wanting them to write something. Asking closed questions means that you will get a YES / NO outcome, which you may not want.

Before you start overthinking your survey, remember that people are busy and time-poor, so the reality is that the simpler it is, the better. Ask a maximum of ten questions, although it's best not to make them mandatory because that can put some people off who may only want to answer specific questions relevant to them.

Use the questions that journalists use . . . Who? What? Where? When? and Why? Ask the key questions:

- What's your biggest challenge?
- Why is that?
- When does this challenge occur?

Even asking just ONE question can be really powerful, if it is the right one that really gets to the heart of what you need to know. So, if you were to ask just one or two questions, what would they be?

For example:

✓ What is your biggest struggle with being on camera?

✓ If you could snap your fingers and change one thing about being on video, what would it be?

If I'm honest, there are some industries that are saturated with surveys and people don't want to respond, while other course creators have huge amounts of help and support from people in their industry. If in doubt, keep it simple and ask ONE question at a time on social media. LinkedIn or Facebook are great places to ask questions on a regular basis.

And if you're really struggling, I find a little 'prize' of a £10 Amazon gift voucher goes a long way!

You've got this!

Here are some software options to consider for your surveys

TYPEFORM

Typeform has a FREE version that has much greater functionality than SurveyMonkey, for example, and also looks good! Yep, it is aesthetically pleasing and easy to create a form. Bingo! You can't customise the URL, unlike in SurveyMonkey, but hey ho, you can't do everything for free. If you are creating your first form, I would look at Typeform.

SURVEYMONKEY

This is the most well-known bit of survey software, although the free version is somewhat limited. You can add branding to ensure the surveys match your business brand. However, to use this tool properly, you have to pay to play. SurveyMonkey enables you to create colourful and engaging surveys, but the downside is that it's not really a viable option when you are first starting out (you have better things to spend your business cash on).

GOOGLE FORMS

Our dear friend Google swoops in to save us once again. This time it's with a free, easy-to-build form that enables you to collect email addresses and easily create a form for your interviewees to complete. It's easy to use and has the simple functionality that we know and love with Google, but it's a jack-of-all-trades form that's designed for everything and it isn't particularly flexible. The form is functional rather than being designed as something unique to your branding.

The upside is that you can collect email addresses on the form, but the downside is that there is no way to store the data so that it is safe and GDPR compliant. Being GDPR compliant is very, very important for your business and if you're selling to the UK and Europe, you need to get on board with it!

But I'm not an expert . . .

We often think we don't know anything, but what have the years of studying, training and working taught you? What know-how and knowledge do you have that has grown, evolved and been nurtured over time?

The best courses and digital products are often very niche; from creating tractor models to running your business better. I've helped people create online courses for ballet, yoga, understanding LinkedIn and even horse whispering!

You *are* an expert in your field, but very often you might not feel like that. When in doubt, ask yourself: 'How am I solving that problem better than others in my industry?'

This question is always tricky because the more confident of us will leap forward with a barrage of ideas, while the shyer creatures will lurk in corners. As an introvert, I am more wallflower than sunflower, so I know how hard it is to claim expert status.

I didn't feel good enough or clever enough for many years because I didn't pass my exams when I was 11 years old. Ever since then I carried this belief that I was a failure. And while I haven't completely lost that negative little voice in my head, I have learned to overcome the self-doubt and disbelief in myself. I know that although I'm not the smartest kid on the block, I can work hard and connect with others and their needs.

To overcome my feelings of inadequacy (that I still have, especially in writing this book), I have Post-it notes all over our house reminding myself that I am an expert. On occasion, if I'm having a wobble, I clean my teeth and repeat to myself, staring at myself in the mirror: 'Lucy, you are an expert.'

My favourite mantra in times of doubt is: 'Lucy, you can F*CKING DO THIS.' Sorry for the swearing, but somehow the 'f' word seems to give me a little potency and renewed power. As I clean my teeth, I use this time to give myself a little pep talk and remind myself of the times when I've succeeded despite the odds.

The negative voice in our heads can often hold us back and stop us from pursuing our passions and following our dreams, but the only thing stopping you from creating a course is YOU. It's not talent, knowledge or ability; it's the willingness to follow through and do this despite your fears and worries.

If you are struggling with your self-belief, I have a FREE guided visualisation at www.makemoneywhileyousleepbook.com/bonus, to help you feel more confident and begin to dismantle your feelings of unworthiness and self-doubt.

Listening to this will help you to rewire your thinking and reprogramme your negative beliefs that you have carried with you in your subconscious, perhaps since you were a child. For example, sometimes we were mocked at school while speaking in class or for speaking about a subject to a teacher, and carried this belief that we are no good at public speaking for many years to come. This can have a major impact on our ability to deliver a course.

Do you want the stories and scripts you created as a child to hold you back now from creating a life you want? If you're ready to change and leap into a new way of thinking, this will help you.

So, download my guided meditation and listen to it as often as you can. I have it on my mobile phone and put it on regularly when I'm going to sleep, out for a run or just pottering around the house.

One thing that I want you to take away from this book is that you don't have to have a PhD in your specialist subject and you don't have to be an 'expert'. You just need to know your stuff, have experience in your area and be five paces ahead of others in the same field.

Let me give you an example. When I first started out in the online world, I hired a fancy business coach who was great at teaching about the online world; however, when I actually needed to get something done, she couldn't tell me the answer because she always hired someone to do the work for her. Now, while I'm a strong believer in outsourcing as much as you can, there are times when you simply can't afford to outsource and you need to just do it yourself. In this case, paying someone to tell you to outsource is a lesson in futility.

My next business coach was someone who was more 'in the trenches' and doing the work rather than doing the hiring. And having someone five paces ahead of me was much more useful and helped me to get my business up and running more quickly.

When you doubt your 'expertise', I want you to remember my two business coaches and the moral of that story. We want someone who is just like us to show us the way.

Cooking isn't my strong point (sorry, Mum). I burn stuff or it just tastes a little *meh*, so luckily my husband does most of it these days. But if I was buying a course to learn how to cook scrumptious meals, I wouldn't want to buy it from a gourmet chef cooking tartines and

Beef Wellington. I would want someone who's sharing healthy recipes that you can rustle up with five ingredients in 30 minutes despite a chaotic life. Why do you think Joe Wicks has some of the best-selling recipe books in the UK?

People want people around them with whom they resonate. And while it is so easy to doubt our own abilities and talents, please remember that if you are consistent with your content and share a message on a social media platform that your audience identifies with, they will come.

My students sometimes worry that there are so many courses and books and resources on a particular subject, so why would someone buy theirs? There are 8,720 million searches that show up on Google about setting up a business – does that mean to say that we wouldn't want to buy a course or a book or pay someone to teach us how to set up in business?

Just because there are many such resources, it doesn't mean to say that I won't buy a course in it. The reverse is actually true. However, I've not just bought a course helping me to set up in business, I've focused on courses that specialise in teaching me how to do something very specific, for example how to use Instagram. So the solution here is that the more niche and targeted you can be, the more successful your offering will be.

Sometimes the fear of being exposed for not being good enough is greater than the reward of creating a course. If you want to do this, but there's a little voice in your head lurking and holding you back, then you have to find a way of flipping your switch.

Start visualising your amazing course. Picture you finishing the course. How will your life be different? What impact will it have on your family's life? How will your business change? Will it mean that you stop having to worry about money or paying the bills? Or will you have more time to yourself and less need to work one-to-one with clients in the juggle? Being able to visualise your amazing future will help you get excited about creating the course and a new future for your working life.

Even during the times when you're shattered from working too many hours, or overwhelmed with your business, or conflicted about spending time with your family, remember how this step will change all this in the long run, and this will help you to stay motivated and on track.

> **Brian Tracy goes to the heart of the matter – www.entrepre-neur.com/article/75648**
> *The ability to find a customer, sell your product or service to that customer, and satisfy the customer so that he buys from you again should be the central focus of all entrepreneurial activity. The greater clarity you have with regard to your ideal customer, the more focused and effective your marketing efforts will be.*

CHAPTER 3

Preparation, Goals and Targets

Why is it that tidying my six-year-old son's sock drawer is suddenly so much more urgent than sitting down to write this chapter?

Aside from his fabulous tractor socks, the reason is that my brain is trying to protect me from the perceived 'pain' of writing – that voice in my head that says I'm not good enough and the stream of negative thoughts that accompany it. However, at two in the morning I'll lie awake worrying that I need to get up and sit down and write it!

Over time, I've learned to be aware of those negative thoughts and push them to one side, and I can now recognise my excuses for what they are so I can actually get on with the business of nailing this!

The same is true for courses. Very often it's easy to procrastinate and delay creating the course because just starting the project is so difficult. The reason for this is that starting a new project consumes more energy than when we know what we're doing, so our brain wants to use its resources sparingly. So, how do you overcome this?

Well, you just need to get going! I know that sounds so obvious that it's a cliche, but sometimes the overall task can feel so overwhelming that we don't actually do anything. Then the life beyond the digital course that we dream of remains unaccomplished . . .

The reality is that once you've started, your brain realises that it's not as difficult as first imagined, and it forms a new habit. Then once you've created this new pattern of behaviour, it is easier to keep going and get that course nailed!

You just need to take that first step.

If you are struggling to actually get going, I highly recommend James Clear's book *Atomic Habits*. It was an incredible resource to me while writing this book. It helped me to recognise where I was procrastinating (mindlessly scrolling on Instagram or discovering all those 'must do' tasks to avoid writing). If you have a lot going on in life AND still want to finish your course, I highly recommend giving *Atomic Habits* a listen while you're out for a run, driving or washing the dishes.

In the book, James says: *'If we want to stop procrastinating, then we need to make it as easy as possible for the Present Self to get started and trust that motivation and momentum will come after we begin.'*

In this chapter, we're going to look at finding your motivation to create the course, your mindset and how you feel about the course, and also your feelings about money and your money blocks. This chapter will help you to get prepared and get planning, and ultimately help you set the revenue goals you want to achieve.

What's your motivation?

Creating a course is all-consuming at first. There will be times when you want to abandon the project and walk away. It requires focus and a willingness to stick to the project even when you feel pulled in many directions. But keep remembering that big dangling carrot at the end of your course-creation journey . . .

What is your motivation? It might be having more time with

your family. Perhaps it is the ability to work from home or from wherever you want in the world. Perhaps you want to step back from your current business and make money while you sleep.

What does creating a course mean to you?

- What is your reason for creating a course?
- Why do you want to change your life and build a course-based business?
- What impact will it have on your life and your family's life?

Understanding your motivation for why you do what you do will help you to stay on track.

We all get distracted and then our plans can get blown off course. How are you going to stay on track despite all that life throws at you?

One stay-at-home mum in the online industry would book herself into a hotel for the weekend to just work on her course with no distractions so she could just focus and get it done while her husband minded the kids. Now, I know that's not possible for all of us (my son wouldn't be happy, for starters) but you need to find a way to get some space to get it done. For me, 5am is my sweet spot. What's yours?

I was about to create a course for *Psychologies Magazine* when Covid-19 struck and we were homeschooling my son. He wanted my attention and I felt pulled in many directions, but I had to stick to the deadlines and get it done. So I got up at 4am every day to have three hours of solid, uninterrupted work time.

Again, I don't necessarily recommend that (I wake early naturally, but even for me 4am was a streeettttch too far!), but you know what works for you, your priorities, your resources and your life. You get to decide how you want to schedule your time and if that means working late, getting up early or booking a week off work and staying in a hotel, then you do what is going to get this course done. You are the creator, and setting the intention to get the work done is half the battle.

Now let's consider some of the key questions in delivering a course. To help you here, I have created a checklist.

What do you need to do to create your course?

Let's get down to looking at some of the detail for your course. Here are some questions to help you get started:

- What timelines are you working to? Do you have a completion deadline?
- What budget are you setting yourself to create your course? Or are you going to try to do as much yourself as possible (without hiring someone or incurring costs)?
- Do you have all the funding available now? If not, can you guarantee those funds will materialise? For example, will you have profits from other revenue streams or apply for government grants or bank loans?
- Do you want to do the filming yourself or hire a videographer?
- Are you involving anyone else in your filming? Children/animals/other people? If you are, are there any other considerations you need to make for filming? Are they available for your planned dates?
- Creating a course means that you have to be chief creator, sales and copywriter guru and also tech wizard. There may be some areas that you decide to outsource. Are you wanting to write all the sales copy yourself or hire someone to do it?

- Will you need PDF workbooks? How are your design skills? Will you need to hire someone or just use Canva?
- Are you wanting to build the sales pages and other tech yourself, or hire someone to do it?
- If you're planning to hire videographers or designers or tech VAs to help you with your course, they are often busy, so have you booked them in advance?

How are you going to sell your course?

Understanding how you're going to sell your course is vital to its success. I see many people create courses and think that the Course Fairy will then magically sell it on. I hate to break it to you, it's not going to happen!

Lots of people build a course and then forget about the process of actually selling it. Business owners get all excited about their course – they create it and sell a few, but it's not as many as they hoped for. Then they think it's a failure and put it away on a digital shelf on their laptop to get dusty and that's the end of their course-selling aspirations.

I have news for you: just because your course does not sell at first does not mean that it's a failure; it's just that you haven't successfully found and talked to the people most interested in buying it.

Your success in selling your course is very often about the groundwork you lay in researching your course, talking to your dream customers and ultimately pre-selling the course to them. Once you've identified your niche audience, you want to reach as many people with those characteristics as possible through social media or Google search. You will hear this statistic a lot from me during this book, but it's so important to remember. On average, about 2 per cent of your audience will buy from you, so that means if you have 100 people on your email list, you might have two buyers. The bigger the size of your social-media presence, the *easier* it is to sell to them . . . (see Chapter 7).

However, before you put this book down and think that you don't have a large social media following so there's no way you can successfully sell your course, press pause on that thought. Just because you don't have an audience, doesn't mean you can't create a successful course that sells.

Having a small but engaged and targeted audience is actually a surprisingly effective way to sell courses and can achieve far greater returns. Just because an influencer has tens of thousands of followers does not always mean that people want to buy from that person, they may just find them entertaining.

You want to establish an audience that is specific to your industry. These are the best type of people to sell to because they know you, they like what you do and they are hungry for your specific product. Once you have established this audience, it is then easier to replicate this using paid advertising.

Here are the key questions to ask yourself (remember, there's no right or wrong answers, it will just help you to know where to focus your energy):

- Are you an established business owner with an email list or are you starting from scratch?
- Do you have an audience on social media? Or do you need to grow your audience? How big is it?
- Do you like using social media? Be honest, if you find it draining, that's okay, there are other ways to sell a course.
- Do you have an analytical brain that enjoys doing research into understanding how best to grow on YouTube, for example? Or is that your worst nightmare?

- Can you afford to pay for Facebook or YouTube advertising?
  Even if you start out at £20?

Earlier we talked about using social media and focus groups to research your course. Now I want you to think about how you're going to take this one step further and pre-sell to this same audience. I want you to start thinking about your customers and how you're going to attract them to buy your course (note: we will cover audience-building in greater detail in Chapter 7).

Growing your social media following is important because the more people who see what you're up to, and what you're selling, the more possibility there is of them buying your course.

If you don't have a large audience, you can try to grow your audience *organically*. This means growing it for free, and on some of the more established platforms such as Facebook or Instagram, this can be difficult.

However, if you are an early adopter of a newer social media platform, you can grow quickly. For example, if you leapt onto TikTok or embraced Clubhouse, you are more likely to grow your audience quickly than if you were on Instagram or Facebook, which are already saturated with users and content. Sites such as LinkedIn, Clubhouse or TikTok are seeing enormous expansion and it is still possible for you to build your audience on these platforms.

I'm an introvert, so I find social media exhausting; I find the engagement and social side of posting and commenting very draining. A couple of years ago, I found the process of engaging in Facebook groups too much, so I withdrew from social media for about a year. Instead, I focused my time on YouTube and Pinterest, because while they may appear to be social media sites, actually the platforms are based around content. I could write blog posts and create videos, then research the best ways for that content to be found on Google. And that was doable. It enabled me to drive traffic to my website and YouTube channel, and from there I was able to invite people to get my free content and then share a webinar training (and sell my courses) on the back of this.

Slowly, things started to build.

When I started selling courses, I didn't have a big audience and I wasn't well known. I had a small amount of money that I could invest in Facebook ads, so we spent £20 and I sold £60-worth of courses. I reinvested that money in Facebook ads and my ad budget grew as I sold more courses and made more money. The more I invested in Facebook ads, the more I recouped into the business.

You can promote your course in a variety of different ways and using a variety of marketing tools. What most appeals to *you?* Is it organic traffic from social media or YouTube, or is it paid-for traffic for ads?

Think strategically to decide how you want to sell your course – is it *organically* through YouTube or Pinterest, or do you want to get found on Google? Do you want to use webinars to sell your course? Or do you want to create a Facebook group to promote it? Or perhaps you want to 'pay to play' and use Facebook ads or YouTube ads?

Managing your time

When it comes to your time, we all have 1,440 minutes in a day, and we each get to choose how we want to use them.

I know life is busy and you're often being pulled in a hundred different directions. I know that you struggle with demanding bosses, the juggle, the chaos and the numerous other reasons that stop you from getting a minute's peace to sit down and focus on your course. But you are here reading this book because you want to get off the hamster wheel and pursue your passion projects and have time for those you love . . .

It is true that creating a course will require MORE of your time while you set it up and go for it, so make life easy for yourself during this startup phase and keep it simple. Focus on the end dream to stay motivated and excited when the going gets tough.

What do you need to think about when managing your time?

- What hours do you have available to plan your course? Are you working full-time? Could you work in the morning for an hour? Or is there anyone to help with the kids?
- For any project, if you think it will take you three hours, DOUBLE IT and build that into the plan. Things always take longer than planned.
- Try to block out time in your calendar for 45-minute sessions so that you can focus and get one task done in that time.
- Work on one element of course creation and then move on to the next.

Key dates plan

When you're planning your course, it's always good to start with the end in mind . . . actually selling it!

When do you want to birth your new baby? When do you want to start selling your course? This is often called your 'launch' date because, like a boat, it's when your course sets sail.

Successful launching on time means mapping out your dates and working out what is realistic and achievable. So the first thing to note is that building a course takes time. Unfortunately, you can't just snap your fingers and get it done.

Give yourself three to four months to create and build your course if you have time to focus with no distractions (no kids off school, or full-time work). But if you have other things going on in your life then be more realistic about what you can achieve and allocate more time to the project). The timescale will also be impacted by the size of the course e.g. a 'signature' course in your business or a low ticket mini-course, which I will talk about further in Chapter 4.

Whaaaatt?! You say. You want it done now? Great! Go for it with gusto and gumption. It can be done if you're focused and determined, but I reckon three to four months works for most people.

You see, CREATING the course is actually, umm, the 'easy' part. Strange as it sounds, sometimes the mechanics of BUILDING your course machine can be more complex. You also want to allow time for writing the copy for sales emails, landing pages and to generate a buzz about your course by promoting it. This is referred to as the pre-launch runway.

Launch Your Course Overview

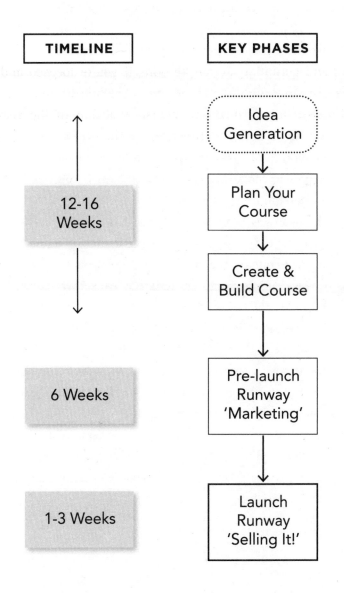

Some key promotional questions

- When do you want to start promoting your course on the 'runway'?
- When do you want to start selling your course?

It's time to look in your calendar and think tactically. Keep in mind your audience – choose dates that will work for them (will they be affected by school holidays or religious holidays?).

Think about launching your course in January or September, for example. August and December are typically quieter months, but you know your business and the way that your customers work.

In Chapter 10 I talk through different launch approaches. To give you an understanding of the timelines involved, let's say I am going to launch via a Facebook Challenge. For this give yourself an approximate six-week lead time to start the 'pre-launch' promotional phase of selling the course and building anticipation and 'nudges' that something is coming. Create content that leads towards your launch. You need to lay the foundations and start planning out blog posts, podcasts, YouTube videos and social media that are aligned with that content.

As I mentioned we will cover your pre-launch and launch runway in more detail in Chapter 10, but for now, let's think about creating a workable promotional calendar for you.

See below for an example that will help you create your launch timetable. and will help you to see when you will actually start selling it! (You can access a version of this at www.makemoneywhileyousleepbook.com/bonus)

Example – Facebook launch timetable	
Week 1-3	Launch promotion begins where you start talking about content that is relevant to the problem you are solving in your course (but you don't actually sell the course or mention the course).
Week 4-6	Invite people to sign up to your training on social media and emails.
Week 7	Classes for people that have signed up to training. Then have a Masterclass workshop (also known as a webinar) where you start selling course (you can repeat this workshop). Cart opens to start selling course for five days.
Week 8	Continue selling course and then close cart.

WHAT ARE YOUR MONEY BLOCKS ABOUT PASSIVE INCOME?

Many business owners – myself included – set up in business because their current way of working was no longer working for them; they wanted to do something for themselves, while having that freedom and getting paid for it.

As business owners, we loved the idea and the freedom of being able to work for ourselves, but we didn't want to be the boss. The idea of doing revenue forecasts or making difficult decisions doesn't always come easily.

Being successful in business does require you to step into your CEO shoes, though, and take ownership of the fact that you are a business owner with a proper business that has profit, revenues and costs.

Perhaps you have struggled for money all your life and you've been raised on the mantra that if you work hard you'll be successful. We can often sabotage our success because we think that we're not worthy of earning this money, we're not good enough to sell or it goes against our family's story of 'hard work'. So we assume that we aren't *good with money* when we set up our business and it permeates everything we do.

Many of us have grown up with particular stories about money, how we are 'not meant to be rich', or perhaps how 'millionaires are *mean* people'.

We take on these stories in our childhood and carry the scripts into our working lives and businesses. My family was very loving, but they would tease me and talk about me as being a *'spender'* and *'bad'* with money. Rich people were *'greedy'* and having money was somehow wrong.

I spent years working in international journalism where I didn't care about my salary or what people earned. But as I grew older, I resented that I was working 14-hour days and yet the promised pay rises were not forthcoming. And when it came to buying a house, I didn't really have any money and I had little to show for my years of hard work.

This was the moment that I decided to take control of my money situation and step out of these outdated beliefs that I was 'bad' with money.

Think about the language that you have been raised with around money. Did you hear these phrases from your family?

- 'Money doesn't grow on trees.'
- 'You don't get something for nothing.'
- 'They're successful and hard-working . . .'
- 'Be good and work hard . . .'
- 'You'd rather be happy than rich.'
- 'Rich people are selfish/greedy/mean.'

When I set up my business, I realised that I was afraid of money; I was afraid to ask for it and I didn't know how to manage it properly. This fear of money permeated my business and my ability to get clients.

So often I would find myself working for FREE because I didn't want to upset the person by charging them my worth. And when I did charge money for a project, I would have to outsource some work and find myself still working for very little profit despite bringing money into the business.

Creating courses enabled me to overcome these fears because I didn't have to do sales calls anymore – the video did the talking for me.

Having now turned over a million dollars, I still find myself struggling with this. Uncovering these deep-rooted beliefs is not about clicking your fingers and hoping they will disappear; you have to do the work to explore these stories you have been told since you were a child.

What beliefs do you still carry about how your family talked about money and success?

- If you don't work hard for it, it doesn't feel 'real' and you didn't 'earn it'.
- You feel so guilty about asking for money that you work for FREE.
- You feel guilty about making money.
- You worry that your ambition is somehow 'wrong' and it impacts your ability to be a good parent or partner.

Perhaps you resonate and connect with some of these beliefs. These stories affected my ability to sell and succeed in business, so I also used Neuro-Linguistic Programming (NLP) and Reiki to help me recognise my blocks and create a new belief system about selling and making money.

The first step to success with money is recognising that you have a money block. Here are some questions to help you decide if you have a money block . . .

☐ Do you find yourself reinventing the wheel or overcomplicating systems?

☐ Do you procrastinate and end up doing things at the last minute or pull an all-nighter?

☐ Do you resist delegating or outsourcing because you want to save money and then you don't take action?

☐ Do you feel like it's cheating if it is too easy?

☐ Do you not feel proud of yourself and fail to celebrate your wins? Do you just focus on the negativity and the struggles instead?

If you resonate with some of these fears, then a course-based business can work for you because it takes you out of the mix, and enables you to automate your sales. Creating courses enabled me to actually overcome these fears because I didn't have to do sales calls anymore – the video did the talking for me.

Strategy alone is not enough, though! It is really important to also work on your money mindset and add more ease and flow into your life and work.

I want you to imagine money coming effortlessly . . . What comes up for you?

Say to yourself: *There's always enough money.*

For more support, download my Money Blocks guided meditation to help you overcome your blocks: https://makemoney-whileyousleepbook.com/bonus

---

Denise Duffield-Thomas, author of *Lucky Bitch* and creator of Money Bootcamp, has these nuggets of insight about our guilt and stories around money:
I think when it comes to making money while you sleep is it feels like cheating for most people. And this is the crux of it: we

are taught that you have to work hard to make money, and you show up for an hour and you get paid for an hour. And so passive income blows that equation out of the water. And so we question: 'Did I deserve it? How did I earn it if I didn't show up for that?'

When I created Lucky Bitch *in 2011, and I was selling it for $10. I would wake up every day and think about the people who bought it, which was amazing. But I felt so guilty about it because I didn't earn that. Although I wrote it, it didn't compute, it didn't feel like it was earned. And I felt like I had to call people up over the phone and read it to them to earn that $10.*

We have grown up with the logic that an hour of our time equals an hour of pay. It feels like we're doing something wrong because we're not 'earning', it feels like we're cheating people. And it feels like we didn't earn it, and we didn't deserve it, so we feel like we have to overdeliver to compensate.

Your skills might be discounted by others in your life, but that doesn't mean you should help everyone for free. You still can offer a ton with your blog posts and social media content – and then, it's OKAY to charge for your personal time if someone wants more from you. I've created hundreds of free videos and podcasts. I've posted 4000+ times on Instagram – yes, a lot of dog pics but mostly with tips on money and business.

Go look at how many times you've posted on your business social media – that is SERVING your community. Don't discount that.

The world isn't served by entrepreneurs doing everything for free – we already do that – in business and in our personal lives.

Money as a concept isn't going away any time soon – MONEY creates a lot of problems in the world right now because

> *traditionally, it's not been in the hands of people who care about the planet. We can CHANGE THE WORLD with more money.*
>
> *I delete anyone who tells me that I shouldn't charge for my work, and you can too.*

How much money do you want to make?

If you want to take your business from a hobby business to profitable and scalable, you need to get your head around the cashflow.

The key questions are:

- What is your course idea?
- What's your revenue goal? (What sales do you expect from it? And remember, sales is not profit.)
- What's your ongoing budget to support your revenue target?

It's ironic that I am writing a book called *Make Money While You Sleep,* because I do not claim to be an expert about money and setting revenue targets.

> Success Coach Emily Williams shares a lot about money in coaching. Read these tips about flipping our money mindset:
> *In order to flip your mindset to believe that you can make money in your sleep, you have to first believe that it's possible. In many cases, it comes from seeing other people do it. As humans, we learn by seeing examples of what's possible. One of the best things you can do for your mindset is surround yourself with people who are doing what you want to do, for example, making money in your sleep. So, learning from mentors who are already doing that. Saturating your mind with examples of others who are making that happen, instead of the alternative outlook*

which is normally saying that it's not achievable. This is true when you are in a group or in an environment that is not possibility-oriented and they don't see that making a lot of money is possible or it is not a good thing to make a lot of money. Getting yourself into an entrepreneurial space that will support you will be an essential step on this journey.

One of the biggest blocks that people have about money is the fact that they believe making money is wrong and they shouldn't be greedy or want more. They should be just grateful for what they have. I realized that you can be grateful and still desire more at the same time.

One of the biggest shifts for me is being able to own the fact that my desires are meant for me. I won't be aware of a desire unless I feel that it is possible for me to achieve this and I am energetically aligned with it. Sometimes it's about being able to admit to yourself what it is that you actually want!

A lot of people have been taught that money doesn't grow on trees, that it's difficult to make a lot of money and really making that shift and asking myself what is the fastest, easiest and most joyful way to bring in the money has been a game changer for me because there is always an easy way to make money. Just developing that abundance mindset and knowing that there are billions of people online who want what I'm selling has also been a game changer. Creating a mindset of ease has been really helpful for me.

When you're creating a course, ensure you're think of the upfront 'project' cost and also of the ongoing fixed costs (such as the software, course-hosting platforms, VA support, etc.); you want to make sure that you are covering those costs and also making a profit.

Setting goals and revenue targets for your course may sound scary and formal, but if you're able to visualise your plan, you're much more likely to nail it!

It's critical to know what revenue you want to make from your course launch and how to allocate your budget. If you're time-poor but cash-rich, you can outsource various elements of course creation. You just have to work out what's right for you.

So remember to keep a close eye on both the revenues generated and the ongoing costs. I suggest you look at this monthly – are you beating 'budget' or do you need to take some corrective action?

It's perhaps not the *sexiest* thing to talk about in this book, but it is vital and there are multiple accounting software packages out there to help you! Quickbooks or Xero for starters.

Creating a course gives you the potential to build a scalable and hugely profitable business but keep on track with those outgoings!

PART 2

Creating Your Course!

CHAPTER 4

Outlining Your Course

When planning your course, you ideally want to decide what kind of business model you want to follow. Do you want to create an extensive signature course that you sell through a launch several times a year? Or do you want to create a signature or mini-course to sell on repeat continuously, without having to do additional formal 'launches'?

When you have an online business, you must establish a way for people to find out what you do. You can do this by creating a launch and make an all-singing, all-dancing party about what you do. Or you can sell your digital product every day. The latter model's upside is that you are selling continuously, which is referred to as 'Evergreen'; however, you do need to ensure you have a steady stream of new customers.

Within this chapter, we will cover:

- Type of course and method of delivery.
- Shaping your course.
- Naming your course.
- How to add a subtitle.
- Outlining your course content.
- What content to include.
- What content to exclude.
- Any other documents you could include.

Let's talk through each model to help you decide what suits your personality and your business best. We'll also map out your course to create a plan that works for you and your business.

Type of course and method of delivery

Within this book, I refer to two main types of courses: signature and mini-courses.

A signature course is a high-value course – generally sold for over £300+ – which is aligned to the heart and soul of your business, and will generally have a good deal of detail. Typically, significant planning, focus and effort will go into creating this course.

Alternatively, you can deliver a mini-course, which will be of lower value and most likely easier to put together, and quicker to digest for the purchaser. This could be a good entry point for a number of businesses, although perhaps less sexy than your high-ticket signature course. By selling my mini-course called Confident on Camera for a low-cost, 'no-brainer' price point, I use a mini-course as a gateway to my other higher-priced products and services.

While you may have an initial preference, as you work through this chapter you will get a better understanding of what will work best for you and your business.

There are two ways to sell your course:

1. Evergreen courses means that they sell all the time, but you offer discounted incentives to buy within a time limit.
2. Live 'launch' of your course, where you might launch every three months, open your cart, sell for a few days and then close the cart. Like deciduous trees, this is a seasonal product where you create the urgency to buy by sheer fact that the cart is

open or closed which can enable you to create a buzz around the product.

Whatever method you adopt, you want to create urgency so that people think they need to buy now rather than dawdling away a few hours on social media without hitting the buy button.

MINI-COURSES

When you create a mini-course, you're essentially selling an afford-able product where people can have a taste of you, to see if they like you and how you teach. The lower-cost product could be anything from £9 to £297 at the lower end, so it's a no-brainer and they don't have to think about the investment – whereas more thought is required by the consumer as the price bracket increases. You can sell these courses day in and day out, and you don't have to trade time for hours once you've created the product.

These are the kinds of products with which I've built my business, and it enables people who are first starting to invest in something right here and now with you.

And you could create a series of courses from £19 and then say 'Oh, would you like this course while you're here?'

For example, think of a waiter in a bar; he'll say: 'What can I get you to drink?' and 'Would you like some olives with that?' And before you know it, that drink has morphed into a few drinks, some accompanying olives, an appetiser and potentially an à la carte meal.

The waiter is 'upselling', and you want to do the same thing with your courses. You are taking someone from the olives to the starter, then to the main course and seeing if they can squeeze in dessert, too.

When someone is buying from you online, they are primed with their credit card in their hand, and now it's time to maximise what they buy from you. More on sales funnels in Chapter 8.

SIGNATURE COURSE

Think of this course as the main dish in your repertoire. You're not offering starters; you're diving into the main course; this is your chunky course that teaches people a considerable amount of knowledge and learning. You are taking your students on a journey and giving them the necessary tools to succeed, or at least giving them a strong understanding of a subject.

Signature courses are generally priced at a higher price point and require a little more connection from you. Because these sell at a higher price point, you can create a launch with 'cart opening' and 'cart closing' every few months. And potential buyers will want to get to know you through social media or Facebook live videos before they leap and make the purchase. Some signature programmes also offer a weekly group coaching-call, that run for a specific time.

The course's price point will help you determine whether it's something that you offer with a live element to your students – via a group call or a one-to-one element – or if you want to just sell the course on automation without involving you and your time. Selling a course for over £1,000 can mean that people are perhaps expecting more time with you, whether on a group call or a one-to-one.

It may be that you charge a higher price point such as £997 or several thousand pounds, and therefore they are making a high-cost, intensive investment with you. If someone has invested a great deal of money to work with you and get the support, they are more likely to do the work, and make it happen!

Of course, it may be that you want to leave your product as a lower price point, such as £297, and then you don't offer any face-to-face contact.

When you take your students through the details of the course in a live environment, being hands-on can be time-consuming. You might want to think about whether this is a good idea because you may not want to trade time for money.

For example, I have a £297 course called Create and Scale on YouTube, through which I teach people how to succeed on YouTube. I have created the video course and workbooks, then people learn at their own pace in a self-study environment and I sell this 24/7 on evergreen without worrying about cart opening or cart closing.

I also have my signature programme called My Course Academy, which I launch several times a year, and I teach people how to create a course. Launching means I can sell this programme at a higher price point, and I am much more 'hands-on', with weekly coaching calls and more involvement in the process. This method is much more time-consuming, but it enables me to show people how to create a course, and I know that they're paying for an investment in my time.

Launching a high-value course with cart 'open' (you're selling for 3-5 days) and cart closed (it's no longer available to buy) can mean that you're on this emotional rollercoaster of feast or famine, hoping for the success of the next big launch. If you love launching and are quite extrovert, you'll enjoy the experience, but if you find it stressful to have to show up and be high-energy for two weeks, it can be very draining.

If you are creating a course that doesn't have a live element, you are not requiring any of your time, so you can sell it on repeat.

You decide what works for you. What feels good?

SO WHAT TYPE OF COURSE IS FOR YOU?

Here are some questions to help you figure out your preferred method to sell your courses, because the more you can plan, the easier it will be to map them out.

I encourage you to write down your thoughts in a notebook or journal. Writing things down doesn't just help you remember, it makes your thinking more effective by focusing on what's important to you.

What are you looking to sell?

Add your notes below or write in your journal or notebook . . .

How much will your ideal customer be willing to pay? Perhaps consider others in your industry. What are they charging for courses? How successful are they?

What price point do you want to aim for to sell your course right now?

Do you want to sell a high-value course where you have a group-coaching element to the programme, or do you want to create a lower-cost digital product, so it just sells as a product and you don't have any live interaction?

What approach most appeals to you right now? And why?

Add your notes below or write in your journal or notebook . . .

Would you like to focus on one signature course or a series of courses?

Add your notes below or write in your journal or notebook . . .

Shaping your course

The rest of this chapter will help you to shape your course and decide on all the elements you need to create a successful course-based business.

Remember to consult your notes about your ideal client from Chapter 2 to answer some of these questions and ensure that your thinking is still on track.

If you have not yet talked to your ideal client, please go and do some research! Use the questions in Chapter 2 to help you. Your course plans will likely change significantly when you know what people need and want.

Once you have the results from your audience research, it's now time to modify your plans accordingly.

So, let's recap ... What keeps your ideal client awake at night? What problem or pain point are you solving in the course (or perhaps it's not a problem, but a desire you're going to satisfy in the course). Tap into the reason that they're going to buy your course right now. What is so challenging for them that if they don't purchase this course, they will continue to repeat the same old habits and patterns and not change their life?

Identify the point where they are now, why they're stuck and why they need your help.

Add your notes below or write in your journal or notebook . . .

Keep thinking about your ideal client and how they're feeling stuck or challenged or in pain. What answers are you going to give them?

How is your course going to solve their challenges and resolve their issues? You want to be sure that you are going to be directly answering this challenge.

How are you going to solve your ideal client's problem or pain point in the course?

Add your notes below or write in your journal or notebook . . .

When you understand your ideal client and what they need, it's much easier to talk their language and make the course a no-brainer for them to buy; they simply must have the course to relieve their pain and move forward.

Understanding where they are right now, and what journey you're going to take them on, is critical. You want to show your ideal client the transformation they will go through in buying your course. Almost like the caterpillar to butterfly, you want to convey that they might feel stuck right now, but soon they'll be in flow, and everything will be easier because they will have bought the course and solved a particular issue that will make life better.

What transformation do you want to see in your ideal client? What emotions/frustrations and feelings are your perfect client going through before they take the course?

Add your notes below or write in your journal or notebook . . .

How do they feel AFTER they've taken the course? (e.g. Where are they right NOW?)

Add your notes below or write in your journal or notebook . . .

```



```

Being able to sell the TRANSFORMATION is the key to selling the course. What transformation are you going to offer your audience? Will you take them from stuck to motivated, or from employee to entrepreneur? Using alliteration can come afterwards, but techniques like this can help you with your marketing, and your course subtitle. For example:

'My course [insert name of course] will take you from burned out and exhausted to brimming with energy and excited about life.'

'My course [insert name of course] will take you from struggling to make a sale to securing six-figure sales with flow and ease.'

Write out in one sentence how your course will take someone from feeling [insert emotion, e.g. stuck/confused/overwhelmed/stressed and attacking the cookie jar] to [success/earning six figures/being healthy/happy etc.].

Write your sentence below or in your journal or notebook . . .

```



```

Naming your course

Naming a course is so liberating! It's that moment when everything seems to come together and it seems to have a momentum of its own.

Until that moment, you can feel as though you're weighed down with the process and the decision. We spent hours deliberating what to call our son. A week after he was born, my son was still in intensive care, and his hospital name tag was 'Lentil' (the size of him when I found out I was pregnant!) – even the hospital documents were beginning to think his nickname was his real name! My husband sat me down in a cafe near the hospital and said we had to decide. Thirty minutes later we had our name!

So, give yourself 20 minutes, set the alarm and get brainstorming! Embrace the 'Done is Better than Perfect' mentality and go for something that works for you and covers all the checklist's critical areas.

When you have the urgency of the alarm clock, it's easier to make a decision.

Your course name should show the course's benefits and its promise (what it's going to do for your buyer). Can you answer what the course is about? If you're stuck creating a course name, try this formula:

[**The thing you solve**] 101: how to go from stuck [**name your problem**] to sorted [**name your solution**].

Using alliteration with the subtitle works well but isn't essential. So, for example, Organising 101: how to go from chaos and clutter to calm and collected.

Don't spend too long agonising over the title. Your name doesn't have to be perfect. You can change it if you don't like it at a later date.

WHAT A COURSE NAME SHOULD DELIVER

There are three types of course names you can choose:

1. The Journey – Results-driven title

Examples:

- 21 Days to Calm Meditation Course
- Create and Scale on YouTube
- Create the Life You Want

2. Searchable Titles – 'It does what it says on the tin'

Examples:

- How to Create a Successful Homestead
- Beginners' Yoga for the Over-50s
- 10-minute Healthy Family Meals

3. Creative and Quirky Course Titles

Examples:

- Lights, Camera, Influence (my course)
- Go Live and Thrive (my course)
- B-School – Marie Forleo's signature group programme
- Spirit Junkie Masterclass – Gabrielle Bernstein's programme

I started out thinking that fun and quirky was the way to go because I like being 'creative', but the reality is that being transparent is more critical than clever and witty.

People need to UNDERSTAND what your course is offering and the OUTCOME of your course.

What course title type appeals most to you?

Add your notes below or write in your journal or notebook . . .

What's the title of your course? (Even if you're still not fixed on a name, write down your working title.)

Once you have decided upon a name, ask yourself these questions.

COURSE NAME CHECKLIST:

✓ Is the name catchy? Go for something that stands out.

✓ Is it as short as possible?

✓ Is my course name memorable? You want a name that is easy to remember.

✓ Does it tell my potential buyers what my course is about? Will it resonate with my ideal customer avatar (see Chapter 2)?

✓ Does it show the benefits of your course? Is it clear? Clear always trumps clever.

✓ Is it different from other courses containing similar content?

✓ Is my course name easy to say out loud? Remember, you will be talking about it on live videos and webinars.

✓ Does your course say what it does on the tin? Sometimes catchy and creative doesn't always work. Ask yourself if you'll have to continually explain what the course is about or if it's simple and easy to understand.

✓ Are there any keywords easily searchable through search engine optimisation (SEO)? Are there any conflicting names?

✓ Is the trademark available? Is it infringing on any existing trade-marks? (Check online and see the section below.) Depending on the type of online course you are creating and the significance of the course name on your branding, you may wish to consider registering the name to protect its use.

✓ Is the course name being used elsewhere? Check Google and Facebook. It's essential to make sure the course name is not in use; sometimes if someone owns the URL it doesn't necessarily appear on page one of Google.

✓ Can you register the domain name – the .com?

✓ Has it passed the Facebook test, and is it available?
✓ Most importantly, do you like the name?

Remember, your course name should show:

• The benefits of the course
• The promise – what it's going to do for you
• What it is about

Just like choosing a baby name, your course title should have meaning and connection.

Domain names

Check the domain name and if the course name is available, then buy it, quick! GoDaddy is a great place to check domain names. Also see if the name is available on Facebook. Check to make sure that a big brand or influencer isn't using the key words / phrase you want to use.

Should you register a trademark?

YES! When you register your trademark, it ensures that no one else has a legal right to use the course name you have chosen. Check the title before you create your course to ensure that you don't make something and then discover that it's not available. If you have to change a name because it's trademarked, it's a lot of hassle (she says, speaking from experience!!). So please do your research and check the course name is available. You can then trademark it when you can afford to.

This can be a complex area, so, if you are in any doubt I recommend you contact a specialist lawyer in your jurisdiction.

I make sure that I register my trademarks in the United States because that's where I do most of my business. Registering a brand in the United States typically costs around 500 US dollars. There are specialist trademark firms you can use that will tend to be significantly cheaper than approaching a more traditional law firm.

Check the US and UK trademark . . . Two sites to consider are:

1. The United States Patent and Trademark Office
2. UK Intellectual Property Office

The art of the subtitle

Use the subtitle to fully explain your promise and what the course will achieve. Show the TRANSFORMATION in the title.

For example, 'Create and scale on YouTube – *create a lead-generation machine that brings you, clients, on repeat'*.

Brainstorm some ideas (and have a thesaurus to hand).

Add your notes below or write in your journal or notebook . . .

Outlining your course

Each course should ideally consist of six to eight core modules that will make up the course framework. Within these modules you can include several videos and additional supporting content. As a rough guide, three to five videos in each module if it's a signature course, and if it's a mini-course, one video per module works. Do what works for you and what *feels* right. Intrinsically trust your instinct here.

To get started, find yourself either a whiteboard or a bunch of Post-it notes and begin thinking about what structure you'd like your course to take.

Give yourself time to plan this out; you don't want to rush, you want to have fun and enjoy the process, too!

Brainstorm the outline

To create your course online, block out four hours of your day and allow yourself the space to let your creative juices run.

Write down your ideas on the whiteboard or sticky notes, give yourself time to brainstorm and scribble down all your ideas.

Use a wall in your house or somewhere where you can spread out! Getting physical space can enable you to gain clarity. Again, don't hurry this process, have fun, play music and allow yourself to be creative! If you find yourself feeling stuck, listening to inspiring music can help me, and I also like to meditate to put my 'thinking' in the right frame of mind so that I stay focused and creative.

If you're using Post-it notes, allow yourself one per module (or training session video) to ensure you capture the key points, which you can expand on later. Map out the key modules, highlight each of the videos and the training needed for each module.

Bullet-point the lesson ideas that come to you in each module. Each course is unique and individual, so it's hard to quantify how many modules or lessons you want to create for each course. It depends on what your course is about, and the price point. As I have advised, a good rule of thumb is six to eight modules; and if you end up creating more or fewer, don't stress about it! The most crucial point is that the course's structure and length are appropriate to the content and price point.

What is the transformation?

What are the critical steps that someone needs to take to TRANSFORM and go from stuck to sorted? When devising each module, ensure that you show the TRANSFORMATION. Ask yourself the following questions.

- How is each module going to benefit the big picture of the course?
- What result will each module achieve for the ideal client?
- Will the module take them one step closer to achieving the transformation?
- Is it *'must-have'* or is it *'nice to have'* information that will move them closer to the desired outcome?

If it's not moving them closer to the desired outcome, rethink the module.

Add your notes below or write in your journal or notebook . . .

Now give yourself some time for the idea to marinate before you start on the next section.

Add your notes below or write in your journal or notebook . . .

Creating your content

Now transfer your ideas to a Google document or somewhere that's safe so that your thoughts don't go missing. The Post-it notes can get jumbled and confusing; that's why it's essential to transfer the ideas to a document.

Allow yourself to add colour and life to the course. People remember stories and anecdotes much more than dry facts, so include the light and shade. Have fun with your course. People are more likely to engage with the fun and learn along the way too!

Now start creating the content for each module. Do a big brain dump to make sure that you've covered everything.

Add your notes below or write in your journal or notebook . . .

If you're feeling confused, return to the creativity of the wall of Post-it notes or your whiteboard. Put on some creative and inspiring music (I find Pura Rasa on YouTube helps).

Then return to your ideal client research in Chapter 2. What transformation does your ideal client want? What steps do they need to take to go from stuck to sorted?

If you're feeling blocked, don't just sit there, go for a walk, or do yoga or something that will fire your creative juices.

Does your course flow?

Now you've done the brain dump, it's time to refine your thinking. Is there any content that doesn't quite fit? Is the content working for you? Answer the following questions in your journal or notebook:

- Are the modules in the right order? Does the learning process feel natural and flow? Talk it through with someone who isn't intimately involved in the course.
- **Are the videos in the right order in each module?** Again, are you in the flow when you share your content?
- **Do your lesson structures flow?** Are your stories and anecdotes relevant?

I find it useful to map out a course plan using Lucidchart or other process-mapping software. This way, you can quickly move the course boxes around. Alternatively, use a whiteboard. In other words, do what works for you to refine your thinking.

The critical point is that you want to create a system and structure that is easy to understand and follow for your students. Ask yourself if the content and modules make sense. If they don't, it's time to refine and tweak.

So, let's refine and prune your content. Think of being a gardener – pruning makes for a more bountiful growth spurt.

What do you need to cut out? What does not align with your course strapline or the course outline? Do some sections or modules go into a level of detail that is not necessary to meet the course's objectives?

Add your notes below or write in your journal or notebook . . .

```
┌─────────────────────────────────────────┐
│                                         │
│                                         │
│                                         │
│                                         │
└─────────────────────────────────────────┘
```

The other side of the coin is that sometimes you can know so much that it's easy to make assumptions about your ideal client. Are you assuming they have some knowledge when they don't? What else do they need help with? You are the expert, but you want them to understand the process and the journey.

- Will they be able to follow along?
- Are you leaving out any key ideas?
- Are you making it too complicated?
- Or are you simplifying things too much?

At this point, I find it useful to talk things through with my husband and also a coach. Perhaps you could talk things through with a friend, coach or someone you trust who can take an objective view of your business. It can help you to explain the course structure and work out what you're missing.

What did you learn and from what?

Add your notes below or write in your journal or notebook . . .

```
┌─────────────────────────────────────────┐
│                                         │
│                                         │
│                                         │
│                                         │
└─────────────────────────────────────────┘
```

Additional documents

I always provide workbooks to accompany my courses. Writing things down doesn't just help you remember, it makes your mind more efficient by focusing on the important stuff.

As well as having a video course, it may be that you want to add some additional documents to help people learn. Some people learn visually, while others learn through listening or kinaesthetically (doing something like writing). Creating workbooks on Google Documents or PDFs enables your students to take notes as they learn. Creating guided meditations can help your students visualise or further embed their understanding. You may want to make a planner, assisting students to map out their time, or a journal to record their feelings. You know what digital products best suit your students and their needs.

You want to enhance the learning journey so that your students take action and learn from you! But you don't need to overcomplicate the process. From your audience research, you know your students and what they need! Some of the mega-big courses from major online influencers that I've bought have felt overwhelming for me when I'm busy. So, keep it simple.

You want people to take action, and you can do this in various ways relevant to your course content. For example:

- Could you add a swipe file (of written sales copy for them to use) if you're teaching about online business?
- Add a digital planner to help them stay on track if you're teaching about nutrition.
- Perhaps you could send a daily email or WhatsApp message for a set number of days.
- Offer a checklist of things they need to do.
- A cheat sheet (or beginner's guide) is always useful.

- An audio meditation can help people to overcome a particular block or gain clarity.
- Perhaps you could also add an audio version of your course so that they can listen while driving/running etc.?
- If you're teaching people to cook through a particular system of cooking or type of food, you could add a recipe book.
- Perhaps PDFs aren't your thing, but you want to create a Google document that people can write in. By simplifying what you're teaching, additional content can be beneficial for the student and provide key takeaways.

Are additional documents needed? What most appeals to you? What would you like to offer people who take your course?

Add your notes below or write in your journal or notebook . . .

Now take a break! Creating your course outline is full-on and chal-lenging! Allow yourself time to let the ideas percolate; pull all your ideas together and read through your notes.

Sometimes giving yourself a day or two to reassess if you're missing a vital area in the course is essential. Be as detached as possible, and think of yourself as your ideal client – what else do they need to know?

Is there anything else that you need to add?

Add your notes below or write in your journal or notebook . . .

Woohoo!

Creating the outline is the hard part, and now you've done that, it's time for a mini celebration! Do something to acknowledge you've overcome one of the most significant hurdles in course creation.

There's a lot of research to suggest that having small celebrations along the way and enjoying the journey means that you're more likely to finish the project. Celebrating the small wins helps you keep motivated and on track. It's been scientifically proven that you release the hormone dopamine, which is most associated with pleasure and motivation if you enjoy the journey. So, when you celebrate the process, you'll stimulate dopamine, which will tell your brain to keep going, then you're more likely to stay motivated and finish your course. So, get celebrating!

CHAPTER 5

Recording Your Course

In this chapter, I will look at recording your course; an overwhelming issue for many is confidence and the ability to create courses and make videos to market them. I'll share some tools and techniques to help with your confidence, then we will look at things to consider when creating your course.

But first, I want to remind you that the most important thing when it comes to creating your course is PASSION – that will carry you through your fears, challenges and blocks.

Passion Vs Confidence

I spent my Saturday afternoons as a teenager selling popcorn at the cinema. When I was lucky, I'd sneak in to watch the latest releases. My favourite of these featured a gorgeous, feisty female who kicked butt, gave the boys a run for their money and seemed to take on the world. Fast-forward a few years, and I'm standing on the red carpet in Paris on a freezing cold December day, my knees are knocking and my microphone is trembling. I'm waiting for this very same fearless female to come and talk to me.

In my head, I assume we're going to be best buddies and have this instant rapport. I'm dressed in a humungous puffer jacket and beanie, looking distinctly walrus-like. She's the A-lister promoting her movie, and I'm in the press pack covering the premiere for TV news. I'm living my dream life working as a journalist in Paris and renting a tiny apartment just off the Champs-Élysées. The icing on the cake is that this megastar and I are now officially best friends, just waiting to happen.

Diamonds are draped beautifully around her elegant neck, and she's dazzling in sparkling sequins and French couture. I've just watched her singing and dancing her heart out in this fabulous old-school musical, and I want to start bopping around the place. The swan-like creature glides down the red carpet towards me, shimmering in her Karl Lagerfeld frock.

I smile.

She stares vacantly.

I ask my question with puppy-dog enthusiasm . . .

She answers . . .

And then I realise: she's frosty, cold and monosyllabic.

From a distance she looks enticing . . . but up close, the ice queen hasn't melted.

More meh than megawatt.

She wasn't present.

She couldn't look me in the eye.

She was distracted . . .

And the honest truth is – she didn't CARE!

Our interview was so dull that it ended up on the cutting-room floor. I'm gutted.

'Cheer up,' says Oleg, my cameraman. 'She's just another human.'

And at that moment, I realised that we're all the same. The makeup, the fancy frocks and the publicists *don't* buy you confidence. Confidence isn't something you're born with, it's a skill that you choose to turn on, and it's something you work at.

In 20 years in TV and radio, I've picked up tricks from incredible camera crews about lighting, from A-lister makeup artists, and interviewed some of the most well-known faces on the planet. While the hair, the makeup and the fancy frocks help your performance on camera, the reality is that it's not about that *stuff* (although I'm not going to lie, having someone to do your face and hair does give you a shot of confidence in your armoury).

Amy Cuddy, in her TED Talk, was right; we can 'Fake it, till you make it.'

However, at the heart of it all is a passion and a mission that will carry you through even if you're lacking in confidence.

That red carpet moment in Paris was just a reminder that if we don't care about what we're creating, your audience will feel it.

Now, if we shimmy gracefully away from the red carpet to you and me in our spare rooms creating our courses, the same principles apply. When you are talking about what you love with enthusiasm and passion, this overrides everything. If you struggle with your confidence, I promise you can exercise your confidence muscles and choose to step into your power.

This is your opportunity to create something genuinely life-changing for so many. Do you want your lack of confidence and the endless stream of mind chatter to be the reason why you didn't go for it and create your passion project?

You get to choose what narrative you want to share with the world. What story do you want to tell your potential customers? A story that you're not very confident? Or the story of how you overcame your fears and blocks and went for it anyway, despite your limiting beliefs and experiences.

When first creating courses, many people have enormous blocks about being on camera, including myself. We worry that we're not good enough or attractive enough or clever enough.

But the reality is that YOU ARE ENOUGH.

Your generosity of spirit will reverberate through the screen when you share your joy and knowledge for something you love.

When you love what you do, and do what you love, it ripples through everything. Your audience wants to feel your passion and enthusiasm. They want you to show up in your PJs and talk from the heart.

They want reality. And nothing is more real than the real YOU!

You have superpowers to share with the world, and you are supremely talented and fabulous just as you are.

Yes, you are enough.

You are enough.

I want you to repeat this and repeat it often.

Stick Post-it notes around your house and repeat that you are enough. This is your time to get on video and start sharing your expertise with the world.

> I have a free guided visualisation to help you step into your confident self and overcome your limiting beliefs. Click on www.makemoneywhileyousleepbook.com/bonus to download.

Lack of confidence or fears about being visible no longer have to limit your dreams and ambitions. I'm on a mission to help you bust past them and create a course-based business that is truly life-changing for you and your family.

And before you start saying that it's easy for me because I've worked in TV for so many years, I'll just share something very personal.

When I discovered I was pregnant with my son, I was just back from reporting in Ukraine and covering the Russian incursions. I was taking my folic acid, dodging dodgy Russian rebels and assuming I would return to my career in TV news after I'd had my baby.

My son's birth changed everything. I had such a traumatic birth that I couldn't leave the house without peeing, and I had severe incontinence. Reporting into the office, let alone a conflict zone, was no longer an option.

So, I swapped red carpets and conflict zones for life as a stay-at-home mum.

I felt very stuck, very lonely and very lost.

I knew that I wanted to do something else, but I didn't feel very employable. Who wanted to employ a former journalist who constantly pees herself?

Looking back now, I wish I'd sought more help for my postnatal depression, but I didn't. The online world became my social life and my community.

I set up my business after my son was born, and my confidence was non-existent. When I first started being on camera, I was worried that I wasn't good enough or pretty enough. I'm an introvert and happy to hide away. I'm the person in the background who would rather do the washing up than have to mingle and do small talk at the party. Being on camera wasn't something that came naturally to me. I spent much of my twenties travelling around the world, and I have about two photos of me from this entire period; I wanted to hide and didn't want anyone to 'see me'.

I thought I was too old and 'past it'. I worried about my enormous eye bags, my skin and my rosacea. I was petrified about what all those old school friends I'd not spoken to in 20 years would think, or if old colleagues would laugh at me. I thought I was too fat, would stumble over my words, go red and people would laugh at me.

We hate seeing and hearing ourselves on video and realising that the version of ourselves on screen doesn't quite match up with the version of ourselves in our head. We worry about what others will say. What if they laugh at us, or it just triggers childhood memories about being 'visible'? We feel naked and exposed. In reality, the camera isn't scary; it's the judgement we fear from making ourselves vulnerable.

Maybe you don't like the sound of your voice, or you get

brain-freeze. We can ask ourselves, what if I don't look good enough? What if people think I'm stupid or incompetent? What if I get brain freeze? Or I sound dull or inauthentic? Or just ramble on?

Perhaps you worry about being visible and being trolled, or someone will laugh at you or write horrible comments. People can say awful things that they wouldn't dream of saying to people in person, but you know what? Most people, in general, are supportive and kind on the internet.

Perhaps you can relate? Our thoughts can play on a loop.

Our childhood memories often trigger our feelings of inadequacy; that time we were speaking in class and we were laughed at, or when we had to perform in the school play. Recognise those feelings and emotions. Explore why you're feeling triggered and delve into that memory.

John Bradshaw's book *Homecoming* was so liberating for me. It enabled me to explore my feelings of inadequacy, comfort my inner child and move forward. If you are struggling with the thought of being on video, spend some time understanding why you have these blocks and fears. (Check out www.makemoneywhileyousleepbook. com/bonus, where I have further exercises to help you.)

Having sold over 40,000 Confident on Camera courses, I know that many people struggle with being on video; I promise that those feelings of unworthiness and inadequacy are not unique. While being on video is stressful, the truth is that the more you practise, the less intimidating the experience becomes.

When we are starting something new, it can be utterly tricky and challenging. Psychologists Andy Ryan and Dawn Markova found that if we draw upon our previous positive experiences and build upon our existing neural pathways, then the new habit is easier to put into action. Think about what experiences can you draw upon to help with being on camera.

Did you train others in your previous role? Perhaps you loved acting in school plays or dancing when you were a kid? Or did you speak at a social occasion such as a wedding when you were scared but it actually went well? Write a list of your positive experiences that you can draw upon.

Ryan and Markova identified three zones where we operate: our comfort zone, stretch zone and panic zone.*

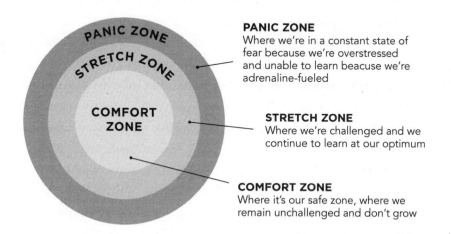

PANIC ZONE
Where we're in a constant state of fear because we're overstressed and unable to learn beacuse we're adrenaline-fueled

STRETCH ZONE
Where we're challenged and we continue to learn at our optimum

COMFORT ZONE
Where it's our safe zone, where we remain unchallenged and don't grow

The comfort zone is where we do things on autopilot without actually thinking about them. Our stretch zone is somewhere that's challenging; we can go on adventures and embrace new ideas. But when we step outside our limits of being comfortably challenged, this can be our panic zone, where we operate from a place of stress. The first time you do a Facebook live, you may feel as though you're doing the scariest thing ever, and you feel very stressed and deeply uncomfortable. But the more you go live, the easier it gets, and suddenly being on live video is just something you do and don't think about.

Confidence on camera isn't something you're born with; it's a skill that you learn. Confidence is a muscle that we can stretch; the

* The Comfort, Stretch, Panic model was first developed by Andy Ryan and Dawn Markova and written about in Andy Ryan's book, *This Year I Will*, first published by Broadway Books in 2006.

more we step out of our comfort zone and into our stretch zone, the easier it will be. The more you step into your stretch zone and consistently create video, the easier it will be to show up on screen.

So, how do you move from fear to happiness and feel more confident about being on video?

You can move to a happier place when you change what Tony Robbins calls your 'state'. Your state is your mental frame of mind, and you can easily change this state and change the way you feel. 'My son can go from tears and tantrums to smiles at the sight of his toy dinosaurs. If six-year-olds can do this, so can we, too.'*

Imagine you are busy working and feeling stressed and then a delivery arrives – a beautiful bouquet of flowers from a dear friend. You would quickly smile and feel so loved! Your state would immediately change. The trick is to recognise that you can choose to move from stress to ease – it's just about your conscious decision to reframe your thinking.

After years of feeling awkward, I finally understood that you just have to put one foot in front of the other and go for it. The more uncomfortable you are, that's okay ... We all feel uncomfortable, but that is not an excuse to hide. You just have to take action. And like any muscle, the more you use it, the more you step into your stretch zone, and the easier it will be.

I opened up my Facebook page, pressed 'go live' and began to talk.

My first video was a nervous splurge of thinking – I hated looking at myself, and I had no idea what to say. I managed to burble my way through it, and once I'd finished, I realised that I needed to up my game.

Being on camera is a bit like dating. In the beginning, you

---

* www.tonyrobbins.com/mind-meaning/how-to-reset-your-mind-and-mood

want to make an effort and look your best, but once you begin to feel more comfortable, you're happy to be more relaxed. Once you've been doing Facebook live for a while, you might not want to bother with doing your hair and make-up, but it will help you when you first start. Now I regularly create Instagram Reels in my PJs, but it's something I wouldn't have considered when I first started.

We're going to focus on the stuff that will help you get confident and make that video.

Why video?

When creating a course, video is one of the key ingredients to make your course pop. You can be on camera or use slides, and I recommend a mixture of the two.

You being on camera enables you to connect with your audience and build a relationship. It means that people are more likely to get to know you and like you, which as a business owner is critical because you want them to buy the course from you and KEEP on buying from you.

We have grown up forming relationships with people on screen; perhaps you spent your childhood hiding behind the sofa during *Doctor Who* or adoring the characters in *Friends*. The brain cannot tell the difference between the person on screen and in real life, so we form the same emotional connections with a character as we do with a real-life person.

And in the age of social media, this is even more pronounced. People think they 'know you' because they've watched your videos, and then they are more likely to buy from you.

I know that I'm talking a LOT about video, but the reality is that many business owners avoid being visible and sharing their story on screen – and they are missing out! Harnessing the power of video is a massive boost to your bottom line.

When I set up in business, I knew that using video to promote my business would be a significant asset in my marketing arsenal, despite how uncomfortable it made me feel, despite my background.

Gradually I began to find my people, and my audience grew. People liked what I had to say, and they clicked . . .

Facebook says you are five times more likely to sell when you use video. I applied my know-how and knowledge as a TV reporter, and the rest is history. And I know that I wouldn't be here today, writing this book or running a million-dollar business, if I didn't do it.

Going live!

If there's one thing you do today, go live.

There are so many benefits to going live and developing relation-ships with your audience. When you go live, it's a great way to prepare yourself for your video content for your course, and it can help you establish your audience. And I cannot stress enough how lighting, make-up and a little preparation will help you feel so much more confident when you first start.

Overcoming your fears around being visible is a crucial component to your success in business. Talking directly to your audience and building a rapport with them – live – can help you shift your products and services. Facebook and Instagram offer you a FREE way to meet thousands of your potential customers with the touch of a button and video. By not taking advantage of the cheapest – and most effective way of marketing your business – you are doing yourself and your dreams a disservice.

Your confidence on camera matters and can impact your bottom line. Are you willing to spend the time busting through those fears and nailing your confidence on camera? And when it comes to your course, the more confident you are using video on social media, the better your course content will be.

No more excuses – let's get visible!

How you feel about being on camera?

- What difference would it make to your life if you were confident on camera?
- What makes you feel uncomfortable and icky about being on camera? What triggers those feelings, and why?
- Now ask yourself how it would feel to overcome your fears? What is more painful? Do you want to stay locked in the past or leap forward and embrace a new way of working?
- Visualise yourself being on video and sharing your expertise. What feeling does it bring up for you?
- When you create your best-selling course, what impact will that have on your life?

Technical tips . . .

Being confident on camera isn't just about the thoughts in your head; it's also about sorting out the tech stuff and finding ways to help with your confidence.

Create your own mini-studio

When creating a course, it's worth thinking about making a mini-studio and building a brand identity.

You don't need a fancy space; just use a corner of a bedroom or even your garage to create your mini-studio. You could create a backdrop with a picture or some shelving. Consider adding plants or some ornaments, or maybe a desk.

Think about adding a splash of your brand colours or using a prop that will help you create an image for your course.

Dating coach Debra Thorpe converted her garage into a mini-studio to film her courses. When neonatal hospital worker Janet Sides was laid off, she turned her parents' basement into a mini-studio to record her 'Shop Your Wardrobe' course.

What equipment do you need?

You can record your course using a more sophisticated camera called a DSLR, but with the advances in technology, your smart-phone is easier to use, and the picture quality is pretty much the same. Remember, one of George Clooney's favourite director's, Steven Soderbergh, created a Hollywood movie using just an iPhone. The newer the smartphone, the better the quality of lens. Don't forget, you may need to increase your storage on your phone.

Some people are more comfortable talking to a laptop. They are used to doing Zoom calls, so this is just a natural next step. You can drastically improve the quality of your video and how you look by buying a webcam. Buying a webcam makes you look ten years younger and seems to smooth over those wrinkles and spots. If there were a way to walk around with a ring light and a webcam over my head constantly, I'd be signing up for that service!

Here are the basics of what to think about, or you can go to https://makemoneywhileyousleepbook.com/bonus to access my Video Guide.

If you're going to use a laptop, I recommend getting a Logitech camera, which is incredibly flattering and honestly makes you look younger and smooths out your wrinkles. If only life could be viewed through a Logitech camera!

DO YOU NEED LIGHTS?

Lighting makes a tremendous difference to video quality. Natural light, with the light source behind you, is wonderful if you have it, but if you are anything like me living in a little country cottage with tiny windows or are trying to film on a grey December day, you need all the help you can get. A ring light or a soft box can greatly improve your video quality and is much kinder to the skin (and seriously makes you look younger!).

This lighting is a good investment all round as it can also be used for Zoom calls to make you look lighter, brighter and generally just better on video.

HOW DO YOU SOUND?

Using the microphone on an iPhone is absolutely fine for a Facebook live, but if you're going to create a course and sell it, you want to ensure there is good audio quality.

Think about getting a Blue Yeti microphone if you are using your laptop and a Rode SmartLav for your mobile phone.

Are you DIY or are you going to hire someone?

If you're bootstrapping, you want to keep it simple and learn the basics of video editing. It is complex and time-consuming – sometimes I just want to hurl my laptop out the window. If you're an established business, or you can afford it, definitely look to hire someone to do your editing.

Worst case, enlist a techie friend/partner/child to help you, it will make life much easier!

What to talk about . . .

Before you create your course content, practise going live with your audience on social media. The more you talk about your content, the more it will flow (and you're promoting the course at the same time!).

When we are comfortable talking about our subject, your performance is better, and it's more interesting for the viewer. You want to take the content out of your head and into your heart so that you speak with passion.

I strongly recommend practising your content on social media so you can talk with ease in your course content. Knowing what to talk about can stop some people from actually creating videos. You may worry about brain-freeze, or perhaps you don't feel 'expert' enough or worry that people won't understand your accent.

I hear these fears a lot from clients, but the truth is that you can overcome these issues.

If you're going on video for the first time, you are stepping out of your comfort zone and into your panic zone. So, before you press that button, prepare what you want to say. It could be you spent 20 minutes scribbling down some ideas for a blog post or email to your list, you could just spend five minutes creating some bullet points.

Either way, you are giving yourself space and time to think about what you want to say. Think about how you can share your experience and knowledge.

If you're feeling nervous about being on video, listen to some music and have a dance before you go live. Dancing releases the stress hormone cortisol.

Practise talking into the camera on your phone. Remember to speak to the lens and not the screen. Perhaps, in the beginning, it will help to put a Post-it note over the screen to hide your face so you don't feel distracted.

When you are doing social media videos, very often you might be talking to yourself. Focus on talking to one person and building a rapport with them. What can you 'give'? What value and insight?

I hate my voice

A lot of clients come to me and say that they hate their voice. It might be that you don't like your accent or the tone of your voice.

I want to tell you a secret . . .

NO ONE – and I mean NO ONE – likes the sound of their own voice, and it has been scientifically proven that we don't sound like the voice in our heads. Scientists have been able to verify that the internal sound that 'we' the speaker hears is different to the sound our audience hears.

When we hear our voice as we talk, we hear the sound carried to our ears through our bones and the airwaves. When we listen to the sound in a recording, it is missing the depth of the low, rich frequencies of sound carried through our bones.

When you hear a recording, you hear your voice without these frequencies, so there's a disconnect. It sounds higher and different, and because it doesn't sound as we expect it to, we, therefore, don't like it.

I remember cringing at my voice when I first heard it, but over the years, I've got used to it. I can't say I like it, but you do get used to it.

Remember, we are much more critical about ourselves than others are.

SQUEAKY VOICE? WHY BREATHING MATTERS

Wish you could stop sounding high-pitched at the end of a sentence? There's a straightforward fix: it's what we do 24/7 without even noticing.

The trouble is that most of us forget to breathe a lot of the time and we shallow-breathe; consequently, we are often depleted of oxygen. As you know, we need oxygen to live, and when we breathe deeply down to our diaphragm (down to our imaginary bra strap), we are utilising our lungs fully, and so our body is getting all the oxygen we need.

When you breathe deeply, you stay calm and focused. It will also help you to sound as though you have more authority. When you breathe deeply, you get enough oxygen to your lungs, enabling you to speak for a whole sentence. When you're starved of oxygen, you panic and operate from your 'caveman' brain, which is your limbic brain. When you're breathing correctly, you are using your cortex, and this is your thinking brain. Operate from here, and you'll be more effective in what you have to say, and you're less likely to get brain freeze.

When you panic, your voice rises. When you stay calm and have a lung full of oxygen, you speak more slowly and the squeak goes away.

Practise mindful breathing before you go live to be calm and look as though you're in control. People will better respond to you if you're relaxed and focused. It will also help your voice to carry more gravitas and authority. If you want to think clearly and sound better on camera, then remember to breathe.

Caroline Goyder, author of *Find Your Voice* and *Gravitas* shares her wisdom:
There's a real secret that will help you ace it on camera vocally. You know the lovely, relaxed conversational style that great presenters have, warm resonant relaxed? The trick is to get out of your head – worrying about how good/bad you are, thinking about what you just said, listening to your own voice, and instead to get your attention into the body – where your voice starts

from. Your voice is exhaled air and it starts in the centre of the body, streaming out of the lungs, powered by the muscles in the rib cage and the diaphragm. Instead of hearing your voice in your head – feel it in your body, When you pay attention to the feeling in the source, not the sound you make, you show up with the embodied presence that is so compelling on camera.

You divert your attention from your head, your throat and into the centre of your body. You then become less of a talking head and start to take on the embodied presence that is so key to finding your voice.

One thing that helps me is to imagine that you are putting your 'brain in your belly'. Or if you prefer to be more like the Chinese with their idea of heart–mind, you might choose to centre your awareness in your heart. All that matters is that your awareness is in your body rather than high up in the head. It will allow you to speak with more flow and freedom and ease, to find that easy present you who shines on camera.

It's all there waiting for you to find it!

If you're speaking a second language on video – bravo to you! As in real life, people will love you for being you, and your people will still fall in love with you regardless of your worries about your accent.

When you're nervous, it may take you longer to process your thoughts. Your two seconds may seem like a lifetime, but to the viewer, it's just a pause.

Offer value and people will listen. You have a great deal to share with the world. It is your time to impact the world.

Ensure that you have some bullet points written so that you've got that reminder if you get brain freeze and panic.

Using a teleprompter

If you worry about brain freeze or waffling and meandering off track when recording your videos, it could be worth checking out the teleprompter apps on your smartphone. You can write a script and use your phone as a teleprompter. The words will flow across the screen at a pace that suits you, and it can help you create informative and concise content.

One of the downsides to a teleprompter is that you lose the spontaneity of just talking, and you can look robotic, so use it sparingly. People want to see YOU, and watching a robot isn't an entertaining experience. Using a teleprompter does take practice, so don't expect to get it right in the first take; just think how newsreaders have spent years honing their craft.

Note: I occasionally use teleprompters for my course content, but I use them far more for my sales videos to sell my courses because I get nervous and waffle around the subject.

Body language on camera

Ever heard the phrase . . . 'It's not what you say, it's how you say it'? Well, it's true, and especially on video.

In real life, people judge people in the first seven seconds of meeting them based on their body language – their smile, eye contact, tone of voice and handshake. On video, people make decisions within the first three seconds.

People are seeking instant social media gratification and your body language matters. Look at the lens (the tiny dot on your phone) and not the screen when you talk. Smile at the viewer, have your shoulders back and be open in your posture.

Professor Albert Mehrabian carried out some research in 1971 that found that only 7 per cent of communication is verbal. That means that the words are only a tiny fraction of what we hear, and non-verbal communication – our **BODY LANGUAGE** – is much more critical. He found that 93 per cent of communication is all about our tone of voice and body language.*

How we communicate:

- 7%: Words (what's said)
- 38%: Tone of voice (how we say the words)
- 55%: Body language

Think about how you watch videos on social media. Do you watch on silent or with the sound on? Look at the videos that go viral; are they a sequence of photos with text, or is the text written throughout the video?

More people are watching video on mute than ever: 95 per cent of videos on Facebook are seen on silent, and with the growth of Reels on Instagram and TikTok, remember it's the captions that count. Using captions on your videos will encourage people to watch your videos. I suggest using Otter.ai or Rev. com for captions.

Get framed . . .

Think about the way you frame yourself in your videos. Note how you might see on TV news an expert talking on Zoom but their head is cut off the shot or they are bobbing about on an enormous screen.

Camera operators use the rule of thirds, where you imagine two

* Albert Mehrabian Nonverbal communication. Piscataway, NJ, Aldine Transaction, 1972.

horizontal lines dividing the screen into thirds. Your head and a little of your body want to be in the middle of the shot and occupy two-thirds of the screen.

Your mindset

Being on the entrepreneurial journey is a rollercoaster of emotions and feelings. When things don't go our way, we must dig deep with our drive and resilience to keep going.

When I first did a Facebook live, I assumed that my old colleagues in television would laugh at me for doing this. I realised I have to push those thoughts aside and focus on my ideal client and what they need to hear from me. Several years on, I find some of them are emailing me for advice on how to do something similar. So yes, it's nerve-wracking the first time you go live, but you know what, it's okay, and it gets better each time you do it.

I don't love being the centre of attention, but I've learned to enjoy sharing my story and connecting one to one with people. Focus on what you can give others, rather than feeling that you have to *'show off'* on camera.

If you're worried that your friends or family will laugh, or your work colleagues will see . . . Well, yes, they might do, but you might be surprised. While some may be a little jealous that you're doing something you've always wanted to do, most will admire your gumption and guts.

Once you've done your video, give yourself some praise! Celebrate this giant leap forward in your visibility. Be careful not to over-analyse and over-criticise yourself. The more authentic and genuine, the better the video! Remember, we all make mistakes; that's part of the realness of it all.

The worries about being laughed at don't go away, but you can choose to put those thoughts to one side and focus on your dreams, mission and tribe!

When I first started in business, I posted my first ever blog post in a Facebook group for mothers, and some women wrote some nasty comments about it. I had an hour or two of being upset, but I realised that they weren't worth my energy or tears. As Taylor Swift says, the haters are always going to hate – let them deal with their stuff and you focus on being you and being brilliant. Don't let your dreams be trampled on by people that don't even matter!

Stay in your lane. Focus on yourself.

Become better.

Rise above.

Am I good enough?

Sometimes we can have self-doubts that we don't know enough, we're not good enough, or we question, 'Who am I to start teaching this topic?'

The critical thing to focus on is 'where you are, right now'. If you are five steps ahead of a beginner, this can be incredibly useful to help people when they're first learning a new skill. But sometimes the coaches who are much more immersed in an area of study aren't necessarily best placed to help those just starting.

You know how Oprah always talks about those 'aha' moments? Well, that's precisely what you're trying to achieve in your content. You want your students to have lightbulb moments where they are pinging with ideas and understand what you're trying to convey. Ensuring they get it means looking at both your expertise and then sharing your knowledge in a way that works for their learning style.

Ask yourself . . .

- What makes you the perfect person to teach your course?
- Write down a list of your accomplishments and knowledge. If you're struggling with this one, ask a friend or loved one to help you. Sometimes it's hard to see our brilliance because it's just our knowledge and we assume that others know what we know.
- What assumptions are you making about other people's knowledge? What level of expertise does your ideal client have in your subject area?

My course-creation recording process

I plan out my content on Word documents or Google Docs and then use this as a basis for workbooks. From this, I plan my videos and the content. I make bullet points for the videos where I'm on screen, including all the key points I want to discuss. If it's very technical, I will use a teleprompter to help me stay on track, but I do this on very few occasions because it's a little more stilted than just sharing my information on the screen.

When I'm talking over slides I'll use Google Docs to create the content for slide decks and then create the slides. I then run through the slides and get someone to check them so there are no typos and it makes sense.

And then I record.

Remember, you can always edit and add in extra content, but it's MUCH harder to add in content after you've recorded. Recording is the LAST THING that I do so that I can always avoid hiccups and screwups. If you don't pre-plan, the editing of your course will be much harder!

Tips for recording:

- Don't overteach in each lesson. Be prepared to prune your content.
- Keep your videos succinct, 5–10 minutes ideally. Don't stress if something overruns.
- The critical thing to remember is . . . Keep it simple!

Your video content

Think about your audience and how they learn – and that means considering visual, audio and kinaesthetic learning styles. Maybe you want to offer an audio version of your course so students can listen while on the move. Remember that people who are hearing- impaired may struggle to listen to the audio and may prefer to download the slides or have captions on the screen (from Rev.com or Otter.ai).

When it comes to recording videos, I record an introductory section to introduce myself and the course. I keep it short. This introduction could be the ONLY time the audience sees you if you're not particularly comfortable on video, and you could use slides for the rest of the training.

Alternatively, you could record an introductory video for about one minute for every section, then combine this together with the slide training content. That way, you can just talk about the content freely for one minute and avoid waffling, but people still see you on screen and then you go into the more focused video content on slides.

Reasons to use slides:

- Can help you keep on track with delivering your great content (and stop you meandering off topic and waffling on).

- You can jam-pack your slides with lots of data, facts and numbers that your audience can easily refer back to.
- To boost your own confidence levels about being front of camera!

You can create your slides on PowerPoint, Google Keynote or Canva. Canva is my favourite tool on the web and is a magical piece of software. You can create presentations, social media graphics, edit and record videos and it is super easy to use. If you're new to the entrepreneurial world, I highly recommend learning Canva and using it to create your slide decks and workbooks.

Recording your content

I record my introduction and the elements where I'm on screen using my DSLR camera. You could also use your smartphone camera or record on your laptop using software such as Camtasia (for Windows) or Quicktime on a Mac.

I then edit using Final Cut Pro, but you can also use iMovie if you are a Mac user, Adobe Premiere or Camtasia if you are a Windows user.

If you are just recording slides, you can also record your screen using Canva, Camtasia, Screenflow (for Macs) or Zoom. If you want to keep it really simple, you can just use Zoom! There are a host of alternative ways to record and edit your content, and technology is ever-changing. The best thing I can say is, again, keep it simple.

I'm a Mac user, so I use Screenflow to record my desktop and record the Canva slides. Then I add this video to the back of the video of 'me' on screen.

Video editing can be very time consuming, so if you can afford to outsource it, do! Sometimes, it is more efficient to outsource the video editing, enabling you to focus on the other parts of the business, including bringing in revenue!

Guided meditations

If you are a coach helping people with their mindset and you want to help your students change their beliefs, a guided visualisation or meditation can be a handy addition to your course.

You can create a script for your guided meditation and record this script on Zoom or using software such as iMovie, Screenflow or Camtasia. You could even use voice memos on your iPhone. You can then edit this audio to remove the umms, ahhs and any heavy breathing, and from there, you can add a piece of relaxing music under the audio track. I like the royalty-free guided meditation tracks that you can buy at EnlightenedAudio.com or AudioJungle. net.

(If you would like to hear one of my guided visualisations to help you with your blocks in course creation, go to www.makemoneywhi- leyousleepbook.com/bonus)

Course creation checklist

Things to consider when creating your course:

- Create one introductory video introducing the course content with you on-screen.
- Include six to eight training videos with the content (these can be slides or a mix of you on-screen with slides too).
- Write out the content for the slides/scripts and PDFs BEFORE you record.
- Be prepared to prune! Less is more: be succinct and try to avoid the waffle.
- Plan out what you want to say in a Word document or Google Doc, then condense this into slides with bullet points. You could

use the longer version of the content for your accompanying PDF workbooks.

- How do you want to record your course? Do you want to be on camera or just use slides?
- Do you want to include workbooks?
- Do you want to include a copy of the slides?
- Would a guided meditation help your audience?

CHAPTER 6

Creating and Hosting Your Course

When I first wanted to create a course, choosing the platform was such an agonising decision. At the time, I was trying to juggle building my course while my toddler son was in childcare for three mornings a week. I knew that I didn't have the time for a technically tricky platform, so I had to go super easy . . .

The trouble was that my business was still fledgling and barely making any money, so I couldn't afford the *'easy and pretty'* version. Instead, I inched ever closer to the *'functional but ugly'* platform. But procrastination stopped me in my tracks for weeks – the paralysing decision of choosing a platform.

Choosing a course-hosting platform is a little like standing in your favourite clothing store and trying to decide what to buy with your budget. Are you a Primark or Prada person? With course software, there is so much choice, and the reality is that it can feel a little bamboozling. And like fashion, the software platforms are constantly updating and changing.

My plan for this chapter is to be your personal shopper, to let you sample a few options and give you an overview of what you should buy.

When you're first starting as an entrepreneur, money and cashflow matters, and when I started out I couldn't afford much of anything. As my business grew, though, so did my options, so I will give you options in different price ranges to see what works for you.

When you choose a home for your videos and course materials, you want to select the best-aligned platform for your business and the system you're creating and, most importantly, how technical you are. If you're not technical, you want a super-simple platform that can enable you to do much of the work without needing a PhD in software, but if you're a little more tech-savvy, the pool of choices broadens for you.

Many of the people I work with are looking to use courses to be an additional income stream for their business or create additional retirement funds. And, just like me, they aren't always the most technically adept. The good news is that regardless of technical background or experience, this is entirely possible for you!

The e-course industry is expected to be worth $3.25 billion by 2025. New platforms and course-creation models are developing all the time, so while giving you a brief overview of some of the software, I strongly recommend that you do some additional research and test them for yourself! I will provide a more updated review at: www.makemoneywhileyousleepbook.com/bonus

Don't just take my word for it, have a play and see what you think will work for you and if you like the software. Many companies have ways to trial the software, so just like buying a new car, go for a test drive.

Also give consideration to the following options:

- Ask your entrepreneurial friends.
- Gather opinions in Facebook groups (beware of people plastering their latest affiliate link suggesting a new product).
- Asking our trusty friend Google is a great starting point if you want to explore the latest options.

One word of caution, sometimes the newer platforms look whizzy but may still have some significant bugs in the system because they haven't been thoroughly tested. Tiptoe gingerly into a platform that is offering lifetime access for a minuscule amount. You don't want your business to be the beta tester for their course platform.

Remember that you can always move course-creation platforms, so you can start small and then move to a more sophisticated and stylish platform when your business is more established, and you have funding from other income streams.

I would strongly recommend going with a hosted platform if you are just setting up your business by yourself. When you don't have a large tech team and try to get various plugins to talk to each other, it can be very frustrating, and there is no helpdesk that you can ring. I recommend all my clients go with a course-hosting platform.

Before we dive into the course platforms, I want you to think about yourself and your business.

What's going on in your business?

What income is your business generating? What are your current monthly outgoings?

Can you afford to pay for a course platform? As a small business owner, you want to be able to afford to pay for the course platform, again and again, every month. So choose a platform that you know your business can afford.

How technical are you? If you're not techie, can you afford to outsource the tech stuff? Bear in mind that you can't always get tech headaches instantly fixed when you outsource and may have to wait several days, so the more you can do, the better it is for you and your business.

As we explore all the course hosting options, look at each of the platforms discussed and ask these questions:

- Which platform is best for your business?
- Which platform best suits your budget?
- How technical are you? Can you afford to outsource it?
- Think about how customers will consume your content – will it be on a mobile or a desktop?
- Will you offer audio versions of your course?
- Or copies of the slide decks you create?
- Perhaps you need to include subtitles or guided visualisations?

Remember, not every content type will suit your course, so focus on the areas that will work best for your audience and help them actually to FINISH the course!

Best budget platform

Teachable

You can use the free version of Teachable. When I created my first course, I started on Teachable – and it was free – yay! However, the free version was for the first ten students, so I sold it to more students and paid from the word go once I launched. Luckily the upgraded version was affordable each month.

Benefits:
It's easy. You can upload and build your own course quickly and start with a free version to see if you like it; this is a comforting place to start when you're first making your course if you're not particularly technical, but want to retain control of your course and how you market it.

Downsides:

It is rather clunky, and the user interface is very unattractive. The sales pages are pretty basic, too. By the time I had finished using Teachable, I was desperate for a more branded appeal with more functionality and options in the sales pages.

Best all-rounder

Kajabi

Kajabi is the Mercedes-Benz of course-hosting platforms; the engine purrs and looks sleek. It has options to use various themes so you can create a more individualised site for yourself. It's easy to add graphics and turn the site into a branded experience that looks like your business.

Kajabi is genuinely an all-in-one option so that you can host your website on the platform, house your emails and build your sales pages and marketing. Many smaller entrepreneurs just use Kajabi for everything and have an all-singing, all-dancing integrated system.

I love and use Kajabi, but I still have my website elsewhere and don't use all the functionality. I have been offered payment to move my courses from Kajabi to another course provider – I declined the offer, and that's how much I enjoy using the platform.

Benefits:

Kajabi is sleek, sexy, easy to use. I love that I can easily create courses and web pages myself without needing to wait for a techie person to sort something out, and it also has a swift and responsive helpdesk.

Downsides:

It's more expensive than some platforms, which was the major stumbling block for me initially.

Business coach Gemma Went joined Kajabi as a founding member. She joined because she was attracted to the vision of the company and its ethos.

'I love the simplicity and ease of the platform. I host all of my courses and membership, and many of my clients also use the platform.

I can easily package up my training so that it is an "experience" rather than just sending someone to a replay for a training on YouTube and Vimeo. It's so quick and straightforward to create a product.

Kajabi also houses my membership, Online Business Accelerator, which has a lot of information and content, but Kajabi doesn't make it overwhelming. You can also buy some customisable templates to use on Kajabi so that your course can look a little different.

I have all of my funnels and sales pages on Kajabi. Once I've created a sales page, I can just easily duplicate it for other programmes, and I can do that in about an hour.

You can also track the conversion rates in an opt-in page so that you know what your audience is doing and the customer journey.'

Best functionality

Kartra

Kartra is a similar price point to Kajabi, and while Kajabi is all about courses, Kartra is all about the sales page and email and has course functionality.

The sales pages are truly excellent, and the email system gives you the functionality of a standalone email system. And these things matter when you are selling at scale. Kartra is the only place I would ever consider moving my course platform to.

I love how you can have the order pages in different currencies, and PayPal and Stripe are integrated for each page.

Benefits:
The email systems and sales pages are brilliant and some of the best on the market. You can create an integrated product that is easy to manage regardless of your technical prowess.

Downsides:
The course functionality isn't quite as good as Kajabi's. Pricing is similar to Kajabi, so it is on the higher side, which is tricky when you're first starting.

Kartra case study: Sheryl Jefferson, Facebook ads expert
Before Kartra, I always found it difficult to keep up with using loads of different platforms to build by funnels and zap them all together. If you edited one piece of your funnel, you had to log in and change the other bits, which took too much time and became confusing.

With Kartra, I love that it's an all-in-one system; landing page, emails, payment system, memberships, etc. All I need to do is log into one place, and I have it all at my fingertips. It's also totally customisable, which is important to me as I don't want people looking at it and thinking it's one of those annoying XYZ funnels!

It's by far the most stable platform I use in my business. And also all the reporting is in one place, which is AMAZING!

MemberVault™

You can use MemberVault™ on your WordPress site to host your courses, freebies and membership site content. One of the criticisms of many course creation platforms is that you can lose touch with your students, and it is difficult to retain their interest in completing the course. There is a free version for up to 100 students, so it is affordable when you start.

MemberVault™ has introduced gamification to encourage students to stay on track, and gives you a real insight into how your audience is engaging with your content. The company has created a system of sales that enables you to tap into further revenue from your existing students, so if you are not a fan of doing a big launch for specific products, this may work for you.

Benefits:
MemberVault™ is all about using gamification at its core to market to your existing audience. This means that you can create conversations with your students and sell naturally to them. It helps you identify your 'hot leads', which just is not possible on other platforms currently.

The free version for 100 students includes ALL the features! And this means you can use this when you start, and it grows with you.

The community of users who use MemberVault™ is very supportive and love their product, and they promote the service to others.

Downsides:
There isn't a help desk that you can immediately call on to support you when you're first starting out and doing everything yourself (unlike some of the other course hosting platforms) so this may be off-putting to some.

Some may say that the look and feel isn't necessarily as slick as some of the other platforms.

MemberVault™ Case Study: **Vicky Etherington**, website designer

It took a while before I settled on a platform to deliver my courses. I tried out Thinkific, Teachable, LearnDash and MemberPress. They were great, but each one had some limitations which I found frustrating. Then I stumbled across MemberVault™. And it was everything I hoped for.

Their free plan gives you access to all the features for up to 100 subscribers, so I used it for my next free Facebook challenge to deliver all the content and replays, and I was hooked.

During the challenge, I was able to see who was actively consuming the content, reward them accordingly (through the gamification features), and follow up directly with those people who were also checking out other products in my MemberVault™ (through their insights of warm and hot leads).

MemberVault™ have worked hard to create a platform that not only delivers your courses, but which also gives your entire portfolio visibility. They refer to this as a binge-worthy marketplace. And the thing that I love about it all is that it feels like a more intimate and personal environment than some of the other platforms, and there are constant prompts to help you improve the experience for you and your users.

One of the features that clinched it for me and made me realise that MV was my forever platform is the one-click link feature (you can provide a unique log in link dynamically to each user which does away with the need for a username and password), and the fact that it integrates fabulously with my checkout cart and my email service provider. It also has an amazing community and support team who almost feel like family.

It is pretty much an all-in-one course/membership platform as it can deliver your courses, freebies, memberships and

> resources, and can take payments. It doesn't host your videos, but you're able to embed those from other platforms such as YouTube, Loom or Vimeo. And it doesn't send your emails, but the integrations are really slick.
>
> It only took me about a month to realise that I wouldn't be moving platforms again and I bought into their lifetime plan. And I'm constantly amazed by the support, the development of the platform and how much I love using it.

Phew! That's the whistle-stop tour of some of the course-creation platforms, but many other options are available. Check out my comparison guide to help you choose a platform that best suits you: www.makemoneywhileyousleepbook.com/bonus.

Have a trial of a few platforms and see what you think. Go and ask your trusty friend Google and talk to other entrepreneurs – see what they like and why.

But don't spend hours on the research; I know how this can be very confusing and bamboozling, and you can spend hours procrastinating and not making a decision. Give yourself a time limit to do the research, then make a decision.

Now we're going to look at other areas you need to consider when deciding how to host your course.

Drip your content?

How do you want to share your content with your students? Do you want them to be able to access a whole chunk of content in one go or would you rather drip-feed the content each week?

The benefit of releasing the content each week is that the students may feel less overwhelmed and take action each week. They can also think that they're getting more support from you.

If you drip the content, it means that you're going to be around to answer questions and be on hand for support. This can work well and increases customer buy-in, and they'll feel that they're getting value for money, but you may not want to do this for a £19 course.

Some students learn differently and like to 'binge-watch' your content like Netflix, and they find it annoying if it's not available because they want the content immediately!

You have to decide what works best for you and your students.

How are you going to support your students in the course?

One of the biggest challenges for course creators is getting students to actually complete the course. You've successfully sold the course, so why should you care whether they do it or not?

First of all, you want students to actually feel the benefits and experience the transformation in your course! You also want to receive glowing testimonials from those who have completed the course and experienced the transformation that your course delivers; having such social proof is really powerful and can go a long way to convince potential purchasers to click that buy button.

Finally, you want students to be able to succeed so that they are more likely to buy additional courses and services. Think about how you're going to support your students with strategies to help them take action and COMPLETE the course, then they are more likely to buy!!

Adding live elements like coaching and live interactions can enhance the experience, but you may not want to include this if it's a low-cost course.

So, consider what's the price point that you want for your course? Does it justify putting your time into working in a group or a one-to-one setting with them?

Create a Facebook group for students

You could consider a Facebook group as a way to build community and enable your students to get further connections and support from you through live Q&A sessions, Facebook live videos and additional engagement. It's also an excellent place for you to further build your relationships with your students and sell to them.

It does need managing and you need to consistently create content. You could set a limit for the time the group is open, though.

Facebook groups can also be a great way to sell additional products and services, and I will talk about this further in a later chapter.

One-to-one coaching for your course students

Offering one-to-one coaching as part of your course is a fantastic gift that you can provide to your students. Having one-to-one support helps with mindset, strategy and particular challenges that students may be facing to ensure they FINISH! Research shows that the optimum way to learn is to include one-on-one support and a group environment where you can get additional peer support. Being in the group gives you extra accountability and makes it fun.

One-to-one services are time-consuming, so you only want to offer this when the results justify your time (e.g. a £9 course probably isn't the place to provide this). You want to make sure that your course is costed to include your time. What is one hour of your time worth? Think big! Do you want to be on a day rate for the rest of your life, especially as your business grows?

Group coaching calls

Group coaching calls can work well with your course offering, and you can do this on a Zoom call or in a Facebook live. A live call enables people to ask questions and is a more personalised response without offering one-to-one calls.

Offering group coaching is time-consuming, but your results are likely better, and it is an excellent way to support your students. Live calls only work for 'high ticket' courses where you have factored this into your pricing. Make sure that the hands-on live call support is talked about and promoted during your launch cycle.

What digital support solutions are you providing?

Your students need accountability and support to keep going and complete your course. There are a variety of ways that you can do this and automate some of the processes.

COURSE COMMENTS
You can enable students to comment on each module on the course platform and interact with them as they progress.

EMAILS
Email campaigns to support and motivate your students are fundamental. Some emails may be specifically written for each module of the course, but you can also set up triggers with your funnels to ensure that they receive an email cheering them on or reminding them to take action.

ACCOUNTABILITY FOR YOUR STUDENTS

You could create accountability partners or buddy support groups to help each of them finish the course. When I do this in my Facebook group challenges it works well, and people build amazing friendships and connections. However, it does need some managing when some students aren't as committed as their partners.

Do you want to provide them with easy access to you through voice tools?

WHATSAPP

Owned by Facebook, this enables you to communicate with students one-to-one on a global basis via voice notes and messages. You can also create group chats. In the coming years, this will be a significant push for Facebook.

VOXER

Voxer is a fabulous tool to send voice messages en masse to up to 500 people and send motivational, supportive messages. The open rate is much higher than email, for example.

SLACK

Slack is a platform to communicate with a team or a group; it enables you to quickly find messages (rather than Facebook, where the algorithm can be messy). You can also share resources, announcements and links to your materials.

Which ways to communicate with your students works best for you?

 One-to-one coaching
☐ Group coaching

- [ ] Events and masterminds
- [ ] course comments
- [ ] emails
- [ ] Accountability buddies through WhatsApp
- [ ] Voxer
- [ ] Slack

Finally, we will wrap up this chapter with a checklist to see if you have all the necessary elements in your course. You can get a PDF version of the following list if you go to www.makemoneywhileyou-sleepbook.com/bonus.

Course inventory checklist

Here are some ideas for course assets to include. Don't worry; you don't need to include everything! If this is your first course, be selective to avoid overwhelm.

- [ ] PDF workbooks for worksheets, checklists and swipe files.
- [ ] Slide decks of your training video presentations.
- [ ] Transcripts of your training videos.
- [ ] Welcome video to join the programme.
- [ ] Celebration video completing the programme.
- [ ] Guided tour of the course.
- [ ] Course wrap-up videos.
- [ ] Intro videos to introduce each module.
- [ ] Audio files of your videos.

What else do you need for your course?

- ☐ Course image thumbnail.
- ☐ Thumbnails for each video lesson.
- ☐ Module image thumbnails.
- ☐ Sidebar image for Facebook group (or podcast/YouTube channel).
- ☐ Logo design.
- ☐ PDF designs (you could use Canva).
- ☐ Slide deck presentation designs
- ☐ Facebook banner image design (if you're planning to have a Facebook group).

You can create a list of all the PDFs, videos, thumbnails, audio files, transcripts and other content you may want to include in your course.

> **Important note**: you don't need to include every type of content mentioned, but it will help if you create ONE place in which you can manage all the content you need to avoid it being a chaotic mess (from someone who's been there!).

CHAPTER 7

Why Building Your Audience Matters

When I first started out in the online world, I wasn't sure that anyone wanted to listen to what I had to say. Getting to 100 people following my Instagram or subscribing on YouTube seemed such a momentous occasion.

Having followers and subscribers does not equal profits, but building your audience can help you to have authority, credibility and customers in your niche. However, remember that hard, cold truth of the online world: 98 per cent of people won't buy from you. Fact!

That shocker of a stat is the reason why if you want to sell online, you need to grow your audience. The more social media scrollers know about you, the more likely you are to sell your courses and digital products to those people.

Yes, of course, some entrepreneurs sell to more than 2 per cent of their audience, and there are always exceptions and pent-up demand for some products, but on average, 2 per cent of your audience is the figure that will buy from you.

Gulp.

But selling online isn't just about bums on seats staring at your sales page and being willing to press 'click'. There's also something more fundamental at play that is often missed. You need to have the right audience.

A targeted audience of raving fans is vital. I've worked with people who had tiny audiences and sold thousands, and I've worked with people who had a super-large audience and sold very few. Unless you are targeted in who you're talking to, your message doesn't land.

So that's why researching who your audience is and talking to your ideal client are key. The more specific you can be in your messaging, the easier it is to build a connection with your ideal customer and the more likely they will buy from you.

So how on earth can you grow your audience in the online world right now?

Back in 2007, when my friend Jennifer, from Healthy Bliss, added hundreds of thousands to her Twitter following, social media was so new then. I remember sitting in her beach house in Thailand and watching in awe as she rode the wave of social media and sold while she slept.

I almost made the leap and went all-in on the new way of working. I quit my job in Bangkok as a journalist and wanted to do what Jen did, and live more, work less. So I went to India to figure it all out. But my bosses in TV news asked me to move to China and report from there.

While I was trying to find myself in India, I stumbled into an ashram hoping for my *Eat Pray Love* moment and met a faith healer called Amma. She meditated on it and then gave me a scrap of paper that said: 'Go to Beijing.' I told my boss, and he said, 'See? Even God wants you in Beijing.'

So I went. China was opening up to the world, the Olympics was happening, and it was a jaw-dropping, awe-inspiring time to be in the country. But my window into the world of social media shrank, and I stayed small. I missed that unique opportunity to ride the wave.

Fast-forward a few years, and I was still working in China and bashing out messages on my BlackBerry to my bosses in New York and London. My colleague – the amazingly talented photographer David Guttenfelder – had an iPhone and would snap photos on it while he was behind the iron curtain in North Korea and share them on Instagram. Instagram followers loved his up-close and personal shots from the repressive state and the photos took off on the visually-led social media site. Fast-forward a few years, and David now has over a million subscribers on Instagram.

Jennifer and David were both 'early adopters'. They embraced the platforms before they became popular. Being early to a social media platform can help you to grow an audience quickly.

So how do you build your audience right now . . . despite the algorithms and regardless of what Mark Zuckerberg does?

In this chapter, we'll hear the stories of exceptional growth from entrepreneurs such as Eloise Head with her brand Fitwaffle on TikTok or Mayah Riaz on Clubhouse. They'll share how they grew their audience and influence on social media because they went all-in early.

I'm going to share some strategies that have worked for me to sell my courses, and I'm also going to include some case studies from successful business owners to help you build your audience and sell your courses.

We will look at all the social-media strategies and audience-building techniques from podcasting to YouTube and everything else in between. You may look at them all with interest and some with horror. The critical thing to remember with social media is that you don't have to do everything, and actually, the opposite is true.

In the beginning, start with ONE platform, maybe two. This feels counterintuitive and the opposite of what you want to do initially, but I promise, less is more. Be consistent with your content. Going deep and focusing on one area will help you to succeed, rather than trying to skim over a larger patch of ground.

But it's scary . . .

I know that being visible on social media makes you feel vulnerable. Who knows what people will say or think? Perhaps someone will write a nasty comment, or what if your old school friend from twenty years ago sees your Facebook live, or that colleague you used to work with 15 years ago sees your post on LinkedIn about your business. It's a leap of faith, and it's uncomfortable, and in the beginning, the thought of a holiday in North Korea is possibly more appealing.

When I first started in business, I was petrified to talk about sales in my business. I remember sitting and staring at the 'publish' button all day before I finally plucked up the courage to share.

Or perhaps you've created a video and then decided it's not good enough. So all that effort and potential sits on your desktop, unused. Fear, perfectionism and anxiety are overriding everything. All those nuggets of inspiration and education disappearing down the digital drain.

It doesn't have to be this way. You don't need to go into hiding. You can build an audience on your terms in a way that works for you. You just have to make the leap and be willing to recognise that if you don't do this, if you don't take action, you and your dreams will not move forward. Your desire to make money while you sleep is just going to be one of those things that you say would be *'nice to have'* in the same way you'd like to win the lottery or drive a Ferrari.

So if you want recurring revenue while you sleep, then this is your wake-up call. Tick tock, it's time to get out of your comfort zone. This is your moment to shine.

Yes, it will feel awkward and icky initially, but the more you show up, the easier it will get. And before you know it, you'll be sharing your stories, connecting and building your impact and influence. What are you waiting for?! Let's do this!

You don't have to share intimate details about your life or reveal your deepest, darkest secrets, but people want to get to know you. And it does require you to share engaging and compelling content consistently – even when you'd rather watch Netflix.

Here are some ideas to get you started:

✓ Share the business heroes that inspire you.
✓ Share books that have motivated or moved you.
✓ Take us behind the scenes in your business.
✓ Describe a life-changing experience.
✓ Tell us about your idea of success.
✓ Share a pain point in your course and how you can solve it.
✓ Share how your course is going to save people time/money.

What's your plan?

Before we leap in and start building an audience, I want you to have a plan for your audience because there's no point posting every day and building an audience if you don't know what to do with them.

Here are four things to consider when building a marketing plan for your courses:

☞ What's going on in your business and on social media?
☞ Define your target market.
☞ Write out your SMART goals.
☞ What's your budget?

What's going on in your business and on social media?

Before you can get started with building your audience, you want to look at where you are right now and what's going on in your business.

What are your social media stats? Analyse what is working in your current social media strategy. Where are you getting the best return for your investment of time and money? If you are established in business, focus on the areas where you have the best engagement and loyal audience.

Using a SWOT analysis – of Strengths, Weaknesses, Opportunities and Threats – helps me get an overall idea of what's working well and what's not. It helps me look at my numbers on social media and know where to focus my energy.

And I should give a little shout out to Albert Humphrey, who came up with this framework at the Stanford Research Institute (S.R.I.) back in the 1960s and early 1970s.

Strengths	Weaknesses
Opportunities	Threats

Look at each social media platform you use and figure out what works for you and what's not.

☞ What is the potential for growth, and what are the threats? (algorithm, time, other businesses).

☞ Who is your competition? What are they doing better than you?

☞ What can you learn from your competition?

☞ Do you need to understand how to use some new functionality on the platform? Remember, the tech giants want you to adopt the latest tools and will reward you with increased views and followers.

☞ I also use this time to look at what people in my industry are doing. How is the current market? What's working for them? And what's not?

☞ Could your course plug a gap in the market?

☞ What sets you apart?

Writing out your answers to these questions can help you to reassess and confirm that your planned target market is correct or if you need to tweak it slightly.

Who's your target market?

As you know, we spent a good chunk of time analysing your target market in Chapter 2; however, it's crucial to constantly reassess and reconfirm who your audience is. Are you still talking to the right people? Or are you setting limits and blocks on your audience?

You can still want to market to a niche audience but also attract other people into your audience. When I first started in business, I talked to mums and as my business evolved, so did I. I now speak to men and women and attract about two-thirds of women, while a third of my audience is men. Much of my audience is over forty and planning for retirement.

And as you get more confidence in yourself and your message, your target audience will evolve.

Write out your SMART goals

These are clearly set goals that help you to achieve specific goals and targets. Sometimes I'm resistant to SMART goals because they remind me of the character David Brent from *The Office* and *'management speak',* but when looking at selling your courses, SMART goals work well.

SMART goals is an acronym for specific, measurable, achievable, relevant and time-based. They were first talked about by George Doran, Arthur Miller and James Cunningham in their 1981 article 'There's a S.M.A.R.T. way to write management goals and objectives'.

And now they have become a buzzword for many managers.

You can use SMART goals in many different ways throughout your business, however I use them to help me with audience building, to keep me on track.

SPECIFIC

☞ What do I want to achieve? (E.g. grow your audience on YouTube.)

☞ What's involved? (E.g. post videos twice a week consistently.)

☞ Why is my goal important? (If you develop your audience, you can therefore sell more courses and create money while you sleep.)

☞ Where does my goal take place? What social media platforms are you focusing on?

MEASURABLE

☞ What metrics are you going to determine if you have met the goal? (E.g. social media numbers or views or email subscribers?)

☞ What time period are you going to use to measure those metrics?

☞ Do you need to add some specific milestones to measure your progress?

ACHIEVABLE

This is about getting excited and motivating yourself to see the big picture! When you are inspired and believe it is possible, you are more likely to achieve your goals as you build your audience.

Is your goal achievable? What social media platforms will you target, and what level of growth are you looking for? If it's not, what is possible? What is a stretch, and what is a leap of faith? Start seeing that the leap of faith is possible. Envision it with your mind and think about it often. The more you visualise your goals and think about them every day, the more likely it is that they will come true.

Imagine creating huge influence and impact on social media and beyond. Imagine your course is a best-seller, how does it feel? Imagine you wake up and check your phone, and you have PayPal and Stripe payment notifications that people have been buying your digital products while you were sleeping. Imagine you are making money while you sleep. This is most definitely possible . . . believe it will happen.

See those goals. Feel those goals. Picture yourself in that situation where you are making money while travelling or spending time with your family. What impact does it have on your family and your life?

There is a saying that business success is 80 per cent mindset and 20 per cent business. Whether it's billionaire and Virgin founder Richard Branson or Spanx founder Sara Blakely, they both practise visualising their goals and believing they will come true.

So do what you need to do to keep yourself excited by your ideas and business. Work on your mindset, read books or listen to audiobooks. When I'm feeling stuck, I listen to *The Law of Attraction* by Esther and Jerry Hicks on Audible, or read Dr Joe Dispenza on *Breaking the Habit of Being Yourself* or listen to guided visualisations on YouTube (a personal favourite is the Pura Rasa YouTube channel).

When you are not feeling excited and passionate about the idea, it won't work. It's as simple as that. Put your energy into the projects that you care about, and no matter how great the odds, they'll have a damn fine chance of thriving.

RELEVANT

How relevant is the goal to the overall objectives of your business?

You know that you want to automate the way you sell so that you are selling over and over again. You are reading this book because you want to make money while you sleep.

Does marketing a course fit with the overall aims of the business? The goals need to align with the company objectives. Take an objective look at your marketing plan and decide if this strategy for marketing will work with the company's overall aims.

For example, if you decide that you like Pinterest because you like making pins and being visual, you need to look at the platform and determine if it fits your objectives. Are you trying to sell the course using Google and your blog posts? Are you trying to sell to women aged 35+? If you are, it could work for you, but perhaps Pinterest isn't the first platform to focus on if you are selling to a significantly male audience.

Does the goal seem worthwhile? Are you the right person to be working on this project? Perhaps you know this is the best social media marketing strategy, but do you need to outsource who actually does the work? Do you understand the mechanics of Facebook ads or YouTube algorithms to harness the platform and sell on repeat?

TIME-BASED

Anyone can set a goal, but in order for your plans to succeed, you want to have realistic timescales to ensure that you achieve your goals. E.g. doubling your youTube audience within 3 or 6 months may seem a realistic timeline.

Ask yourself specific questions about the goal deadline. If not, what can be reached and accomplished within that time period, or consider is the time period reasonable?

Knowing your marketing plan will help you focus and stay on track rather than spray painting a variety of social media platforms.

In Chapter 10, we will look at a variety of different strategies to sell your course. The critical thing to remember is that you don't have to be on every social media platform and try to skim the surface of them all. In fact, please don't! Choose one or two ways of connecting on social media and focus your time and energy on those. Choose platforms that light you up and you like.

Also, think about the algorithm. Trends and social media platforms come and go. Remember Myspace? It seems a lifetime ago! Look at what is the 'new' platform of the moment and decide if it is right for you. Early users of a new platform are more likely to build an audience quickly, so it's easier to get traction, so those who embraced TikTok or Clubhouse early on, are more likely to succeed.

However, just because you're NOT an early-ish adopter does not mean that you cannot succeed on a social media platform. Remember that a social media platform is social. If you are consistent, show up, and connect with others in a fun and engaging way, they will want to know more about you and what you do.

What's your audience-building budget?

When I first started in business, I worked three mornings a week on the business and tried to juggle everything. I found social media exhausting and draining, so I knew that I had to work smart.

I built my audience by getting found on Google from my blog posts and YouTube videos.

But that only took things so far. To grow in the online world, I had to establish a bigger audience pool.

When I got my first client, I was lucky enough to re-invest in the business on Facebook ads, and that helped me grow my audience because the ads put my freebie in front of people who would want to buy my products and services.

I will be candid here. Building an audience through Facebook ads has been my significant success in this area. Using this method changed the trajectory for my business, and I wouldn't be here writing this book, being a columnist in *Psychologies Magazine,* or building a million-dollar business without harnessing the power of Facebook ads. It is a leap of faith, and it's scary because you don't know if it will work or how best to ensure it works. And along the way, I've quite possibly paid the wages of several well-paid execs in Facebook.

If you have a marketing budget for your courses, it gives you options to consider how to sell your course on repeat.

When you first start advertising, the thought of paying money to ensure that your digital product or course gets seen is a scary prospect because you don't know if it will work. And as a small business owner perhaps your partner or family will question what you are doing.

Before you leap into spending a lump of cash on Facebook or YouTube or Google ads, learn how the systems work and know what you're doing, because otherwise you are flushing money down the drain and lining Mark Zuckerberg's pockets. There are lots of great courses and memberships that can teach the basics of advertising on Facebook. And if you find it complicated, see if there is someone you can hire or pay to do your ads.

But – and it's a big but – using advertising is only one way to build your audience and sell your courses . . . and we will talk about organic methods to grow your audience later in this chapter.

Building an audience

So now you have developed your plan, goals and worked out your budget, let's dive into the audience-building strategies . . .

Remember that stat – 98 per cent of people won't buy from you.

Yep, all those people that you've so lovingly cultivated, talked to, befriended and spent hours commenting on their posts. Yeah, those people. Well, they likely won't buy from you.

Despite your best efforts, they might comment on your post, but they might not be bothered to type in their credit card and part with their hard-earned cash for you. As you grow your audience, your pool of potential buyers just gets bigger.

We all start with a smattering of followers, and a few likes. And gradually as we share more, talk more, we build our audience. And if you're at the beginning stages of building your audience, it will happen for you too.

And that's why reaching new audiences is crucial to build your online business and sell your course, but it's not the only answer.

I once posted a photo of my son and one of his toy tractors. One of my community commented and told me he had built a course-based business teaching people how to make model tractors. Now, there's only a small fraction of people in the world who want to build model tractors, but they are a committed, passionate and thriving community.

In the online world, there's a marketeer phrase, 'There's niches in the riches,' and it's so true. You don't need to sell to everyone, just find your niche, build your audience and sell. Sounds easy, doesn't it?!

There is a beauty in going down a really specific route with what you teach. It means that you don't necessarily need a big audience to make a profitable course. I can honestly tell you that an engaged audience of 5,000 that is willing to buy is more lucrative than an audience of 100,000 that likes your content but doesn't regard you as someone they buy from.

Growing your audience

I started out building my audience with a Facebook group for 300 mums. I created posts and pictures with Canva and I shared blog posts in the vain hope that someone would want to buy from me. I had no clue what I was doing, and I didn't even mention the fact that people could buy from me.

Cultivating an audience of buyers took time. After lots of false starts and faffing, I finally found my social media feet. I would create videos for YouTube and then create blog posts for Pinterest that included the videos and using this method enabled me to attract thousands of viewers to my videos and blog posts, without having to spend hours engaging and commenting all over the place.

But my story isn't unique. There are thousands of small business-owner-worker-bees buzzing busily around trying to attract an audience and make a living.

So, how to do you go from invisible to viral?

How do you breakthrough from just about being seen to a scroll-stopping, stand-out, internet sensation?

How do you create content that people want more of? And actually want to pay you for it?

In the rest of this chapter, I'm going to share stories of do and daring on social media. From 60 million views on TikTok to million-dollar businesses, I know that some of these stories will seriously inspire you. It may also send you shuffling back to your sofa and giving up on passive income before you've even started.

I want you to remember that we all start somewhere. Building an audience takes time, persistence and perseverance. Learn from what works, what doesn't work and stay consistent. If there's one thing that I've learned in growing an audience and talking to these successful business owners, it's that consistency is key. Keep creating, keep going and don't spread yourself too thin.

Dig deep on one social media platform and don't go wide. I know it's so tempting to want to do EVERYTHING that I talk about in the rest of this chapter. Believe me, as I write this, I've just had a conversation with my husband along the lines of . . . 'oooh, I should do more TikToks, or perhaps I should learn to like Clubhouse.' But the reality is that you can't do everything and when you try to do everything, you will set yourself up for failure.

Stick to one platform!

Focus on one or two social media platforms and go all in. Spend your time, energy and enthusiasm.

- Which social media platform most appeals to you?
- Where does your ideal client hang out?
- Where is the best place to grow your audience right now?

Have a read of these incredibly inspiring stories to decide which platform best suits you and your business.

FACEBOOK

Love it or loathe it, there are 2 billion people on the planet using Facebook every month. And while the numbers of users logging on from North America and Europe is declining, and the algorithm isn't perhaps as friendly (so your posts don't always get seen) it is still a very popular place to hang out.

Facebook groups are an incredible way for you to connect with your ideal clients and customers, get to know them and ultimately sell to them. You can nurture relationships, chat to them on Facebook live and build connections that just aren't possible on other platforms in the same way.

For your Facebook group to succeed, you want to create a community where you're asking questions rather than broadcasting information. Open-ended questions work well, and try not to just talk about your course content.

I have a community of 5,000 entrepreneurs wanting to get Confident on Camera. I'll pre-prepare a series of posts for the month, then schedule them so it is easier to manage the group. I'm also careful to ask lots of engaging questions: 'What type of dog shall I get?' is one of my most commented topics (even when my husband is allergic to dogs and it probably won't happen!).

Ruth Kudzi is brilliant at creating friendships and social networks and she took her real-life skills and created safe, nurturing Facebook groups, which enabled her to build a hugely successful coaching business.

Ruth Kudzi, founder of Optimus Coach Academy:
how Facebook groups helped me to grow my business:
Facebook groups have been pivotal to me in growing, nurturing and converting clients in my business.

In 2016 when I started my business online I had my very first Facebook group: career-change mums. By the end of the first month I had nearly 500 members, and I had converted my first clients by showing up and giving value at the time with a focus on confidence and mindset.

I started to grow it by posting about the fact I was doing free training in other Facebook groups where my ideal clients spent time (at that time it was mainly mum groups), and I created a lead magnet all about confidence which had people join the group. As we grew I encouraged my existing members to share and built the reputation through speaking at various events, as well as by consistently delivering value and training.

This group grew to nearly 5000 members over three years (and went through two name changes as my business evolved – finally being called the Rebel Collective) and helped me generate hundreds of thousands of pounds in revenue. As we grew we started to use Facebook ads to help grow the group through creating a lead magnet with the group sign-up being on the thank you page: this helped us to grow our list as well as our group.

At the end of 2019 I closed down this group as it was no longer aligned with my ideal client, and in the last 18 months have grown a new group of over 5,000 people, called the Coaching Community, and this has helped me generate over £1 million in revenue. I was able to use the same strategy by really getting clear on the ideal client and delivering value and training in the group as well as supporting the growth with Facebook ads.

I have also had many pop-up Facebook groups often for launches which have helped me build and nurture relationships. The key for me has always been about being really clear about who the group is for and what people will get from being in the group. At the start I used to offer exclusive training for people in the group, though over time I have reduced this, however, I do share more personal posts and we engage with our potential clients in there: I find they are a great place for people to see if they like your vibe and to build and nurture relationships before people buy.

INSTAGRAM

More than a billion users frequent Instagram's videos and images each month, and it's a lovely way to while away time procrastinating (especially when I should be book writing). It's also a fabulous way to connect with new clients and sell your courses.

If you are just starting out on Instagram, you want to try to be an early adopter of whatever Mark Zuckerberg and his team create. So whether it's I.G.T.V., Reels or Stories, it's best to learn it, jump on it and embrace it.

Using Reels has helped me to gain hundreds of new followers, and it's a fun way to be creative.

Sam Bearfoot is one of the funniest people I've encountered on Instagram and her content always makes me giggle. She's grown her audience by simply being herself. Here's her story . . .

When Lucy asked me to share my story around how I grew my business on Instagram I had to think about exactly where I was going to go with this. Sure, I could talk to you about hashtags domination, influencer shout-outs or how to get an increased click-through rate to your website, but those are all sexy side effects of one thing . . . Great content!

So how do I do that, you may be asking yourself? Well, this requires a little back story if I may . . .

In 2016 I pivot from a 10-year health business after having my little boy and even though I had to rethink my business because I had become a mother the truth was, I was exhausted from it all. You see I had done all the things. Half a million times downloaded podcast; radio presenter for UK Health Radio that reached a quarter of a million listeners each month; 40 thousand followers on Twitter (because that was the place to be then) and a regular spot in some very well-established newspapers to boot.

All that fancy pants, as I like to call it, was a big fat lie, though. I had created a version of myself that I thought the public wanted and after keeping up that persona for a decade I was so over it. So when I decided to pivot, and this is the juicy bit that I REALLY want you to take on board here because it's what will separate you from the masses in 2021 and beyond, I promised myself one thing. If I was going to do this, give up on the 10-year business I had worked so hard for to turn my hand at something completely different, I was going to do it as me! 100% warts and all, authentic Sam.

I can tell you that as scary as it was in the beginning it is the single most empowering thing I have ever done, and it translates into everything I do now. Being my uncensored self is what makes me unique and to my surprise (at least in the beginning) it's also what my audience love me for.

On a social media platform like Instagram, standing out is hard when you are being pre-programmed to blend in. 'They' (that's the Internet Illuminati, as I like to call them) will tell you that you need a beautiful feed, you'll need to write content like The Joneses and you'll need to fit in and kiss the ass of every 'influencer' out there to be successful.

What I will tell you about being successful on Instagram though is this ... The single thing that makes great content stand out above the all the others is to be YOU. It's your very own superpower that no one ever will be able to copy, and it's magnetic as F!!

Create whatever and however you want and not how it's 'supposed' to be done.

Oh, and one last thing, when you do and you get that twinge in your gut that tells you it's scary, post it anyway. Trust me, that feeling you know as fear, is actually the magic that makes your social media come to life.

LINKEDIN

Forget the old days when LinkedIn was for posting your CV and the domain of recruitment agencies, LinkedIn is now all about the content. The site wants you to share, engage and create conversation.

And the way that the algorithm works means that your posts and comments are more likely to get noticed than on some other platforms. I get a steady flow of clients asking me about my products and services just through the power of organic marketing.

The beauty of LinkedIn is that it's for everyone. It's no longer the domain of the stuffy corporates. But remember, it's perhaps like the early days of Facebook – to encourage engagement, you need to ask questions, post daily and stay consistent.

One of the people that I can credit with showing me the light on LinkedIn is the fabulous Lea Turner. Her story shows that right now, you can still have phenomenal success on LinkedIn.

Lea Turner, LinkedIn growth coach: How LinkedIn helped me stay afloat in the pandemic and build a business . . .

Pre-pandemic Lea ran an audio-transcription business. As the world went into lockdown, her work dried up and she began teaching people how to use LinkedIn.

I was hesitant and clueless when I first logged into LinkedIn. I had a small business that I wanted to grow but zero marketing budget. I had 400 connections and no idea what to say.

My first posts got zero engagement. Nada. Even a rogue tumbleweed would have been welcome! Probably because I was trying too hard to sound smart, successful, professional – all things that aren't really 'me'!

I quickly learned that being my real, weird self was my best chance at standing out from the crowd on LinkedIn, so I embraced it.

My following grew exponentially, hitting 10,000 followers in the first two months, without using any growth hacks or engagement groups. People resonated with my story. A lone mum to a little boy trying to grow her tiny transcription business, having fun and sharing the highs and the lows of her journey towards a better life for her little family. And with that came more than 60 inbound clients and I had to hire a team to support all the work! When Covid hit, everything changed, and my business collapsed. What else was I good at that could make money?

By that point I had 30k followers on LinkedIn after just six months. I started charging £99 per hour to help other small businesses boost their visibility and attract ideal clients. I became so booked up I had to increase my prices – which blew my mind! My follower count continued to rise organically as I consistently posted, replied to comments, supported other people's content, and embraced good humour and authenticity in everything I did online.

In the first 12 months from starting LinkedIn training I have hosted more than 250 1:1 training sessions, dozens of business training sessions, live workshops, sold-out webinars, and created and sold hundreds of content resources. I've even just released my digital course (with Lucy's expert help). I now have an army of over 85,000 followers who support and encourage me in everything I do.

But the most life-changing thing of all is that after six house moves in five years due to being in rental properties, I can finally buy me and my son a house of our own and provide security for our future.

LinkedIn is a powerful platform. If you log on just to brag about your business or sell, sell, sell, you're missing out on so much. This is a community of exponential opportunity. People want to support one another and see them succeed and are ready and willing to help those around them.

LinkedIn is not B2B or B2C, it is human to human. And those who show their humanity on the platform are the ones reaping the biggest rewards.

CLUBHOUSE

Clubhouse is one of the newer kids on the social-media block and, unlike any of the other platforms, it is all voice-based. The beauty of the audio-only platform means that you don't have to put on makeup or even get out of bed to participate. And perhaps that was a major appeal during a global pandemic.

I have to confess that I tried the platform once, spoke in a room and quickly realised that it wasn't for an introvert like me: I was terrified! But if the idea of using a voice-based app appeals, there is huge potential on the platform. It's one of the fastest ways to build an audience and also establish your authority and expertise.

Pre-pandemic, Mayah Riaz was a Celebrity Manager and known as PR-to-the-Stars, but when the UK went into lockdown because of Covid-19, she pivoted her business and started coaching entrepreneurs to harness the power of publicity.

Clubhouse was her perfect platform to connect with hundreds of entrepreneurs and build her audience.

Mayah Riaz, publicity coach. How Clubhouse helped me to build an audience . . .
I had heard so much about Clubhouse towards the end of December. My work is as a Celebrity Manager and in PR, so I haven't been using social media to get clients but I did have a personal presence on it. However, I have recently pivoted my business and teach entrepreneurs how to do their own PR, so for

this side of the business, social media is really beneficial, but even then, I haven't used it hugely.

So when the new social media kid came on the scene, at first I totally dismissed it. However, in early January out of curiosity, I gave in and decided to see what the hype was all about. A good friend of mine sent me the invite and I joined straight away. It took me a week to figure out how to use it and what was going on. But after that, I quickly became addicted to it – which took me by surprise! I was on the app from the breakfast room at 6.30am and then in the American rooms until 3am! I loved it because it was audio and you show up as you, without needing hair and makeup to be intact or thinking too much about what you put out there (i.e. no filters needed, no editing). You use your voice and you hear other people's voices – it just felt very authentic. I connected with some amazing people and then further enhanced those relationships via WhatsApp and Zoom.

When I started on Clubhouse in January 2021, I didn't have a game plan – meaning that I didn't have a website in place and didn't create a lead magnet like many had. A lot of my Clubhouse connected with me on Twitter and Instagram and I soon found my Instagram was inundated with messages. I had literally hundreds of DMs and followers (even though my Instagram is private). The DMs were centred around my PR work and how people can work with me. I had to hire a VA to work through my messages, as they had gone so crazy and I didn't want to be ignoring anyone.

I wasn't taking on any one-to-one clients at the time, and when someone asked if they could work with me, I referred them to my PR membership. I realised this was something I wanted to promote more of and be more proactive with. So I began hosting my own PR rooms three times a week. After each room, I would get a handful of DMs on Instagram to join my membership. I decided to make it easier, I would have a link in my bio where *people could just join if they wanted to. This was a great move, as I would go to bed and wake up seeing people from around the world had joined my PR membership – so I was truly making money in my sleep. People had heard me in a lot of rooms, they knew what I was about, they heard the tips I was sharing and they wanted more. By having a link in my bio where they could learn more, it made it easy for them to work with me.*

I have clients from all over the world that I work with and many of them have come via Clubhouse. I have found it to be the best and most converting social media app. This is because they hear you on Clubhouse, then follow you on Instagram where they can see more about you from your photos and videos and engage with you on a deeper level via DM – as at the moment, there's no direct messaging facility on Clubhouse.

Tips

If you haven't tried Clubhouse, don't dismiss it as another social media app. Start exploring and using the app. The more you use it, the more you will see how it could work with you.

As soon as you're on Clubhouse, fill out your bio. You want to seem like a real human being rather than a bot. But also, this is useful so when you're in a room and other people are checking you out, they know what you're about.

When you're on the app, go into other rooms. Raise your hand and go on stage to join in the conversation. If you want to be noticed, sitting in the audience isn't helpful. You want to be on the stage engaging in the conversation.

Have at least one other social media platform connected to your profile, so that people can connect with you and stay in touch.

Remember, when you're on the stage, don't sell. No one likes being sold to. Contribute, share value (which is an overused word on Clubhouse) and people will see what you're about. They will know if they need what you do.

I wouldn't recommend starting your own rooms straight away – you need to build a following and the way you do that is join in the conversation so people know if you're worth following. So that when you create a room once you have a following, it will show up in people's hallway and they will be alerted to you starting your own room. There's nothing more disheartening than not having anyone in your room because they don't know about it.

YOUTUBE

When I started out on YouTube, I thought that it was just about posting video and I said to myself, I can do that. I've worked in video for so many years. But the reality is that it's about so much more than the video. Remember, Google owns YouTube, so it's a search engine for video. And for you to get found, you want to show up in search.

YouTube is a little like school. There are the kids who don't work at all, yet are straight-A students, and then there are the majority, who have to work hard to do well or fail.

So for most of us – me included – my YouTube growth has been slow and steady. It's a platform I love, and I love that my videos show up in search categories for years afterwards (unlike in the world of 'social media').

I've seen people explode their audience on YouTube and reach seven-figure businesses with rapid results, and one of those people is Gillian Perkins . . .

Gillian started in the entrepreneurial world young as a music teacher. After selling her successful music business, she came into the online world wanting to live more and work less. I remember the days watching Gillian on Facebook, trying to stand out. And then suddenly, boom! She was everywhere on YouTube. One video had garnered her thousands of subscribers quickly and tens of thousands of views and her business took off. She was the straight-A student who studied the YouTube algorithm. Her channel now has over 25 million views and she now has over 500,000 subscribers and growing.

I first started on YouTube as a hobby and this was in 2013. It started just a hobby because I was interested in making videos for fun. I saw others making beauty videos and I just liked watching those videos a lot. So, I thought that was something I could make videos about and I knew there was an opportunity to make a living out of YouTube. That sounded really cool but I wasn't really expecting that to happen. It was really just supposed to be a hobby. So, I did that for about 3 years.

My channel wasn't growing, but at a certain point it finally did start growing. I had a few videos take off and got several thousand views. And it was cool but it made me realize that I didn't really like the videos that I am making and I wasn't very proud of them. It was not the topic that I wanted to be known for. So, I shut down that channel.

I was still really interested in being a YouTuber. But I knew that I needed to think through things more and do more research so that I can figure out how to make my channel more successful and how I could make better videos.

I got into research mode and I kind of put YouTube on a back burner. I started working on my marketing agency which was the business I started at the same time that I stopped my YouTube channel.

I worked at my marketing agency for the next year and a half.

And I was also researching YouTube at the same time. Then, as I was trying to figure out what the best marketing strategies were for me to get clients and also to help my clients, I remembered that I get a fair amount of exposure and comments on YouTube, even though I didn't have any good videos at all. And I thought it could work for my marketing agency.

So, I started making videos about marketing and online business. And that channel took off really fast and grew to about a thousand subscribers in just 3 months. And then at that point I started earning money from it. The first month I earned $113. Then the next month, I earned a couple hundred dollars and the next month several hundred dollars.

By about month 6, I earned about a thousand dollars. And that was around the time I had the income from my marketing agency, a little passive income I generated from other business ventures and now also this thousand dollars amount that was growing quickly from YouTube. My husband quit his job and I worked on YouTube and my marketing agency clients.

So, yes, that's why I started there basically because I saw it as an opportunity to get a lot of visibility and exposure for my business.

I knew that in order to grow more, I had to become a student of the algorithm. I studied the algorithm for hundreds of hours and figured out exactly how it worked. We analyzed, me and my small team, thousands of videos and channels and the data on them to figure out exactly what the algorithm liked, what it didn't and why some videos succeeded and others didn't.

It was a lot of time, a lot of research, but you just need to be a student of the algorithm.

When you're making your videos, think about how long your video is and capturing viewers' attention. I really focused on trying to make my video as enjoyable to watch as possible and also as search friendly as possible so that they would rank well in YouTube search. I also used some key collaborations to get a little bit more exposure and grow my channel even faster.

YouTube is my number 1 source for leads. It's my lead generation source. It's where almost all of my customers originally find me. And if not directly from YouTube, it's because of YouTube.

Prior to my YouTube channel taking off, I didn't really have any audience at all on other platforms but thanks to my YouTube audience growing, I have been able to grow about 14,000 Instagram followers and I have a couple of Facebook groups with over 10,000 people in them and it is completely 100% thanks to YouTube. I didn't have any other way of getting exposure other than that.

I have also grown my email list to over 90 thousand email subscribers and it's one of my most valuable business assets. My email list is how I make the majority of my sales.

People watch my educational YouTube videos and in the video I offer additional free resources that they can get if they sign up on my email list. After they sign on my email list, they go through an automated sales funnel that promotes a webinar. If they watch the webinar then I pitch a product which includes a series of follow up emails.

Sometimes for example, someone finds me on Instagram, or on Facebook first, or perhaps on Pinterest, but the only reason that I have any clout there is because I was able to grow my YouTube channel first and just grow my audience significantly and then that audience transferred to these other platforms.

Here are four top tips for growing on YouTube:

1. Have a focus for your channel. It doesn't have to be one specific topic, it has to have some sort of focus, some main

theme, or a person in mind that you are making your videos for. Try to be cohesive with your content or else you're going to really struggle to know what to make your videos about and you'll feel like you're all over the place. And your people won't subscribe because they won't know what to expect from your channel. So, first off, have a focus.

2. *Keep the viewer engaged! Your videos need to be fairly fast paced. That doesn't mean that you need to talk super- fast. It doesn't mean that tons of things need to happen although more going on in the video is better. But you need to be bring in variety throughout the video so it's not just talking to the camera. Those videos can perform well but it's difficult and it's more of a gamble with that. Just have something changing in your video in the first 30 to 60 seconds: whether that is showing a clip of what you're talking about or moving to a different location or something new starts happening. Or you add some text to something. But add in a twist and a change every 30 to 60 seconds to make the pacing a little bit quicker and keep the viewer engaged.*

3. *Show, don't tell. Either use very descriptive language to describe what you are talking about or actually show us. Use props or do it, don't just talk about it. It makes your videos a lot more dynamic and a lot more interesting to watch.*

4. *Become a student of the algorithm. Learn how the algorithm works, learn what it wants and don't try to like to spread yourself too thin on too many different platforms. Just focus on YouTube if you want to grow on YouTube and learn how the algorithm works.*

PINTEREST

I first discovered Pinterest when I was renovating houses. It was this wonderful pool of images and inspiration.

It took me a few years to realise that actually I could harness the power of Pinterest for my digital courses and products. I now use Pinterest to drive traffic to my website and from my blog post, and people sign up for my freebies and ultimately my courses and products.

Remember that the pin is key. Create colourful, engaging pins with a strong call to action. Use tools such as Tailwind so you can re-schedule your pins so that they are re-pinned again and again and you can reach millions of viewers.

> Rachel Ngom teaches entrepreneurs how to grow their audience on Pinterest:
>
> *First, let's talk about why should you focus on Pinterest.*
>
> *Pinterest works differently than other social media platforms, like Facebook or Instagram. The idea isn't to broadcast images or ideas to followers, rather to save content, ideas, or products for later, which makes it the perfect marketing platform.*
>
> *Research shows that large amounts of Pinterest users use the platform to research purchasing decisions before they buy. 87% of Pinners have purchased because of Pinterest!*
>
> *Pinterest is a huge driver of traffic! Pinterest accounts for almost 94% of all of my site traffic, over 34,000 viewers a month! What's pretty crazy to me is that I have over 50,000 followers on Facebook, and only 14,000 on Pinterest, yet Pinterest obviously drives way more traffic.*

Create boards targeted to your audience (with the right keywords)

Pinterest is a search engine! Name the board something that people are actually searching for. Instead of saying 'My Favourite Recipe', maybe use 'Easy Gluten-Free Dinner Ideas'.

As an example, one of my clients is a fitness coach who focuses on intermittent fasting and macros.

I suggested she create boards around those topics, so her board titles are: Intermittent Fasting for Women, How to Track your Macros, IIFYM Recipes, and she's creating more to go with her theme. What's cool is she's already at the top of the Pinterest search for intermittent fasting!!

Since a large element of my audience are female entrepreneurs, some of my boards are: Female Entrepreneur Tips, Pinterest Marketing Tips, Apps for Entrepreneurs, Social Media Marketing Tips, Inspirational Quotes for Entrepreneurs, Branding Tips for Female Entrepreneurs, etc.

What is your main focus, and what boards can you create to go with those themes?

To find out what people are actually searching for on Pinterest, start typing in the search bar. What pops up are the actual keywords that Pinterest suggests!!

Design visually appealing pins that are share-worthy

I am obsessed with Canva.com for creating images on Pinterest!

When creating a graphic, make sure the font is legible, and have text on your image, including keywords. Pinterest can actually scan the text on your images, which can impact your rankings. Finally, be sure your graphics are long and skinny. Use the Pinterest graphic image on Canva.

Tell people what you want them to do in the pin description (give them a call to action!)

Here are examples of pin descriptions:

Example 1: Have you ever heard of intermittent fasting? Ever wonder what intermittent fasting is? Essentially, intermittent fasting isn't dieting at all, it's just eating in a condensed window. For some people, intermittent fasting is going without food for 12-36 hours. Repin and read the ultimate guide to intermittent fasting for women.

Example 2: OMG calling all PEANUT BUTTER lovers!!!! These are KETO Peanut Butter Fat Bombs. These keto peanut butter fat bombs were so good!! Have you ever tried fat bombs? This was my first shot – and I know that I'll be making more keto fat bombs in the future! Fat bombs are a super easy way to get your healthy fats in . . . and they are delicious!! Pin now, try later!

Don't just pin something just to pin it. What do you want people to do? Give them that call to action!!"

TIKTOK

One of the platforms that has just exponentially exploded in growth in the last few years is TikTok. Not without controversies about ownership, the early adopters of the platform have seen their audience and revenues skyrocket.

TikTok does appear to be about funny dances and pointing, but actually it's so much more. You can offer value, entertainment and training and grow your audience within a short space of time.

Eloise Head from Fitwaffle has grown her follower base to over 2 million and garners millions of views on her videos. Her videos have been viewed over 60 million times and has the kind of numbers that a TV broadcaster would be happy with!

Tell us about your story on TikTok . . .

I first downloaded the app when it was called Musical.ly because I wanted to put some background music to a video of a choco-late-covered banana. I didn't know much about the app at the time and I realised once I downloaded the video that it had a watermark on, so I thought, oh well and didn't revisit the app for about a month.

When I went back onto the app, the video I posted had over 7 million views and I had gained around 20,000 followers! Now, I wish I had kept up the momentum and continued to post regu-larly on there, but it wasn't a priority at the time so I would just post the occasional food video.

In August 2018, the app changed over to what it is today, TikTok. As I saw the app gaining popularity, I started to post more regularly to it, showcasing indulgent foods from restau-rants and how they are made. Although that's quite different to what I post on the app today.

How did you grow there?

When the UK went into lockdown in March 2020, I started creat-ing short, simple recipe videos. I posted these every day without fail to Instagram and TikTok. I posted a video of a three-ingredi-ent Oreo fudge and it took off, gaining around 2 million views on TikTok.

During lockdown, while everyone was furloughed or working from home, baking became hugely popular and so did my reci-pes, with some videos being viewed over 47 million times, result-ing in a big boost in followers. At the time of writing this, I have 2.1 million followers on TikTok.

How has it transformed your business?

TikTok has allowed me to reach and connect with an audience I would have probably never reached via the other social media platforms. It's also allowed my videos to be seen by the masses and be exposed to people all over the world.

I have been presented with huge opportunities from TikTok, including large brand deals, features in hundreds of press articles across the world, and something else really big, which I can't talk about just yet.

How has it helped you to grow on other platforms?

When I first started posting recipe videos to TikTok, I didn't put the ingredients on the video. The ingredients list for the recipe were all listed on my @FitwaffleKitchen Instagram page.

Therefore, I would encourage my followers on TikTok to head to this Instagram page for the full recipe. The FitwaffleKitchen Instagram page grew incredibly quickly during lockdown from zero followers in April 2020, to 575k in July 2021.

What are your top tips for growth on TikTok?

1. *Look at other successful people within your niche to see what they are doing well. Break it down to figure out why they are doing well and implement this into your growth strategy.*
2. *Content is king. It doesn't matter how good your growth strategy is if people don't want to watch your videos. If you have a video perform really well, work out why it did and use it as a template for future videos. If a video doesn't perform well, try to figure out why not.*
3. *Be consistent. If you have great content, but you only post once a month, or you post regularly then give up, you're never going to continue to grow. Post consistently, figure out what works and keep going.*

4. *Lastly, adapt. The world and the platforms are always changing. Don't be afraid to change your strategy quickly to keep up and stay relevant. While posting a particular video may have performed well six months ago, it doesn't mean it's still relevant and will perform well now.*

Keenya Kelly teaches business owners how to grow on TikTok, she shares these tips for stellar growth on the platform:

5 Tips for TikTok growth

1. *It's important to understand the 'culture of TikTok'. It's an entertainment driven platform so even though you may be growing a business there, you need to add in some creativity that can be seen as entertaining.*
2. *Keep your videos at 15 seconds or less. The algorithm loves when your video is viewed all the way to the end, which causes your videos to be pushed out on the For You Page longer.*
3. *Periodically, jump on some of the daily trends. Trends are what make the TikTok world go round. You don't have to dance or act goofy, but use the trends as creative inspiration.*
4. *Keep your descriptions short and catchy. With the character limit being 150 it's important to leave room for your hashtags.*
5. *Post often. The more content you post the more your content can keep circulating days, weeks and months down the line.*

PODCASTING

Whether you're driving or pottering around the house, listening to a podcast is increasingly popular. And the best thing is that you too can easily create a podcast.

It's relatively simple to record and build an audience of raving fans, but there are some must-do tips to take your podcast to chart-topping.

Anna Parker-Naples is a podcasting expert, business coach and host of the *'Entrepreneurs Get Visible'* podcast. Anna stumbled into podcasting and soon realised her background in audio was a perfect fit.

I came into the online space in 2017 and my goal was to reach lots of people and change lives and empower them to achieve success – whatever that meant for them. I was struggling to know how to build an audience and someone suggested I try podcasting.

I have an audio background and had a recording studio, so it was a no-brainer. My podcast was live within 24 hours.

I knew the tech, but I didn't understand about podcasting and I didn't understand how to use it to build my audience. And I didn't understand the little things that go on behind the scenes to build a successful podcast, versus one that's just out there. I didn't understand how to promote it and build leads from the podcast. So I was really proud of it, but totally clueless.

I was looking at a lot of successful entrepreneurial podcasters who were saying they were earning millions off the back of their podcasts and I couldn't work out what I was doing wrong because my audio was top quality.

So, I went to learn everything: every article, blog, course and book. I realised that I had missed a unique window at the beginning to promote my show, as well as lots of keywords and tagging that goes on behind the scenes in the podcasting directories. And I wasn't using it for search engine optimisation, so I wasn't using it to build other facets of my business.

As my audience was growing, people were finding out I had an audio background and asking me 'How can I create a podcast?' 'How do I record audio?'

I resisted it for a while until I read a book about podcasting in my parents' back garden. It was so badly misinformed about the audio side that I remember saying to my parents, 'Why hasn't someone written about this?'

That was the start of it. So I started teaching people about podcasting, and I decided that I didn't want to have an average podcast, I wanted to have one that was an undeniably successful one. So alongside launching my first course, I launched a podcast and I was always a week ahead of my participants. And that became an international, very successful podcast and it has consistently stayed in the top one percent of global podcasts.

It knocked things like Tony Robbins and Gary Vaynerchuk off the top spots in the charts here and in the US. And as a result, when I started that podcast my first self-published book was being released. As a result of the podcast success, the book was then a success and I didn't have a very big audience at that point.

It's basically the success of that show over the last, coming up for, 20 months, that has completely transformed my business. You know, I was not really making much money back then. And now I have a multi-six-figure business that's very comfortable. And for me, that's because of the quality of the show, understanding how the podcast space works, but also the connection with the audience. And it makes it very easy

> *for me to bring people into other parts of my business.*
>
> *I now have a very strong Little Black Book of contacts that have become my peers, connected as a result of the podcast.*

A few things to remember about social media . . .

- ✓ Building an audience isn't easy. Sometimes it's frustrating. There will be algorithm changes, or the social media platform may close down your account or block a video for some unknown reason.
- ✓ You don't 'own' your social media audience, you're just renting the followers. You want to own your data and that means emails, so it's really important to get your audience to download your freebies and join your email list.
- ✓ Don't forget to drive your audience from your favourite platforms to other places; for example, I use YouTube for lead-building and then use Facebook groups to nurture that same audience.
- ✓ Give yourself a break! Sometimes social media can feel over-whelming. Use apps to restrict the hours you spend scrolling aimlessly on social media and so you log on with purpose and intention (and then log off!).
- ✓ When you first start out on social media, it's scary being visible. You have a message to share with the world and we want to hear what you have to say.
- ✓ I'm always my own worst critic, and I've a hunch that you feel the same way about yourself. You don't have to be perfect. You don't have to be a perfect size 6 and have the social media following of Kylie Jenner. Just be yourself and your people will gravitate to you.
- ✓ You may worry that the trolls will come knocking. And while there is always the odd nasty out there, if you project

positive energy, it will rebound back to you. If someone is nasty, remember those inspiring words of Michelle Obama: *'When they go low, we go high'* and just send them a little blessing and press delete. Their issues and triggers are not your problem.

Where do you want to put your energy?

The internet has given us so many incredible opportunities to connect, make money and build truly global communities. Now little you from your spare room or kitchen can become a content machine and generate an army of raving fans.

The challenge for you is to go big in one place – the question is, where?!

* Where do you want to put your energy and passion?
* Where is best suited to your ideal clients?
* Where do you like to hang out?

Go for it! You have a story to share. So let's connect on social media. I'd love to hear your thoughts about this book!

Cheering you on all the way!

CHAPTER 8

Selling Your Course – Sales Pages That Sell

You have a passion and a project to share with the world. Your talents and capabilities transcend you. Your fears and blocks about selling and money are not a reason to limit you from creating the life you want.

My purpose and mission are to help you see that you can create true wealth for your life and family. What impact would that have on your family if you had the financial freedom to live where you choose, work how you liked and didn't feel chained to the old ways of working? This future is now. It's your opportunity to go for it! You just have to be open to the possibility.

The world is shifting fast, and those jobs that once required human hands and brains are disappearing. I remember back in 2012 when I was still a journalist, and my old company announced that a robot (AI – artificial intelligence) was writing financial news stories. It was a glimpse into the future.

Technology is incredible. We can now use the wonders of social media to connect with people across the world and use our stories to sell our ideas and make money while we sleep. All you need is your laptop (or phone) to build an audience and unleash your creativity.

But there is ONE thing that holds so many back from actually building a successful business. What stops people from selling? It's the fear of rejection. Those questions in your head: *'What if they say no to me? What if I'm not good enough?'*

I know. I've been there. And very often, I'm still there.

But for your online course-based business to succeed, I must remind you of something, and perhaps you've not considered it before. The reality is that while I can talk strategy and funnels and the tech stuff non-stop, there are two key things fundamental to your business's success:

1. Your mindset and willingness to do the work and show up even if you find something challenging. Being in the online world requires you to dig deep, do the work and recognise your blocks and limitations. Just because you had a launch or created a product and it didn't sell, does not mean that it will not be a long-term success. You just have to keep working at it.
2. Study the data! Keep tweaking, testing and refining your sales pages until you get the leads, then convert the leads and the sales flow. Then analyse the metrics and study what is working and what needs adjustment.

I've learned to sidestep my fears about selling and build an automated system to sell for me. Learn this, and you will create a whole way of living for yourself and your family. And you'll open a whole host of possibilities and potential.

This is YOUR time. What's stopping you?!

Success Coach Emily Williams shares these tips for successful selling in the online world:
Perhaps the biggest quality that contributes to success in the online world is persistence.

Really just trusting whatever that you desire is meant for you and continuing to move forward towards that goal really helps me. See it in black and white terms. If I want it then that means it's meant for me and it's possible and I don't have to question it.

Now, it might not happen on my timeline but it will happen if I continue to move forward and take that action and really implement the law of cause and effect.

Adopt an abundance mentality. A lot of people think that because the person offers the same thing as me then that person has all the clients, not recognising that there are over a billion people online. So there's more than enough for all of us to go around.

The 'not-so-secret' formula

If you were looking for one secret ingredient that would help you Make Money While You Sleep, this chapter is perhaps the oil to grease the cogs that you need to build your very own lead machine. So buckle up, we're making a sales engine that sells on autopilot.

Your audience is the fuel into the engine, and the sales page is the automated machine that works while you are off living your life. And the more refined and tweaked the page is, the better the engine will run. We will talk about refining your machine later, but I want you to listen up, take note and see that your little side hustle from your spare room doesn't need to be just that.

Your sales page is crafted copy on your website or online sales platform that enables you to automate your sales process from start to finish. You can reach thousands of people and influence so many lives just from the funnel or sales page that you create. This is your opportunity to play big from the spare room and compete with the real players – even if you struggle with the selling stuff!

One of the best things about the online world is that you can sell even if you hate selling. When I first started as a small business owner, I struggled to sell. I used to have sales calls and spent so long with the client that I'd give the training session for free. I once spent four hours on the supposedly 15-minute taster session!

It's supposed to work like this: you have a sales call with someone, attempt to sell your products or services, and then your customer says that three-letter magic word: 'Yes!' The trouble is, for me, I feared actually selling to people, I didn't offer them my services and I was afraid of rejection. I gave away all my value for free because I didn't value myself and what I do.

To sell successfully, I embraced a variety of tools, from mindset to sales training. I began to see selling as a service and an act of generosity. You have something that other people *need,* and it will transform their life and their business. When it is truly life-changing for others, the fear of selling goes away.

Those blocks and limitations fall away when you have that mindset shift and see money as something genuinely transformational. To help me sell, I took some sales workshops and had hypnotherapy sessions to help me bust through my blocks around selling. When I am selling during a big launch, I have reiki sessions to help manage my energy. Everything is energy, including money, so you want to be operating at your most positive level!

The book *Go-Givers Sell More* by Bob Burg and John David Mann is well worth reading. I love this quote from the book:

> *Sales is much like farming: you prepare the soil with care, you choose and plant the right seeds, you stay faithful in your watering, weeding and cultivation – and God and nature do the rest. But you do have to plant and cultivate.*

During this chapter, I will show you how you can plant your successful digital harvest. We're going to cultivate that sales page, nurture those leads and build your successful lead machine.

Imagine a small flower shop on the high street of a local town; the owner would decorate the facade and possibly paint it so that it is light and inviting. The shopkeeper would decorate the window to stop you in your tracks, and you are compelled to take a look. A digital store is no different. Your Facebook ad or social media post is the scroll-stopper that intrigues you so much that you just have to stop and read. And then you're invited to go ahead and click the button and 'learn more', which is the real-world equivalent of going inside the store.

You click on social media or an ad to find out more about a product or service and arrive on the sales page. The sales page succinctly sells the product and is the automated machine that powers your online business. It is also known as the 'funnel'. It is also referred to as a 'landing page' if you offer a freebie to entice people to sign up to your email list.

Just as you would try to enhance the customer experience in the real world and decorate the shop, display your wares creatively, add light fixtures and a place to pay, you do the same in the online world. Think about your retail experiences – shops that have been so attractive that you just couldn't help but browse, then before you know it, it turned into a buy. And then those shops that just felt a little awkward; the intimidating salesperson, the poorly laid-out store or they didn't have what you were looking for, but you don't know exactly what you were looking for, and something just didn't appeal.

Just as big-name retailers spent millions decorating their stores and understanding the psychology of their customers, the online world is just the same.

Your sales page is an experience for your customers. Your clients want an attractive page that is simple enough to keep them on the page without being 'too much' and overly decorated to scare them away. They want to connect with the copy and feel attracted to you. Just as in the real-world shop, you want them to decide what they're going to buy. Instead of moving to the cash desk, it's all about that 'click'.

What is a sales funnel?

A sales funnel is just fancy marketing speak for the journey your potential clients and customers go through to buy from you. The funnel is often made up of several steps of different products, each with their own sales page, that the potential customer can purchase. These steps vary depending on your course price point and sales model.

When you first start, you might use a sales page on your website and need to manually send your customers a link to PayPal. As you develop your business and your audience grows, you may look for integrated solutions that help you talk about your product or service seamlessly online with integrated payment systems such as PayPal, Apple Pay or Stripe.

There are many sales funnel software systems, a.k.a *the tech*, including ClickFunnels or Leadpages. This kind of software enables you to automate the process of taking large numbers of clients on a journey through your funnel from potential customer to buyer, using integrated sales pages, payment systems and post purchase welcome emails.

Copywriting for your sales page

But before we start metaphorically building your sales pages, we need to craft some copy. Understanding the psychology of selling and how to create a sales page is vital to your online business success because it's your shop front.

Think about a flower shop on the high street; it has divine pink peonies that we can't help but stop and smell. Imagine if you went into the shop to buy the flowers and it was dark and dingy – you might think twice because it wasn't a good buying experience. Or imagine that the sales assistant was rude to you? You'd leave, right? But if the person in the shop was warm and welcoming and then showed you some gorgeous pink roses that would match the peonies, you might say yes to those too.

Your sales pages are the shop in your sales funnel, that you decorate, and the words you say on the page are how you connect with the customer. How you decorate it, what you say, and the sales formula will impact your business's bottom line (more on sales funnels later in this chapter).

Sales copy is the words you use to sell your products and services. When I first started, I thought, *'I can do this; I've been a journalist for 20 years.'*

Big no. No.

Sales copy is an art and a different style of writing. Copywriters are some of the best-paid writers on the planet; part wordsmith, part psychologist and part salesperson, they can craft copy that makes people part with their hard-earned cash for what you are selling. As soon as you can afford to hire a copywriter, I would suggest that you consider that even for one project because there is a language and a nuanced way of writing that means your products and services are more likely to sell, and your profits will increase. But when you first start, hiring a copywriter most probably isn't an option, and it wasn't for me either, so I'll show you how you can get going as you work through this chapter. Yay!

First, you want to think about why people would like to buy your product. Is it something they need (and want), or is it a scroll-stopping desire that they will have once they discover your service?

What are you selling? Do your customers know they need your product or service? Why might they desire your product? And what's your hook to attract people to your product or service?

As Simon Sinek says in his compelling TED Talk, *'People don't buy what you do; they buy why you do it. If you talk about what you believe, you will attract those who believe what you believe.'*

Crafting your copy

When it comes to creating copy, you want to develop a relationship with your audience to build the know, like and trust factor. The more you understand your audience, the easier it is to create copy that talks to them!

If you just say that you want to talk to women aged 35 to 45, that doesn't mean anything. But if you say that you want to speak to menopausal women in their fifties who want to start a business, or a mid-thirties woman who is on maternity leave and is feeling lost, or talk to stuck 25-year-olds who've had their first job and realised the world of work sucks, then that is much more specific. The more targeted you can be, the better it is for your business.

Go back to your audience research that you conducted. Transcribe the notes from your interviews with potential clients. And if you didn't bother to do this research, I recommend that you have some discussions with your ideal client or customer now. Asking them about their pain points and what they need will help you understand the marketing language you need to use. You may find yourself using phrases and vocabulary from these calls. Focus on their pain points and what they need and also look at their desires. What could you present to them as the future that would make them ultimately buy your course?

If you're struggling for interviewees, you could look at the language people use in the reviews on Amazon for books that are targeted at your ideal client.

Objections

Make a list of objections that your ideal client would have to buying your course. These are reasons that may stop your potential buyers from actually clicking the 'buy' button. Maybe they don't want to purchase because:

✓ They're too busy and don't have time.
✓ They can't afford it.
✓ It's not for them.
✓ They're not experienced enough.
✓ They're too experienced.
✓ It's too technical for them.
✓ They can't see what makes this offer different to other offers out there.
✓ You aren't offering a guarantee or a refund policy for product.
✓ The price isn't clear.

When you are crafting your copy, you are solving a problem. Share testimonials of clients who had one or more of the objections, and people who struggled with an issue and how they overcame it, or tell your story in a way that overcomes many objections.

You might have seen sales pages that are crazily long in the online world. Despite the fact that very few people fully read the copy on the sales page, you want to make sure that you cover all those objections to ensure that you're answering the questions for the people that DO read it!

Things to think about before crafting your copy

Here's a list of questions to help you when we get writing.

☐ What is the name of your course (or membership)?
☐ Who are you talking to?
☐ What is the title of your course?

- ☐ How many modules will there be? Are there any particular features that you need to mention?
- ☐ What do you currently charge for the course? What is the regular price?
- ☐ Is there a price plan for your course? What are the payment plan options, if any?
- ☐ What bonuses are you offering with your course? Are there different bonuses at different times (e.g. early bird bonus or cart-closing bonus)? Write down the names, details and value of these.
- ☐ Who is your ideal customer to buy this course (or membership)? Describe the person that will benefit from purchasing this course.
- ☐ What makes your course unique or different to other people's offerings? Perhaps you have a unique experience, or you're targeting start-ups, people who can't cook, or an older demographic.
- ☐ What is the niche you're targeting to sell your course?
- ☐ What makes you an authority in your area or niche? Write out a brief biography and some accolades BUT share a bio that is written to sell the course; this is not a time to start writing your CV.
- ☐ What is the specific result your ideal customer or client will gain from this course?
- ☐ How quickly will they see results or experience this outcome?
- ☐ What has stopped your customer from getting it done and moving forward in the past?
- ☐ What is the most significant pain point your course solves/helps them do/achieve?
- ☐ How does your course solve their pain point or problem? Or perhaps it doesn't solve a pain point but creates a desire.
- ☐ Think about the course's most significant problem/pain point or desire – what is the most crucial benefit of your course?
- ☐ In a sentence or two, how would you present/describe your course to your ideal client with respect to how it benefits them?
- ☐ Why act now?

☐ What kind of support is included with your digital product or course? (Facebook group/WhatsApp group/Zoom calls/emails, etc.)

☐ What are your customer's objections to buying your course? List as many as you can (e.g. can't afford it, time, is it for me?, I'm not an expert, I'm not advanced enough, this is too advanced, I'm not very technical, I'm too old, I'm too young and inexperienced, my husband says no, etc.).

What's your writing style?

What will your customers connect with: punchy and *'bro'* marketing? Softer and more feminine? Or do you want to write the *'Queen's English'*? It might please your mum, but will it fit with your customers?

What are your brand traits? Do you use humour on social media? For some brilliant examples, check out @girlwithnojob or for business examples Chalene Johnson @chalenejohnson or Sam Bearfoot @iamsambearfoot on Instagram.

Perhaps you are *'educational'* and teach 'how-to' content – for some great examples, look at Keenya Kelly @keenyakelly who teaches all things TikTok (on TikTok and Instagram), Janet Murray @janmurrayuk, Boss Babes on Instagram @bossbabes, Gillian Perkins on YouTube or Stefan James (founder of Project Life Mastery) on YouTube.

Maybe you are *'spiritual'* – for some inspiring examples, look at Gabrielle Bernstein or Jessica Huie @Jessica_huie_ or Deepak Chopra @deepakchopra or Russell Brand @russellbrand on Instagram.

SALES PAGE

In the sales pages, you want to include the following areas:

HEADLINE

Include a big headline statement or question that will hook people in. Talk about a pain point or a challenge. Make it stand out! These are THE most important words on the sales page. It will make people decide to keep reading or click away.

For example:

Get XXXX [no #1 result] without the [biggest struggle your ideal client will have in attempting to go for this].

OR

Did you know that XX% of [insert industry e.g. start-ups or marriages] fail within the first XX years?

SUBHEADING

This is your statement that further supports your headline and shows the transformation.

THE PROBLEM

Go into the pain point and challenge of your customer. Tell a story of difficulty and struggle. Acknowledge their reality right NOW and the struggle they are facing. Think about what keeps them awake at night. What annoys them about their situation? What's their biggest frustration?

For example, *'After years of learning, studying and reading [insert all the learning you've done], I've discovered the #1 most effective way to [insert desire, e.g. study for exams / house train a puppy / manage my relationship with my kids].'*

'Even if you've [insert specific story on struggles x 3] . . .'

'It's not too late to . . .'

'Yep, I promise, it's not too late to turn everything around.'

'How do I know this?'

Then introduce your experience. Either you have struggled with the same problem and talk about how you got out of the challenge or say how you've helped others to overcome this challenge.

FUTURE THINKING . . . THE DREAM!

This is where you present the possibility of the future if they solve this pain point. What do they secretly desire?

You could start with the words 'Imagine if you could' or 'Wouldn't it be nice to . . .?' then present a list of examples where you can get the buyer to imagine what life would be like if they overcame this problem or challenge.

Use words your ideal client would use and make it so that they feel you are talking directly to them!

For example, imagine if you could:

- **Break the endless pattern** of [insert pain] and replace them with techniques that ACTUALLY [insert the action, e.g. gets your dog to . . .].
- **Stop using** [insert things people do to avoid the problem, e.g. stop watching TV and start enjoying being at home with your partner].
- **Go to bed each night feeling** [insert emotion about way you've handled the day].
- **Enjoy** [insert things your ideal client would dream about doing].
- **Feel** [insert emotions such as calm or confident e.g feel more confident in meetings] **about XXX situation** because you've learned [insert your ideal client's transformation, e.g. the ability to speak up in meetings].
- Easily [insert the desire, e.g. launch a business or potty train a toddler].
- **Insert more dreams/emotions.**

And all just by taking this ONE course and applying the methods inside.

THE OFFER

This is where you transition to writing about the secret formula that is the number one ingredient that that has helped you to achieve these results . . . all just by taking this ONE course and applying the methods inside.

What if you could start seeing results before [insert timeframe]?
What if you could go into [insert timeframe] with a [share your secret formula] that made you feel [insert emotions]?
What if this was the best time investment you ever made in your XXX journey? (Hint: I've heard these exact words from other [insert who your people are, e.g. course creators/mums/couples] after completing this course!)

Name your offer. Include a brief summary of the offer and say what they'll get:

☐ Show the video lessons and tools they'll receive.
☐ Share graphics of the course modules.
☐ Will there be a live training element?
☐ Will there be a Facebook group?
☐ Will there be one-to-one support or a WhatsApp group?

Share some specific features and don't tell them about the ingredients, then say what the transformation will mean to them. Explain what the transformation will be and what makes it unique.

Bold out the benefits so they stand out on the page.

Share some additional bonuses that buyers will get when they buy the course (only do this if it's a higher-cost course). And again include the transformation.

Include the value of each item (e.g. value £300).

THE PRICE

Now it's time to talk about the 'investment'.

You can convey the value if they pay in full rather than instalments, or you could jump right into the 'assumptive close' where you could say something along the lines of . . .

This course normally costs XXX . . .

But you can have it right now for just XXX! [half the value].

As soon as you register, I'll send you an email with all the details and a link that gives you immediate access to the course.

Enter your information below NOW to get the course!

Then include a call to action (CTA) button to get the sale. Have bright CTA buttons that stand out and say something like:

'I'm ready to XXXX [result]!

GUARANTEE

This is where you offer a guarantee. This is the reassurance for the customer that this is a legitimate product.

It is entirely up to you and what you are comfortable with; you could offer 14 days or 30 days guarantee or no refund at all, although that may put off some potential purchasers.

I'll talk more about refunds (and guarantees) in Chapter 11.

CREATE SOME URGENCY!

You want people to make a buying decision right now, even if the course is for sale all the time. Tell them it's available for a limited time, or there are just three spots left.

For example:

For A Limited Time Only Get [name of course in full with subtitle] For Just XXX [insert price]!

NOW INTRODUCE YOURSELF

It's at this point that you introduce yourself. You're not just selling your offer, you're selling YOU. Tell them why you are the person to be teaching this course. Share your knowledge and expertise.

This is NOT the time to pull out your CV, this is the time to sell again by sharing your story and experience in your subject. So, say how your course has had such amazing results for these students, then share testimonials and social proof. If you've just created the course, that's why it really helps to get feedback from beta testers who are testing the product, or people who have had one-to-one training with you or attended a training that you've given.

Sprinkle screenshots of social media comments showing how incredible your course is and how fabulous you are.

Include video testimonials if you have them (you may not have them when you're first starting out).

TELL THEM WHO THIS COURSE IS FOR –
AND WHO IT'S NOT FOR . . .

List people that this course can help and why it can help them, e.g. *'This course is for go-getters who want to streamline their XXX.'*

Then list the people that it can't help. For example:

This course is NOT for people who don't want to work smart or want the easy way out.
This course is NOT for people who don't get [list transformation].

FAQS . . .

This is a section where you can list all the possible questions that your ideal client might have about your course and their objections:

✓ Share your brand values and what you stand for (perhaps your anti-racism stance or environmental credentials).

✓ Will this course work for XXX person who's struggling with . . .?

✓ What if I need to take a break during the programme?

✓ Will this course work for non-techy people?

✓ Will this course work for people who aren't qualified in XXX?

✓ Will this course work for people who are OVERqualified in XXX?

✓ Does this course answer the key questions about time, money, technical ability and confidence about a problem?

SUMMARISE THE COURSE

This is where you round up everything that you've talked about. Most people skim a sales page and don't read it. They will read this section.

• Remind them of all the great stuff they're getting.

• Talk about the problem and the solution.

• Have a final Call to Action (CTA) to invite them to join.

• Present them with a choice . . . This is your last chance to hook them in – these words matter.

And then they click through to the order page!

If you would like to access this outline in a PDF, go to www.make-moneywhileyousleepbook.com/bonus.

And just as a reminder, you want to be relatable and understandable. Don't use jargon or words that won't mean anything to your client. Why say robotics when you could say put your business on autopilot?

Share the transformation. What are they going to LEARN? What BENEFIT will the course bring? What differentiates you from competitors in the marketplace?

Why does your customer want this transformation?

Erica Lee Strauss is one of my go-tos for copywriting and she supports students in my Make Money While You Sleep membership. Here are some of her copywriting hacks:

Writing a stand out sales page can intimidate even the savviest entrepreneur – and most confident writer! – but it's a must-know skill for online course creators who want to sell with ease while catching their beauty Zzz's!

When you do it 'right', a sales page will 1) paint a clear picture of your ideal client's biggest pain points (where they are now), 2) paint an equally vivid picture of what they desire (where they want to be) and 3) explain how your course can uniquely transport them from point A to point B.

While that might sound like an order taller than a three-pump venti caramel macchiato with extra drizzle at Starbucks, you don't have to wing it. Here are my top tips for writing a sales page that sells:

1. Craft a killer headline. Your headline is the most important copy on your sales page. Use these precious words to grab attention by focusing on your reader's biggest problem or biggest desire. In other words, your headline should speak to what your clients desperately want, or desperately want to get rid of – or both!

Example: 'Write a succinct sales page that actually sells' (big desire), 'Stop second guessing every word on your sales page' (big problem), or 'Write a sales page that sells – and stop second guessing your writing skills forever' (both).

2. Use your ideal client's language. It's easy to talk over our client's heads because it's the way we talk. Instead, describe their problems and desires the way they do. This not only makes your sales page easier to read and understand (yay!), it also makes your reader feel deeply seen and understood – and more likely to buy.

Example: You're a relationship coach who teaches clients self-love so they can attract relationships. Do your ideal clients desire 'self-love' (and use that language) or would they rather 'find their soulmate' or 'stop dating crappy people'? Bonus tip: Swipe your ideal client's verbiage directly from Facebook groups, surveys & discovery calls or other interactions.

3. Focus on benefits, not features (or your methodology/process). While it's wonderful to have a signature process & to pack your course with fun features, they don't ultimately sell your offer.

Example: Turn a feature-driven statement like, '20+ hours of unique content on positive psychology' into a benefit-driven statement like, '20+ hours of unique content on positive psychology designed to turn you into a more confident speaker in 4 weeks flat.' After each feature, complete the phrase, 'so that they can . . .' to get to the benefit.

4. Talk about yourself. If you want your reader to snap your offer up with confidence, make sure to include a section with your unique story, background & credentials (or anything that makes you uniquely qualified). This will build that sweet know, like and trust factor so people feel safe (and justified!) buying from you. Don't forget to include a photo, too, because this is the internet, and people want to know you're a real human (and not a #catfish!). (And the same goes for photos – aka mockups – of course materials.)

5. Add a FAQ section. Most people won't devour every word on your sales page and that's okay! Add a FAQ (or 'Frequently Asked Questions') section to ease pre-purchase jitters. People reading this section want to find reasons to justify their purchase – so give it to them! (Humans buy for both logical and emotional reasons – and the emotional stuff we've covered by now!)

Common FAQs include: 'Why does this cost [X] amount?', 'How much time will this take?', 'Can't I learn this on my own?' and 'Why should I trust you?'

6. BE SPECIFIC. Do any of your sentences feel a bit 'blah'? Add a proper noun, color, texture, numbers, or anything related to the five senses to spice it up.

Example: 'You're burnt out' becomes 'You wolf down dinner at your white Ikea desk everyday, can't concentrate for more than three minutes before needing a "TikTok break" and don't have the energy to keep up with anything (save for decades-old episodes of Keeping up with the Kardashians*).'*

Now it's time to get writing!

I know how difficult it is to actually get writing for your sales page. Most of my students would merrily trot along learning and then give up when it came to the sales page. I realised I had to change the format. So, I introduced a 'Get it Done' workshop where they craft the copy and go through a workbook just like this copy here.

Having deadlines to write to and the support and accountability helps you to actually move forward.

In writing this book, I struggled with my procrastination and I started running every day (errm, okay, granny running), but it helped me to focus and stay on track. And while I ran, I listened to James Clear's *Atomic Habits,* which helped me recognise how I could hack my systems and habits.

Set yourself two hours and just write out your plan. Yes, you may feel like you want to scroll aimlessly on social media and raid the fridge, so make it easier for yourself. Hack your procrastination and put your phone in another room or do whatever it takes to give yourself that space and clarity to write.

When you know that you have something happening (you have to pick the kids up from school or have drinks at 5pm or an exercise class booked), it can make you more productive because you feel you have to get it done before the activity. Create that momentum so that you start.

Once you start, you are on a roll, and it's easier to keep writing. The brain struggles to start something new because starting new projects consumes so much energy. Once you are in flow, it's easier!

It doesn't have to be perfect!

In the beginning, it might be scratchy and messy, and that's normal. You can tweak and refine as you go. But it is much better to have something than nothing.

Remember, *done is better than perfect!*

Just get writing! Some people will write and it's a flurry of perfect sentences. I'm more of a scrappy mess that gradually turns into something that someone else would want to read.

What if your grammar or writing isn't perfect?

Just because your Year 7 English teacher didn't like your story doesn't mean that you can't write about your course on a sales page. (Grammarly is this AMAZING resource that can give you a gentle nudge if you're not making sense.)

Sales pages aren't a thesis for your PhD; it is a way to get people to buy your course or digital product. You want to tell them what it is and why it can help them. Writing is like everything else; the more you do it, the easier it gets. My first sales page was hilariously awful!

Reading the words out loud will help you to make sense and help with the flow. And if you're struggling because this is just not your thing, that's okay. Don't beat yourself up about it.

If you are really struggling with the copywriting, you can look to hire a copywriter, but for most people this isn't an option when you first create your course. If you are an established business with various income streams and pressing deadlines, this could be worth considering.

Remember: you are going to tweak and refine your sales copy when it is in the page in your funnel. You are going to tweak the wording when you are looking at your figures and what's working in your online business. Your sales page copy is a constantly evolving process.

Now we're going to shift gears and talk about the tech needed to support your sales pages, i.e. the sales funnel. This is the next stage for you in the process of creating your course!

What sales platforms are best for you?

The critical thing to remember is that you can start small and move as your business grows (this isn't buying a house that you will live in for the next 20 years).

Your sales page will start small and scratchy, but in time it will become slicker and fancier. Which software you use also comes hand in hand with choosing where you will host your course. Some course-creation platforms have an integrated sales page (Kajabi or Kartra or Teachable). Or you can also buy a standalone sales page platform such as ClickFunnels or Leadpages.

To make the best decision for you and your business choose software that fits seamlessly with your course platform.

I personally use Clickfunnels for my sales pages, but if I'm honest, I recommend Kajabi for a simple integrated solution. There are many software-hosting platforms and I've compiled a starter's guide if you go to www.makemoneywhileyousleepbook.com/bonus to help you decide. Do your research, test the free trial demos and see what works for you. Perhaps also talk to other entrepreneurs and ask for feedback about their favourite platforms.

The tech can be the biggest headline and limitation when it comes to building an online business. Once you crack this, the possibilities are endless. Embrace the sales systems that work for you.

Fear of tech?

Funnels and tech can feel overwhelming and prevent many of us actually moving forward. I'm not going to pretend that you will understand everything, and I'm also going to tell you there will be days when you want to throw your laptop out of the window. In the beginning, I remember building a landing page and having a blue splodge that I just couldn't get rid of, and it's soooo frustrating when you can't figure it out.

However, your tech challenges are not a reason to not build a business that works for you. Start small, don't overcomplicate things, and do your research! Use platforms that work for your business, are user-friendly with a support desk to help you out when you feel stuck.

If you want more help deciding what platform is right for you, go to www.makemoneywhileyousleepbook.com/bonus to see what platforms I use.

One potential option when you feel you have sufficient cash in the business, or other revenue streams, is to outsource some of the tech. Reinvesting some of those revenues is a great investment allowing you to focus more on your areas of strength and build your business. If you are looking to outsource, you can search on many social media platforms for VAs – 'virtual assistants' – or 'tech VAs', who will help you navigate the tech. I have two tech VAs who I work with, and I adore! I realised that while I learned to do the tech it wasn't the best use of my time, as something simple could take me hours, and sometimes fried my brain! Instead, I send them a WhatsApp message asking them to help me with something, it takes them an hour, so I can get on with the business of serving my customers and creating more products. It means that I'm in my sweet spot of creating, I'm not overwhelmed with a mountain of tech, and it's a more effective use of my time *and* my business works properly because the tech is seamless. You don't have to know everything in the digital world to run a successful online business.

By hiring someone, your small business can also impact lives and change futures. That is the beauty of this globally interconnected world.

Don't use your fear of sales or writing or tech to be an excuse why you don't take action! If I can do this, you can too!

There's a saying in the online world: 'new levels, new devils', and it's there for a reason. As you grow as a business, you will embrace new challenges, things won't work out as you want them to, people will upset you, the tech will fail, but that is not a reason to press pause on your dreams.

You are here reading this book because you are dreaming of opportunities and possibilities. You know that you have this nugget of an idea, and you just need to make it become a reality. This is your chance to create meaningful change in your life and your family's life.

This is your time! Now do the work!

CHAPTER 9

Master the Masterclass!

A masterclass is another fancy word for your webinar training or sales presentation. When I started selling, I was a disaster! I would create these presentations, give lots of value and 'teach' people a ton of stuff and then stick a 'would you like to buy?' at the end, and, sadly, very few people bought.

A webinar is a way of selling your course and nailing your webinar is key to the success of selling your course. I always suggest working on your webinar BEFORE you get too involved in the launch process because this is so important to your success! Then you can tweak while you're in the promotional phase of the launch.

Regardless of how you decide to sell your course, using a webinar sales presentation is usually at the heart of your sales strategy. Whether you are selling via an evergreen webinar (and selling all the time) or you are doing a launch with a webinar, or you're creating a Facebook challenge in a Facebook group, you will be putting a sales presentation at the core of what you do.

However, you don't have to create a webinar for a mini-course because people probably won't want to spend 30 minutes watching a webinar sharing why they should spend £19 on a mini-course.

First . . . a little pep talk

But before you say, *Lucy, that sounds really icky*, I want you to know that I too struggle with the selling . . . I get it; I've been there. And I used to hate creating webinars.

In this chapter, I am going to show you how you too can create a webinar. And while it's maybe not something you love to do, you can get immense satisfaction from nailing your webinar format and creating something that is going to help you to make money.

'But, Lucy, why do I have to even bother doing a masterclass?'

Masterclasses or webinars are important because you are more likely to successfully sell when you use one. A live or pre-recorded webinar is a virtual way of 'pressing the flesh' and enabling your customers to get to know, like and trust you.

If you send a customer straight to a sales page for a £27 course it will still mean that they buy from you and you don't need to worry about doing a webinar. But if you are selling a course for £300 or above, a webinar is essential.

One of the most important things that I can recommend with creating your masterclass is to practise. You will be scrappy initially, but the more you get used to selling to a live audience and talking about a subject, the easier it will be.

The first one you do will feel terrifying, and that's okay; we've all been there.

Like everything, the more you do, the easier it gets. And we will talk more about your presentation skills later in this chapter.

We can all have this voice in our head that tells us we're no good at selling and useless at getting people to buy from us. But the reality is that if you want to create a business and enormous potential for your family, you have to learn to sell. Being in business is about selling your goods and services, and as uncomfortable as it may be, you have to learn to do it.

But before you immediately respond with *'this isn't for me'* I want you to honestly answer these questions: Why are you reading this book? Why are you contemplating creating a course?

It's because you are sick of doing things the same old way and getting the same outcomes. You are tired of being on the working treadmill, trying to pay the bills, hit deadlines, do the shopping, keep the house tidy and make ends meet. Perhaps you're working in a way that's not helping you – you're juggling the merry-go-round of school drop-offs, racing to work and racing home to meet the kids, cook dinner and then bed. You're feeling exhausted and over-whelmed and want some direction and purpose in your life.

You keep being told it's about finding the balance, but it's not; it's about getting off the endless cycle of bland and boring monotony.

Or perhaps you are running a business that is sucking the life and soul out of you. You are juggling everything with business and the family. You know there has to be a better way.

I want you to go back to your passion and purpose. Why do you do what you do? What motivated you to create a business in the first place? What did you hope to do and achieve?

You are here because you want more for your life.

- ☞ Do you want to spend the rest of your days doing what you're doing, or do you want to do something different?
- ☞ Do you want to create extraordinary opportunities and possibilities for yourself and your family?
- ☞ Imagine if you could work from anywhere and not have to be chained down by work?
- ☞ What experiences do you want to have? Where would you like to travel to? What's on your bucket list of countries and adventures?
- ☞ What do you want to be remembered for in the world? For being someone who was around for your family? Or for being the person who was always in the office?

☞ How would it feel to be around in the holidays for your kids? Or take the grandchildren to Disneyland, or have incredible experiences with them?

☞ Imagine if you could volunteer for organisations you care about and spend your time doing things you love. Or change your corner of the world.

If you continue to stay stuck in the old ways of working, you will stay the world's best-kept secret. You won't get to fulfil your passion and purpose, instead, you settle for mediocre. And you don't get to impact the world with your message . . .

You are here reading this book because you want to create a new way of working. A way where you get to work on the projects that you love, with clients that you adore, and you get to choose the hours that you work.

Selling your course is your opportunity to share your experiences and learnings with the world and truly impact lives. You get to help your clients solve a problem and make a change on a massive impressive scale.

Let's reframe your webinar (or, if you prefer to call it, masterclass) as a service. You are offering people something to help them overcome their problem. You are helping them by making something available that is going to be transformational and life-changing.

And when you see the benefit and the goodness that you can create in the world when you share your message and methods, what have you got to lose? Do you want to stay stuck doing the same old thing, or do you want to step into new ways of working?

Creating a webinar isn't 'comfortable', it is stepping out of your comfort zone, but it will enable you to transition to a new way of being.

When you throw a stone into a pond, the ripples radiate outwards. Throwing the stone requires effort, but the waves spread out across the water, changing the shape and form of the pond. Creating a webinar is sending ripples across your industry. It's an effort to throw that stone into your pool of contacts and invite them along, but the changes can be genuinely transformational.

Let's start creating those ripples and changing things up!

Webinars help you get clients fast! Why? Because you are creating a space to sell what you do in a controlled way. People spend 30 minutes and more listening to you, hearing about your experience, and your offer opens a doorway to new possibilities. All you have to do is create that path to the sale, which means infusing the sale throughout the webinar.

Remember how I said I first screwed up when I was selling with webinars because I would stick the sale on the end? Sprinkle mentions of your course throughout the slides so that it's a seamless transition.

When you focus on yourself in selling, it can feel uncomfortable and icky. What if you were to focus on the transformation in your students? When you can focus on how it will help others, it makes it easier to sell. And from there, you can sell with confidence because you are selling with an energy of love and gratitude.

Focus on the transformation of your clients, sell with love, and it becomes easier!

- Think about how your clients will feel when they achieve their goal (and can visualise the transformation).
- Start getting excited about how lucky you are to speak up and share.
- When you show up with an attitude of gratitude and service, how will you feel when you speak to your audience?

Perhaps the biggest lesson in creating a webinar is that this is not a job interview where you have to rattle off your experiences and list of achievements. This is a time to tell stories that connect and make your audience feel that if you can do it, so can they!

Your story wants to touch people's hearts and connect with them at a soul level, so they feel that 'yes, we're the same!'. You think about how you connect with someone at an event or a social gathering, and you talk about TV or kids, and then you talk about what you do, and gradually they say, 'oh, I need some help with this.'

Your social media posts are about the social niceties so that they get to know you and you connect. The webinar is to explain what you do and how you can help them. The emphasis is on THEM and their transformation!

Entrepreneur Seth Godin once said, *'When in doubt, raise money from your customers by selling them something they truly need – your product.'*

Let's get your webinar nailed!

Your story

When our ancestors were roaming the plains and deserts, they entertained themselves by sitting around the fire and telling stories of fighting lions and escaping through the jungle. Storytelling is one of our oldest forms of communication, and it's how we navigate and understand the world.

While we no longer have to fight lions or hide from wild bears, we still connect with our view of the world through storytelling. Stories give us all the feels, from tears to terror. I remember hiding behind the sofa when *Jaws* was on TV. Or how I sobbed when Rachel came back for Ross in *Friends*, and how I wished I could hang out in Central Perk with my besties Rachel and Phoebe for a coffee.

---

* seths.blog/2012/06/before-you-raise-money-assets-and-expenses

We grew up sitting on the sofa and watching stories play out on TV. Now, in the age of the influencer, YOU are Rachel or Joey. You, as a small business owner and course creator can entertain, inspire and influence.

Your stories build connection and sell who you are and what you do. Throughout your social media and your webinar, you want to have a couple of signature stories that you share. These are your stories that convey the transformation you have been on, and you make these stories relatable to your client.

You tell these stories repeatedly and reinforce your brand message, what you care about, and what you stand for.

I posted this on LinkedIn recently:

I started my business because I couldn't physically go back to work for health reasons, and I knew that I wanted something more.

My little boy was a baby, and he got Hand, Foot and Mouth.

And then so did I.

It allowed me to think and figure out what I wanted.

And so I started while breastfeeding my son by writing blog posts on my phone.

I didn't have all the answers, but I knew that I wanted to pursue my passions and create change in the world.

What's your WHY?!

Why do you do what you do?

In this post, I'm connecting with my audience and sharing why I do what I do.

Why do you do what you do? What inspired you to get started? What was your biggest driver? What is the pain point that kept you awake at night and connects you to your clients?

My incontinence was a significant factor in leaving my career in journalism and starting in the online world. But if I were sharing my story with the Professional Golf Association, I wouldn't necessarily start with that story because it perhaps wouldn't resonate with an audience of golfers. You want to tell stories that connect with your participants.

What do they need to hear in the webinar? What stories will help them see what's possible?

Write out your signature story – this is a core story at the heart of you and your brand and connects to the webinar. Stories trump facts because they are easier for our brains to digest than facts. Think about it, would you like to read about online marketing, be shown a bunch of statistics, or read a story about someone's success in the online world? For most people, we prefer to read a story than a spreadsheet.

Stories are also part emotion and psychology and part narrative. Think of the brand stories of Bill Gates building his first computer in his parents' garage, or Sara Blakely selling Spanx while in full-time work. These stories are almost folklore in legend.

Your story creates a connection between your brand and potential buyers and helps them see that you (Ordinary Jo or Joe) overcame these hurdles to build a business, and it has enabled you to scale successfully.

You want to share what you are willing to do to help your clients get the best results and possibilities. Your signature story is about weaving a little magic into the narrative so that it's as though you've had your brand put through the Hollywood blender, and now YOU are the superhero.

Now, imagine if your story moved your audience to buy; how would that feel?

Do a Disney on your life!

When you are crafting your stories, you want to use the narrative arc. This is the classic method of storytelling in three parts that you can steal from Shakespeare and Disney and add to your webinar – obviously I'm not saying you want to talk all Shakespearean and steal his actual words, but you can use the process.

Act One: Think of a Hollywood movie; you have a regular guy or gal who is ordinary and unaccomplished and struggling in his or her day job. You set the scene of your old life and the frustrations and challenges. You sow the seeds of struggle.

Act Two: You are failing. Nothing is working. You've lost everything, you're so embarrassed, your family thinks you're a mess . . . you're [insert your story and the hardship and challenge] and then you discovered this XXX [insert the secret formula or way of working] that changed everything. Now you have a way out . . . you start climbing out of the hole. You take us on a journey with you.

Act Three: You keep climbing out of the hole. Each day it gets easier, even though it's still a struggle, and you reach the summit! Everyone loves you. You are the star, and you get the guy or girl. How did you achieve all this? Our unlikely hero has some soul-searching and has to dig deep, but in the webinar you share that this would not have been possible if you didn't follow your unique three-step process [insert what feels right to you: unique formula/system/way of being]. You've learned that if you follow your particular system that is special to you, then life is much better, and you can create massive success on your terms.

How often have you heard those kinds of stories? Take note of people using those stories in the online world. What stories resonate? And what stories are annoying? Start reverse engineering what works and what doesn't work.

Now it's time to create your story. You can use this in your marketing and messaging.

Donald Miller's book *Building a Story Brand* is a great place to start if you need additional support.

What is a core premise?

Your core premise is one sentence that will explain what transformation you are offering and gets the audience to question and shift their way of thinking. The core premise is the backbone of your webinar, for example:

> [*vehicle e.g. Using TikTok*] is the fastest/most effective way to get [*result – client wants: e.g. Build an Audience Right now*]

> OR

> [*vehicle e.g. Trying the Keto Plan*] is the fastest/most effective way to get [*result – client wants: e.g. Shift those unwanted pounds*]

Now it's your job to prove this statement throughout the webinar! You want to focus on your ideal client's desires, resistance and objection and get them to shift their thinking.

As you create your webinar, ask yourself: *'Are they ready to commit and shift their thinking?'*

Then tune into your client's problems and objections. What is stopping them from buying this course? How can you get them to think differently?

Business growth strategist, Christina Jandali loves launching and has built a multi-million dollar business thanks to her launch strategy. Here are Christina's tips . . .

The biggest mistakes I would say when it comes to launching is thinking that people want to actually buy your course, your coaching or whatever it is that you are selling.

They don't want to buy your thing, they don't want the delivery of it, they just want to solve their problem.

> *That means that we have to clearly articulate to them the transformation and the pain and the solution. If your mistake is just selling them what you want to sell, selling the features of the programme, it's not going to convert. You've got to sell people on the emotions and the possibility – the after result – of what they are going to create.*

What's your client's problem and how do you overcome their objections?

Connect with the ideal client who is going to buy your course. What are their biggest problems? Where are they right now? What do they need to hear from you? What are their most significant objections to buying your course?

We covered this earlier, but let's recap on some of your ideal client's key objections. Perhaps they'll say . . .

- ☞ I can't afford it.
- ☞ I don't have time right now.
- ☞ I don't have the right knowledge.
- ☞ I'm not good with tech.
- ☞ I need to check with my partner.
- ☞ I'm not ready yet.
- ☞ Is this course too advanced for me?
- ☞ Is this course too introductory for me?
- ☞ I'll wait until I'm ready to do XXX . . . or I'll wait until I've reached XXX success . . .

Think of some objections as to why your ideal client may NOT buy your course. What excuses will they give? What objections will they offer?

Write out all the objections that your client will have. Go back through your notes from your interviews with ideal clients, and you may find some more objections.

In your webinar, you want to use stories to overcome every objection that your client may have. So get clarity about the objections and dig into these. Use stories that you may have (or that your clients have) about overcoming the objection.

Use the Hollywood story method that we talked through earlier to overcome the objections. Show how they were struggling and that it wasn't working, then how they reached a crisis in their work (or their relationship or business), and found a solution.

The solution was your three-step formula (your secret formula within your course) that showed them how to solve the pain point you're offering.

Sprinkle case studies and testimonials of your student success strategies throughout your webinar. Screenshot comments from students on your social media to show how fabulous your course is and include these in the webinar.

Use this strategy to overcome every excuse that your potential clients will throw at you for why they don't want to buy. Your job is to convert their doubt into a sale BEFORE you've even said what you're selling and how much it is.

Once you have identified your potential students' objections to buying your course, you want to tap into these and overcome them. You could say something such as: 'I'm going to introduce the three biggest myths about [insert your student's desired goal from the course].'

For example: 'I'm going to introduce the three biggest myths when it comes to healthy eating at home.'

Then you can explore each of these three myths. This is your opportunity to overcome their objections that they don't have time, or they aren't qualified or whatever are the key reasons your client gives that would stop them buying the course.

Pre-selling to your audience

Use testimonials to convey your client's transformation throughout. Share how client X went from struggling to successful (and if you don't have clients yet, use your testimonials from beta testers).

Use your stories to overcome each objection. When you list your client's objections and problems, you can use your client's testimonial stories to show how they've successfully achieved their goals and got results from doing your course.

Ask your audience to say YES throughout the webinar. From the small questions such as *'are you having fun?'* or *'do you want to make money online?'*, if they say yes to the minor stuff, they are more likely to say yes to the big decisions and buy from you.

Bonuses

Bonuses are the additional programmes and courses that you can drop into your course as 'add-ons' to sell it. These are not the core content of the course but are complementary to the course.

You could create an extra mini-training or offer an additional workshop. You could offer swipe files (marketing speak for copies) of your email templates or a 21-day planner. Or you could create social media templates to help people post on Instagram, a guided visualisation to encourage them to meditate and relieve stress, or perhaps a 21-day journal to help them track their food intake each day.

Whatever you do, you want the perceived value of these bonus products to match the value of the course.

Crafting your webinar title

The webinar title should be catchy and have a hook. You want to draw them into wanting to know more.

Show your potential clients what's possible and use the all-important word 'without', so it's without overwhelm, stress or difficulty. You want to make them believe that this is achievable, this is possible, and that you and they are just the same.

Examples include:

☞ 'How to use YouTube to build a lead machine to sell on repeat *without* spending hours on social media.'
☞ 'Grow your audience on LinkedIn *without* having to send lots of sleazy messages.'
☞ 'Cook easy and healthy family meals *without* spending a fortune.'

You are offering a solution and using the word 'without' to remind them that they don't have to do something that may be an objection stopping them from taking action.

Christina Jandali shares some top tips:
The topic title is going to get people to watch it but the most important part of the webinar is actually not the content. Yet this is the part that people will spend the most time, effort and energy on and is not the part that matters.

Focus on what happens earlier in the webinar before you get to the content. When it comes to having a webinar that sells, you have to regard it as a metaphorical bucket of water with a bunch of holes in it. When you're pouring the water in, you're piling on information, giving them great value and content in the webinar, but it's just going through the holes.

Before you even get to the core content that you're going to teach, you want to make sure that you address the elephant in the room and talk about the mistakes and the beliefs that people have that prevent them from being open to receiving what you are about to share.

At the beginning of the webinar, call out the false beliefs that people may have that may prevent them from purchasing. Your job is to reframe and flip those beliefs and help them get a fresh perspective. Once they are open to seeing the possibility, then you can share your core premise:

What's the one thing that, if they believed it, would make their success inevitable, would get them to become a buyer?

You are warming them up and creating a demand and hunger to consume what you're sharing.

The webinar close

When you 'close' your webinar, you don't want to wait until the last five slides to sell. This is your time to share your offer with your audience, but you are not having to 'sell' at this point.

As I mentioned before, you want to sell throughout, so it means that you don't need to do the hard sell. You are using your storytelling to overcome objections and you should do this seamlessly throughout the webinar. Sprinkle your sell in the webinar so that it doesn't feel icky and salesy.

Then you can share your final slides in a seamless transition and make your audience an offer to which they can't help but say YES!

As you prepare to close the webinar, you want to ask questions that your audience have been primed to say yes to, such as:

'If there was a way to get my system for [insert your solution to the problem your course solves], *would you take it?'*

'*What will happen to you* [and your family if relevant] *if you keep* [doing the thing that is causing you pain]?'

'*I can't guarantee what your outcome is going to be, but what I can guarantee is the cost of your inaction, the cost of you not moving forward, the cost of not doing what you desire* [insert adjectives].'

Then tap into the three reasons why they are watching the webinar and what solutions they are seeking, and then, and only at this point, can you share your offer and talk about your course.

You could say something like, '*Then [name of course] is right for you.*'

From there, you can again overcome those objections by saying:

'*Even if . . . you [list objection 1] or you struggle with [list objection 2] or [list objection 3].*'

Now is your time to talk about what the course offers, share each of the modules and explain how best it will help your audience overcome their challenge.

Go through each of the modules in your course. Share a taste of what they'll learn, but you don't want to teach or overwhelm. Share the 'what' but not the 'how to'.

Imagine if you were buying a brand new house that hadn't yet been built. You would look at the plans and architectural drawings. The builders would most likely produce a 'showhouse' for you to go and see and imagine how your house might look.

You want to do the same thing for your students. Walk them through the sales page, the order page and the buying process, so they know what to expect. This will help convert your students into customers.

Your final slide should:

- Include a summary of the course and what they'll learn.
- Include all the bonuses and the value
- Outline the total value of the course and the bonuses.

- Share the cost of your course in big, bold letters or payment plan.
- Offer a FAST-action bonus, so they sign up within the next 20 minutes.
- Share a URL of your sales page that is easy to remember and type.

Finally, if it is a live event, wrap up the webinar with a question-and-answer session. When you start to answer those questions, leave your final slide on the screen as you answer the questions.

Prepare some questions that you want to answer in the Q&A. think about what objections need answering. What questions do your students need to know: perhaps it is about payment plans, or the length of the programme or whether there is a guaranteed refund?

Just like at an event where no one wants to go first, people feel shy about asking questions. Prime a biz bestie or your assistant or friend to ask some of these questions to get the ball rolling. Once someone asks a question, others will also ask their questions.

If it is an evergreen webinar, ensure you have covered off these questions and objections in your presentation

This is your opportunity to talk through people's objections and support them in making a decision.

When someone buys your course, name them and praise them! Say how it's incredible they are taking action and joining you on this journey. You're here because you want to get off the hamster wheel.

Your webinar design

Canva is one of the most incredible tools for a small-business owner, and they also have beautiful designs for webinars.

One of the benefits of using Canva is that you can create amazing slides that look well designed, and you can add photos that are already part of the Canva system. They have a vast image library, and the photos are great. You pay $1 to download each image, but actually with the webinar option on Canva you don't need to download anything; you can use Canva and press 'present' on the software.

If you use PowerPoint, Keynote or Google Slides, you can use their templates and import your own designs. The templates within the systems are good but perhaps not as stylish as Canva. You would then need to upload images from an image library.

You can use free stock images from online sites such as Unsplash or Pixabay. These have lovely photos, and you can download these and then upload them to your PowerPoint presentation.

Types of webinar

As mentioned at the beginning of the chapter, there are different types of webinars, and essentially your approach will be driven by whether your course is being sold using a live launch or evergreen model (and we'll explore these options in more detail in Chapters 10 and 11).

In terms of your webinar, it can be as technical or non-technical as you like. In creating a webinar, you want to think about where you are going to host the video. And in the online world, there are lots of options for how you can distribute your webinar.

LIVE WEBINAR OPTIONS

You can do a 'live' launch of your webinar. This means you are invit-ing people to come and watch your training and hope they buy from you.

You could just create a live event on Zoom, Facebook, LinkedIn or YouTube and invite people to come and watch the training. You could then go live regularly to present your webinar, or do it once a month for several months to test what works for you. This is a low-tech option that also garners sales.

EVERGREEN WEBINAR OPTIONS

'Evergreen' (as opposed to a live seasonal launch) means that it never goes away and you can get people to watch your recorded webinar all the time.

You could create a recording of your webinar and then upload this to a video sharing site such as Vimeo or YouTube, embed this on to a page on your website and invite people to watch it. Or you could use webinar software to host your webinar and send out an auto-mated sequence of emails. We will talk this through in more detail in Chapter 11.

Both of these systems are great ways to sell your courses. A *live* webinar is more work, but being live means the audience will connect with you and the rest of the audience, so this is the best place to start when you first get going.

Critical mistakes in a webinar

So, as I have said, when I first started, I would give these enormous training sessions about getting found using social media or being more confident on camera. I would give, give, give away content and information, then invite people to buy from me.

It didn't work.

In a webinar, you want to share some content and help, but in a webinar that sells, don't share ALL the details. Avoid the 'how-to' content and instead focus on the transformation; otherwise, this will detract from the sales.

This chapter has been about understanding the core themes of the webinar and knowing what matters.

If you take anything away from this chapter, please remember these magic ingredients when crafting your webinar.

Five things to remember in a webinar:

1. Get clear what your core premise is for the webinar.
2. Spend time crafting out a strong title. Remember, you want to offer the dream/opportunity/core premise and then promise that this is deliverable without [stress/expense/insert your keyword].
3. Use your testimonials to cement the transformation that you want to show throughout the webinar. You are making your content irresistible and selling throughout rather than just having the content and then surprising them with a sale at the end. Lead your content so that your audience is saying YES throughout! Saying yes to your offer is just the next step.
4. Map out your storytelling and ensure that the heart of your story moves your audience, inspires and offers perceivable takeaway value. Build connection and credibility and sprinkle your testimonials throughout.
5. Ensure you address the audience's objections head on when it comes to your 'close', just see this as an extension of your storytelling and let the testimonials do the talking for you. You have tapped into a problem that your audience has and shown how your offer will help them solve this. This is your time to share it!

CHAPTER 10

Launching Your Course!

Think about a significant event you have had in your life, from giving birth to getting married. With either of these particular monumental life experiences, lots of unseen work goes into preparing for the event. Having a launch for your course is a little like this too.

Launching your course is your new baby. You've spent months preparing for this; perhaps you've decorated the nursery, you've gone for scans at the hospital, bought the baby clothes and spent hours planning, imagining and nesting.

Before I had my son, I spent so much time dreaming of having a little baby and holding him in my arms. The nursery was decorated, the pictures hung, the cute onesies bought. And there's a significant part of me that thought it would be the glossy, curated image of motherhood that I'd seen in the movies.

Motherhood was such a joy and a wonderful blessing, but it also brought struggles with postnatal depression and incontinence. I didn't expect to go through a traumatic birth and struggle to walk down the street without weeing. I didn't expect the days of delirium from lack of sleep, the worrying if my son was eating right, and the delicate balancing act needed to navigate across the parental tightrope and the never-ending rollercoaster of emotions.

Sorry if that's slightly too much information, but I want to put a launch in context. You will imagine that you will get this incredible six-figure launch and make a pot of cash. And you absolutely can do! But like any new baby, there are teething problems along the way.

During this chapter, we will cover the highs and lows of launches, and hopefully you'll learn to love them!

Launches are an incredible way to get your course out into the world and make sales – and bring a welcome cash injection into your business. But this book is about money while you sleep so I will also be showing you how to turn your launches into evergreen; when you move a new product from a live launch to evergreen is absolutely your choice. It's your business, your rules so go with what works for you! Launches can result in more profits, but, but, but . . . they can also be so sucky, overwhelming and stressful (SOS) that many people vow never to repeat the experience.

There are many moving pieces and a great deal to think about. Launching is about exciting your audience and creating a demand (and level of scarcity) in the eyes of your audience so that they know they have to act now to buy before it goes away. And hopefully that gets your audience motivated to purchase from you right now, rather than thinking, *'I'll buy that next month'*, and then never actually getting round to purchasing.

This chapter aims to help you navigate the world of launching successfully to kick off your course creation with a $10K launch or better!

What are you launching?

Courses come in all shapes, sizes and prices. And while there are a variety of price points, there are two easy ways to think about launching your course: a mini-course or a signature course.

In Chapter 3 I gave an overview of launching your course. In this chapter, we're going to look in more depth at launching your signature or mini-course. Once you've mastered the launch, you can then decide to move to an evergreen model where you automate your sales day in, day out (which we'll cover in Chapter 11) and sell while you sleep. Or you can choose to rinse and repeat the launch formula several times a year.

Whatever way you decide to sell your courses, it does help to start with a launch and create a buzz about your course.

The table below shows some of the key differences between signature and mini course launches.

Signature course launch	Mini-course launch
Your course sells for upwards of £297–1,997. Note: you can go higher than this price point, but if so you want to maybe add in a sales call in your automated process, so that your customers get to talk to you or someone in your team.	Your mini-course sells for about £19–297 price point.
The course is not entirely finished, and you test and tweak as you go. By live testing, you can verify your audience's needs.	The course is finished, and there's typically no cart close and instead, you will use urgency and say that this is a limited one time only (OTO) offer.
With the pre-launch you are marketing the course for at least six weeks ahead of the launch using your social media and email. If you don't have an audience or you want to attract new audiences, you can use Facebook ads to build your audience ahead of the launch. Then, once they're on your email list, you can market to your audi-ence through email marketing to warm them up.	You sell to your audience on social media and email and also use Facebook ads to drive cold traffic (e.g. an audience that doesn't know you) to the offer.

The signature course launch is what I use to sell my course creation programme – My Course Academy – and this is what you see more established people in the online world doing, such as Marie Forleo and Jeff Walker. You want to position yourself in the marketplace and create a buzz about yourself and what you do.

The mini-course launch often sells at a lower price point – such as a $19 for a course or a template pack. It's usually a smaller launch as you develop the funnel and test and can use paid advertising to attract customers. The benefit of this system is that you don't need ANYONE on your mailing list to get started. This can help you grow an audience, which is how I grew my audience by thousands.

The mini-course method works fabulously for me, but I come with a word of caution. If you don't have a strong following and are principally using paid ads, be careful to ensure your marketing spend does not outstrip your forecasted revenues. Set your marketing spend, start small and as you sell, reinvest some of the profits into more ads. Track your income as you sell courses and don't exceed your budget.

What's your plan to sell your courses?

When it comes to selling your courses, you want to have a plan as to how you're going to sell it. Answer these questions honestly:

☞ Do you have an audience?
☞ Do you have a budget to run ads and market them to your audience?
☞ How much time are you giving to your live launch?

Revisit the plan you put together in Chapter 7, and if you skipped over it, I implore you to go and think about your strategy to build your audience. The more strategic you are, the more successfully you will grow.

KEY DATES PLAN

When you're marketing your course, it's always good to start with the end goal in mind . . . actually selling it!

It's imperative to look at the dates for your launch if you're going to sell your a course that way. Mapping out your time is vital. How often do you want to launch – every three months, or perhaps twice a year?

Look at the year ahead and decide how you want to spend your time. Remember that the pre-launch cycle is about six weeks to market your course.

Once you've created the content for your launch, you can then rinse and repeat the content in forthcoming launches. As you know, I'm all about you creating passive income and getting that freedom in your life rather than feeling chained to your business, but when you've set up the launch process, and it works well, you can replicate your launch strategy a couple of times a year if you choose. Remember, you are testing and tweaking in the future rather than reinventing the wheel every launch cycle.

It's entirely your choice how often you launch and whether that's one, two, three or six times a year. However, if you decide you love the launch cycle (and the ability to generate significant profit from launching), plan out your dates well in advance. Avoid special holidays, and remember that September and January are often very popular times to launch.

Your yearly calendar could look a little like this:

January Launch?	February	March
April Launch?	May	June Launch?
July	August	September Launch?
October	November Black Friday promo	December

Go to makemoneywhileyousleepbook.com/bonus to get my launch plan.

Before we talk about selling your courses to your audience, I want you to think about your numbers and how you will tell your audience (and potential clients and customers) about your course.

How much revenue would you like to make from your course in the next 12 months?

(Note to self here: be bold, ambitious but also realistic! I want you to get excited here and visualise what's possible!)

Based on that number, how many students will you have to sign up to meet that target?

How many launches would you like to do this year – 6, 5, 4, 3, 2 or 1? Note: 6 is a lot, so you'd need a strong team to help you keep launching! But there is no correct answer; it's just what feels right to you and your family.

How much money would you like to make from this launch?

If you've previously launched, look at what's worked previously while selling your programme and launching:

• Where did your audience come from (paid-for advertising or social media?).

- How many sign-ups were there to your challenge?
- How many attended the webinar?
- Do you still have a viable webinar that you can repurpose?
- What was the conversion rate of people that bought from your webinar?
- What was the conversion rate from your sales page?

What's your launch strategy?

Remember, there are two key ways to sell your course. You can launch it every few months, make a big celebration of the fact that you're selling your course, and run training to promote the course.

Or you can sell the course on evergreen; which means you are constantly selling the course using Facebook ads or YouTube ads or through some other kind of marketing strategy to be continuously selling.

We will cover live launches in this chapter and cover evergreen launches in Chapter 11.

When it comes to selling, consistency is critical. We often try something for a few weeks and then think it's not working, so we try something else. But if you are a gardener, you know that you plant some seeds, water them and have to give them time to grow. You wouldn't then dig up the roots every couple of weeks to check they are growing.

Whatever strategy you decide to use to sell your courses, whether it's social media or YouTube or selling to corporates, you go with your gut, do your research, and once you have made your decision, go with it, stay consistent and allow it to bed in and work.

Please, pretty please, don't try to do everything. You have my permission and recommendation to focus on one or two methods of audience-building that excite you and skip the rest! When you skim the surface of social media platforms and don't invest time and energy, the results will show up.

There is zero point posting for a week and then giving up and trying a new platform. Social media doesn't work like that. You have to be consistent and create content that your audience wants.

Don't be a dabbler. It's a waste of your time and energy and it's utterly unsatisfying because you won't get the results you want!

And if social media isn't your thing . . . I understand. Instead, find something that does work for you to build your audience – whether that's getting down to the data on YouTube or selling to corporates.

Are you throwing spaghetti at the wall?

There's absolutely no point lobbing spaghetti and hoping that your audience will bite. As a small-business owner, you have a finite and quite possibly limited budget.

Think of the world's big brands – such as McDonald's or Coca-Cola – they spend millions talking to their customers every year through adverts and marketing. But they don't just wing it; they have a strategy.

As a small-business owner you need a strategy because you need to understand who your customer is and how to talk to them. You simply don't have the budget or the time to throw marketing spaghetti, hoping that some of it will stick. Your small budget and time can go a long way if used cleverly.

The first and most crucial step is to know your audience. We talked this through in some detail regarding courses in Chapter 2. If you haven't spent the time talking and researching your audience, then it's well worth investing the energy.

The best way to understand what your customer needs, wants and desires is to talk to them. I've tried various methods, from having one-to-one video chats with some of my ideal clients to sending an email to my email list and offering whoever completes a survey a £10 Amazon voucher.

Sometimes you might know the demographics of a person – their age, where they shop, where they live, how old their children are – but you don't get under their skin. If you've got that research from your interviews with your ideal clients, this can be really helpful to help you gauge your audience's beliefs, attitudes and interests. Used alongside the usual demographic studies of age and gender, this can help build a more rounded audience profile.

For example, is your ideal client more Waitrose or Asda? More Primark or John Lewis? What do they feel about various issues of the day, from politics to health?

When I worked at a big UK radio group, they would regularly invest in audience research and focus groups. What did the audience really think of the presenters? Would they consider listening to this station?

We make decisions about a video ad within the first three seconds of watching.

We make decisions about a text ad just by reading the headline.

We make decisions about a presentation or webinar within the first three minutes of watching it.

This is our unconscious brain just doing its thing and making a decision about someone or something.

Unconscious bias is often described as social stereotypes or prejudice about particular groups or a person. Consumers will make judgements based on age, dress, skin colour, hair, tattoos, whether they have kids or not and – whether we like it or not – ethnicity. Your audience is searching for someone who they can relate to.

Perhaps you made choices about someone on Instagram based on their sense of dress, or if you relate to their story, or you found their voice annoying. The conscious brain is just trying to justify and rationalise the seemingly irrational decision that you've made.

You, as a marketeer, have to decide how you want to navigate this. For a long time, I worried that I wasn't young enough or the right fit on social media, and I used this as a reason to play small. But then I realised that the people who wanted to buy from me were buying from me because they identified with me and the things I struggled with. I started seeing my struggles as a strength and something that my audience identified with.

Your voice and message will resonate with your audience too. You don't have to be perfect, and the more time you spend on social media, the more your brand voice and message will evolve.

My lovely friend Lea Turner positions herself as the outsider on a sea of corporate voices on LinkedIn, and this has played to her advantage to attract others who also might feel like they don't fit in on that platform.

In her book, *We Should All Be Millionaires,* the fabulous Rachel Rodgers talks about how women make up only 10 per cent of the world's millionaires. She uses social media to openly challenge the structures and systems that make it difficult for women to wield the economic power to create lasting equality. She uses this as a rallying cry to encourage wealth in all communities and backgrounds regardless of race, gender or sexuality.

Instagrammer Sam Bearfoot has me howling at her comedy reels and combination of tutorials about Instagram and navigating life.

When you talk to your audience, they will resonate with you because they connect with you, identify with you, and feel like you're a friend. Meet your audience where they are at.

Audiences that convert

It doesn't matter how brilliant you are, how talented you are, how much you know; if you don't have an audience to sell your course to, you'll get zero sales. The rest of this chapter will focus on showing you ways to sell to your audience and how you can establish connections if you're just starting.

Building an audience to sell an online course is not optional; it's a must-do for you to decide how best to develop YOUR audience.

I know I bang on about this one, but on average 2 per cent of your audience will buy from you. That means, for every 100 people that you have on your mailing list or in your Facebook group, about two people will buy your product. But as I explain in this book, there are always exceptions to the rule; have an engaging audience and you can smash those stats!

So finding a constant flow of new people to buy your courses and digital products is paramount to your business's long-term success and viability. And when you're first starting, that can feel overwhelming and send even the most confident into a cycle of fear.

Remember, we all started somewhere, so in the beginning, keep it simple.

We will talk this through in more detail later in this chapter, but there are many different ways to sell your courses, and I'll share some of the approaches I've used and those of my clients and friends in the online world.

We're talking about ways to sell your courses and build your audience. Some of these methods may appeal – and some won't – go with what feels right to you! When you put your passion and personality into your audience, you will enjoy it and make friendships, and the results will multiply.

The wonderful thing about the online world is that ANYONE, and I mean anyone, can harness the power of social media, Google search, podcasting or paid ads and sell their knowledge and know-how. This is not just the domain of big business; the small guy can compete with the big guys and be regarded as a powerful force and movement for change. The reality is that if you are willing to take the leap and invest time and energy (and perhaps money in digital ads) on Instagram, Facebook, YouTube, LinkedIn (or wherever your audience hangs out), then you can create a system that pays for itself.

However, remember that while numbers on a social media platform are helpful, followers does not equal profit. Followers is a vanity metric, and it is not a symbol of your ability to create wealth. You want to have an audience that wants to buy from you. Just because you have 50,000 followers on Instagram who like watching your reels doesn't mean they will buy from you. A smaller, targeted audience is usually much more likely to buy from you and want to deepen its relationship with you, so don't feel disheartened by vanity metrics.

It is also super important to take people from the social platform to your email list. Because at the end of the day, if you say something that the social media platform does not like, it will remove you from the platform. And before you say, 'that only happens to Donald Trump', it doesn't.

It could be that you are offering people a freebie and taking them from the social media platform to your PDF or to sign up for your quiz. In getting people to join up to your mailing list, you have a way of communicating with them, regardless of what happens with the algorithm on your preferred social media platform.

Live-launching your course

When it comes to promoting your course, you want to build a buzz about it. You want to tell everyone about it and create an event. One of the easiest ways to do this is to tell your followers and email list that you're holding a training, sharing valuable insights, then invite them to buy.

It's that simple! But it can be full-on, so the more preparation you do for your launch, the better it will be.

There are two methods I favour for a live launch – Facebook Challenge or a series of webinars. I will talk you through each of these and you can go with whatever works best for you. Note: both methods work for either signature or mini courses, although the key difference is that for a mini course you may elect not to 'close cart' but continue to promote on an ongoing basis, creating scarcity and a 'One Time Offer' (OTO).

SALES METHOD #1: FACEBOOK CHALLENGE

With my high-value, signature course, I create a pop-up Facebook group, then I invite my ideal customers and clients to join the training.

Here is a high-level overview of this approach.

Challenge launch plan	Timescale
Pre-launch – share content relevant to your launch and tap into a pain point but don't talk about the actual launch. Go live on your Facebook business page or wherever you promote your business.	Start six weeks ahead of the Facebook challenge.
Promote challenge – start talking about your challenge and ramp up content on social media.	Three weeks ahead of the challenge.

Send emails to your list and invite people on social media.	One week before the challenge.
Send daily emails inviting challengers to join the training. On the day of the masterclass, send three emails to each person.	Week of challenge.
Send daily sales emails for five days after the challenge ends.	Cart open – sales promotion kicks in.
Cart close day when you stop selling – send three emails telling people it's going away.	Cart close.

When I first live-launched on Facebook, I allowed myself six weeks ahead of the challenge sign-up to prepare and create content to launch with gusto. Think of it as a runway, and you are in pre-launch. You want to give the plane as much fuel to take off, then when your course is ready, you'll fly.

The purpose of the challenge and cart open and cart close is to create a limited window where people can buy the course before it disappears into your digital vault. The opportunity to buy the course will end on the final day of your launch when it's cart closed. During this time, you'll promote the course and create urgency and scarcity . . .

I love selling via a Facebook group challenge because you can have fun, and I don't feel like I'm 'selling'.

You can plan three- or five-day challenges that work well. The shorter the better because it's hard to keep up the high-energy momentum. The critical thing is to promote the challenge, have some fun while offering some training and then sell the course in a webinar.

The final date of your Facebook challenge is the day you start selling your course. You offer free webinar / masterclass training and share value and then sell.

WHAT DATE WILL YOU BEGIN YOUR LAUNCH?

It's time to look in your calendar and decide when to launch. So let's get tactical! Keep your audience in mind . . . choose dates that will work for them – will they be affected by school holidays or religious holidays?

When planning your cart open date, remember that it's essential to allow for the six-week promotional schedule outlined above to promote the Facebook group challenge to your audience and then sell to them. You need this time to warm up your existing list and remind them about your expertise and value, and you also want to invite enough quality participants to join your group challenge.

Pre-launch runway

You want to generate a buzz to promote your course.

There are several phases of your launch: pre-launch, announcement of your training, the training and then your sales sequence selling the course. We will break down each of these sections.

Remember the plane taking off analogy? So, at this point, the content is taxiing around the runway a few times; it's looping around trying to get more passengers before it builds up enough momentum and speed to take off. You need to do the same thing with your course. You create a pre-launch runway to attract more passengers and build up that speed to propel you forward.

Your runway is made up of six weeks of warming up your audience to your content and then a week of launching where you are putting lots of thrust into that marketing machine for lift-off in your launch. Create a ton of content on social media and send it to your audience on email, warming them up ahead of launching the course.

The pre-launch phase is your opportunity to tell people what you do and create a breadcrumb trail that leads to your course. You want to start sending out two or three emails a week about something relevant to your course and offering insight, inspiration and training.

At this point, you are saying that you have something exciting coming, but don't give all the details about the course. Also, post on social media regularly and take the same themes of content. You want to share value and help people see the transformation in learning what you will offer them.

For example, suppose you are selling a course called *Using Pinterest as a Small Business Owner*. In that case, you want to share some of the basics about Pinterest (perhaps setting up a business profile or creating a Pin on Canva). You want to share why Pinterest is a good return on investment for business owners, and you want to show the transformation in your business (and blog traffic to your website) by using Pinterest. And sprinkle testimonials throughout.

So, the key three areas you want to focus on are:

☞ Basic training and insights (don't share all your magic).
☞ Show the transformation.
☞ Why learning the process you share in your course (but don't talk about the course at this stage) is a good idea (and include testimonials to back this up).

In your emails, follow the same thing. Think about creating two to three emails per week that offer insight and inspiration to your audience. You are NOT selling. You want to warm people up so they remember who you are, what you know and why they like you.

We will look at email in more detail later in this chapter.

Keeping Up with the Kardashians – what can you learn from Kim and co for your launch?

Love it or loathe it, reality TV is really popular. Whether personalities were on *The Kardashians* or *Love Island*, audiences think they 'know them'. Kim, Kylie, Khloe and the rest of the Kardashians can sell billions of dollars' worth of products and beauty lines because a host of teenage girls (and grown-ups) identified with them and wanted to dress like them and be them. It took the TV personality to a whole new level and made them feel so 'real' and someone the audience could connect with.

The online world of course creation is no different. Kim and co. have shown us that sharing our lives and talking about what we do – and genuinely connecting – is very valuable and lucrative for our business.

Think about the online world. We're swimming about in a sea of nameless faces and people that aren't really 'real'. And then someone offers us the chance to connect and get to know each other more. You leap at the opportunity!

I know I keep saying this, but launching is a lucrative way to promote your online course. Yes, it's intense, but offering a webinar means that more people are likely to buy from you if there is free training to warm them up and explain what you do rather than just being presented with a sales page.

You can get to know them and build a relationship with your ideal customers – just in the way that the Kardashians have done so successfully to sell billions of dollars of products.

Creating a Facebook group challenge

Creating a Facebook group challenge enables you to bring an audience together in one place to watch your training. For those three, four or five days, you are the star. You are the person that your audience wants to learn from and hear from.

You are sharing your insight and knowledge and warming up your audience and answering their questions. On the way, you are selling your course to them and opening them up to the possibility that your course or programme can help them.

Creating a live experience in a Facebook group, will mean you are more likely to sell and get a higher conversion rate.

So how on earth do you invite people to your Facebook group challenge?

ANNOUNCE YOUR FREE TRAINING

You have been warming up your audience through the pre-launch. Now, about three weeks ahead of the Facebook challenge, tell your audience on social media and email. You want as many of your ideal clients as possible to know about it, sign up for it and ultimately buy your course.

Start by inviting people on your email list and your organic followers on social media to join your training. Quizzes are a great way to hook people into your email list and then invite them to sign up for your free challenge.

When you have the budget, running ads to promote your free training works well. I run Facebook and Instagram ads to get new people to sign up for my free challenge that will ultimately promote my signature course. And I have used ads to grow my audience when I didn't have an audience . . . It's your budget; decide if you want to use ads to drive an audience to your challenge.

You want to talk about your training and share how you're going to help people. What transformation are they going to see?

Create a landing page so that they can sign up for your training. This is a web page on something like Kajabi or Leadpages that is selling your freebie. You want people to feel compelled to sign up for your free training because it sounds brilliant and just what they need.

Here's some copy to get you thinking about your landing page:

Ready to go from XXX [insert pain] to
[insert solution / desire]. Get my
[insert name of free training] to help you . . .

**Join the FREE 4-Day Challenge [insert date] that
transforms XXX [insert pain] into [solution].**

<<< Join now for FREE! >>> (button)

In the [**name of challenge**] Challenge,
here's what we'll cover over the next four days . . .

✔ Why it's more important than ever to XXXX
✔ How to get XXXX
✔ How to get crystal-clear about your XXXX
✔ What NEVER works in XXXX . . . Bypass all of my biggest mistakes and get on the fast track to success

---

You can also go to makemoneywhileyousleepbook.com/bonus to get a sample landing page and to see mine in action.

PROMOTE YOUR FREE TRAINING ON SOCIAL MEDIA

As part of your pre-launch runway, you want to get people excited about your content. You want to share what you're up to and tell them that you're working on something exciting.

Show them behind the scenes in the filming, in the course creation . . . but don't tell them precisely what it is. Just give them a
sneak peek into your world.

Think Kardashian . . . what do they do when they're promoting
something? They show the behind the scenes for the photoshoots,
the makeup and the prep. You want to do the same thing for your
course.

Ensure that you're promoting your free training on social media.
Tell people about it and often!

☞ Tell stories about how you've gone from XX [pain point] to
successful you and what you did to get there.

☞ Talk about your mindset and how you manage the challenges
that come with success.

☞ Share your struggles and what you've had to overcome.

☞ Talk about your inspiration and what motivates you.

☞ Share some tips for helping people wanting to learn from you
(don't share too much, just one morsel at a time).

OVERCOME OBJECTIONS

Creating a list of objections is one of the stepping stones to your
success. If you're able to help people overcome their blocks, fears
and doubts about buying, even at the Facebook Challenge phase,
then it's much easier to sell it.

As someone that fears selling, this was game-changing for me. It
helped me move from the block and dread about selling, cover all
the objections in emails and my Facebook group challenge. So, when
I got to the selling stage, all I was doing was talking about the offer
without having to do any selling. It felt sooooooo much better, and I
didn't feel awkward and stumble.

You want them to join your training to ultimately buy your
course, but they will have many reasons why they can't possibly

purchase the course right now. Your job is to overcome these objections and chip away at them so that they have no excuses left . . . they just realise that they NEED your course, when you come to actually sell it.

Make a list of all the pain points that your audience has and the reasons that might STOP them from buying the course. For example:

- Too much money, can't afford it.
- No time.
- I need to ask my partner.
- Am I ready yet? I'm not good enough to do this . . .
- Is this right for me? Am I too experienced for this . . .?
- I'm not an expert.
- I'm not good with the tech.
- I'm shy on social media.
- I don't have a business.

When you start analysing the pain points for your ideal client and the reasons or excuses that they will give you as to why they don't want to take your course, it is YOUR JOB to overcome them.

You want to promote your training on social media. Create posts that talk about the training and posts that overcome the objections. For example, write a post saying, 'When is it the right time to learn about XXX?' or 'How I learned to XXX'.

Your list of objections will help you to overcome your ideal client's excuses and help you to sell without feeling awkward or sleazy. So if there's one thing you do today, create that list of reasons. That is a checklist that I will refer to a lot in this chapter.

Let's make your first £10K course with a live launch!

So now let's plan your Facebook group live launch in a bit of detail. I will give you the blueprint to create your £10K course with a live launch.

You need to spend some time planning out what you're going to share. Don't do this as a last-minute thing – have this set up a couple of weeks ahead of the challenge, at least. I plan my challenges several months before the actual event.

Ahead of time, you want to do the following:

☞ Plan a 'runway' of content to promote.

☞ Create a least three weeks' worth of social media posts to share with your audience every day.

☞ Send an email every 2–3 days to your audience with relevant stories and info.

☞ Create a Facebook ad (if you're running ads).

☞ Set up a landing page so that people can sign up for your challenge.

☞ Send five emails the week ahead of the challenge inviting your audience to join up.

☞ In the week of the challenge, send emails reminding people to come and join the challenge each day – one in the morning and one 30 minutes ahead of the training.

☞ Prepare your webinar.

☞ Create your sales emails to go out.

☞ Think about prizes to include in the challenge.

What should you include in your Facebook challenge?

When it comes to planning out your Facebook challenge, you want to, first of all, decide what do you want to 'teach'.

Your students and participants will be learning from you. But you don't want to replicate what's in the course; you want to share some of the steps to think about BEFORE they step into the learning zone in your course.

So, for example, if you were teaching how to grow your business on Instagram, you would introduce some of the basics, such as creating a Reel or what kinds of graphics and videos work best.

Create a task for your audience to do every day. You want to do something connected to your course that will enable you to share your knowledge, and so that your audience will see tangible results.

Or if you are teaching people how to get more engagement on Facebook, you want to create a challenge that will show them something, so there's a transformation without showing them all the secrets of your course. You want to give them an insight into what's possible.

You want to also think about your list of objections that we've just discussed in the previous pages. Use this list to help you decide what you need to discuss. What subjects do your students have blocks about and want help with? How best can you help them?

If one of the objections is *'I don't have time to do this right now'*, then you want to talk about how your training is going to save your clients so much time.

Perhaps an objection is about money and *'I can't afford this'*, so talk about the potential to create wealth and save so much money within your training. The more you can overcome the objections, the more successful you will be.

I suggest running the challenge from Monday to Wednesday/ Thursday and having the masterclass on the last day (avoid a Friday or a weekend).

Plan out three, four or five days of training within your group challenge. Here's a sample to help you.

Day 1 Challenge: *[e.g. update your Instagram headshot so that it looks like this . . .]*

Share a story that will help people to understand how they need to move from XXX to YYY.

Include a transformation and how you can overcome an objection when you follow this story.

Remember – show the what and not the how. Then ask yourself, what takeaway will your audience have? What transformation will they receive?

Day 2 Challenge: *(e.g. update your Instagram bio so that it's like this . . .)*

Share a learning or a transformation that will help people to see how they need to flip a particular mindset or learn to think differently, exercise differently or see things differently.

Remember – show the what and not the how. Then ask yourself, what takeaway will your audience have? What transformation will they receive?

Day 3 Challenge: *(e.g. create your first Instagram Reel . . .)*

Share an obstacle that you've overcome and show them they can overcome this challenge too.

Show the transformation. What does this look like? Tell them what they need to be aware of but not how to get there. What takeaway will your audience have?

Day 4 Training – the masterclass

On the final day, you want to include a masterclass where you are selling people your course and shifting mindsets.

Revisit the webinar framework in Chapter 9. Work on your webinar a couple of weeks before you get to the challenge.

You could share your screen in a Facebook group, or you may prefer to invite people to come to a training on a Zoom call, so it feels more intimate.

Use the specific outline given in Chapter 9 for more details for crafting the content, pain points and how to successfully sell your product using this formula.

Conversations that convert!

During the challenge, you want to nurture relationships with your potential clients and customers. Send them personal DMs and welcome them to the training.

Ask them how they're doing, see how you can best support them and help them. You want to use their name, create a relationship on any connections (e.g. 'Oh, I see you're from Edinburgh, my husband's family are from Edinburgh too . . .) and ask open-ended questions.

You want to create a conversation. From that meaningful interaction, you may be able to nurture your ideal client from a lead in a Facebook group to someone who buys from you!

Continue to nurture relationships. Try to reach out before the challenge officially begins, and then keep those conversations going during the challenge. Ask them how they're getting on and if they need help with anything.

Sending your audience emails . . .

PRE-CHALLENGE EMAILS:

You want to invite your audience to join the challenge. Send them an email every day for five days in the week leading up to the challenge.

In these emails, you are selling the challenge and not selling the course. You are giving them reasons why they're going to see such a transformation and learn from you. You're sharing your knowledge and expertise, but you are not selling the course.

CHALLENGE WEEK EMAILS:

During challenge week, send an email every morning reminding your challengers to take action on today's activity. It's an email that offers a transformation and shows them what's possible if they take this step.

You want to show a new version of the future to your students to show what's possible for them when they read your stories (or your clients' stories) of transformation.

Also, send an email one hour or 30 minutes before the training begins. For example, if you're starting your session at 8.30pm, send an email at 7.30pm reminding people that it will start in an hour (or 30 minutes later).

Your email schedule will look a little like this:

Monday:

Email 1: 7am (or whenever is best for your audience in their time zones).

Email 2. 7.30pm (reminding audience of upcoming training in an hour).

Tuesday:

Email 1: 7am (or whenever is best for your audience in their time zones).

Email 2. 7.30pm (reminding audience of upcoming training in an hour).

Wednesday:

Email 1: 7am (or whenever is best for your audience in their time zones).

Email 2: 7.30pm (reminding audience of upcoming training in an hour).

Thursday:

On the day of the masterclass, send out FOUR emails.

- 7am: Email saying, woohoo, I'm so excited, the masterclass is here! Here's the link to join.
- 7pm: It's the masterclass later. Do you have everything you need, have your notebook ready? Here's the link to join.
- 8.25pm: Join us in five minutes; the masterclass is starting!
- 9.30pm: Your first sales email goes out.

The masterclass day email structure is somewhat different because you want your audience to come to the training. If they show up to the session, they are more likely to buy from you.

When people watch my training, I have a 60 per cent conversion rate that will buy from me. When they read my emails, my conversion rate is 5 per cent. So, as you can see, the success of your launch depends on getting people to come to your training and buy into you. Make it as easy as possible to turn up to the training so that they can get to know you, watch your webinar and hopefully buy from you.

Remind them to turn off their phone or do their best to avoid distractions. If your audience has kids, perhaps ensure that they've got the kids in bed before the training begins. You want as many bums on seats turning up to your webinar. If you can, using software to text your audience is a great way to remind them to show up!

Prizes, prizes!

When you're running a challenge, you want to encourage people to join the challenge and then stay for the masterclass. Giving away prizes is a brilliant way to keep people interested and focused.

People like to win goodies. I give away equipment to help people with the course, but I've known people give away holidays and handbags.

I also include a *'challenge bingo'* game so that people have to listen out for keywords during the training, and if they type 'bingo' at the correct time, they win £25 Amazon gift vouchers.

Go to www.makemoneywhileyousleepbook.com/bonus to get my launch checklist.

Sales method #2 – webinar launch

I'm often asked how I can launch a digital product without using a Facebook challenge. Some people dislike Facebook or don't like the intensity of a live launch in a Facebook group.

As an alternative, you can follow the webinar launch method. You have the six-week runway where you create content and trainings that inspire, educate and showcase what you do. And then, three weeks into the runway, you invite people to a series of webinar trainings.

This process is less intense because the launch element runs for two or three weeks, for example, you could run a webinar training on a Thursday, and the following Tuesday and Thursday and then invite people to join the waitlist to be the first to know when you are opening your course for sale.

You could run the webinar training several times during your launch cycle then 'open cart' from Monday to Thursday the following week.

The launch timetable would look something like this:

Webinar launch schedule	Actions
Week 1 Pre-launch begins on the runway	Create social media content that educates, supports, inspires and motivates. Talk about the topics around your course but don't talk about your course.
Week 2	Keep building momentum with your content. Offer value so that people get to know you and like what you do. Start building anticipation and 'hinting' at something that's coming. Create content that leads towards your launch. You need to lay the foundations and start planning blog posts, podcasts, videos and social media aligned with that content.
Week 3	Invite people to join the masterclass training that starts the following week.

Week 4	Final promotion to get people to join your master-class and start the masterclass on Thursday. Nurture the relationships and DM people to see if they're able to join the masterclasses.
Week 5	Repeat the masterclass on Tuesday and Thursday and then invite members to join the waitlist to get in on the action for the course.
Week 6	Cart open for four or five days e.g. from Sunday (or Monday) then the cart closes on Thursday at midnight.
Lift-off!	Open course to students.

Your launch schedule

To map out your schedule, let's work backwards and allow for six weeks . . .

- When do you want to start opening the doors to your course?
- When is the cart close?
- When is the cart open?
- How many webinars will you do, and when?
- On what date will you start promoting the webinars?
- On what date will you begin the pre-launch promotion?

The principles outlined in the Facebook challenge method in reaching organic and paid for traffic, frequency of pre-launch emails, and addressing objections apply equally when following the webinar method. The key difference is you are swapping a live Facebook challenge for a series of webinars. Remember also to revisit Chapter 9 that looks at content and delivery of successful webinars and go to makemoneywhileyousleepbook.com/bonus to get further help with this.

Sales emails

When you've finished your masterclass/webinar under either launch method, you want to send an email immediately telling people that the cart is open and include links to your sales page so they can purchase your course.

You want to include the following features in your emails:

☞ Testimonials and success stories of past students.
☞ Graphics to show how the course will look.
☞ Bonuses.
☞ What they'll get in the programme.
☞ Share the transformation.
☞ Include the price of the course.
☞ Later in the launch cycle, you may also decide to offer details about the payment plan to increase excitement.

Include testimonials and screenshots of client praise about your course in the sales emails, but don't just sprinkle in testimonials. You want to tell your audience why they are important and what it means to them.

Imagine you are buying a box of Betty Crocker's pre-prepared chocolate muffins. They don't sell the list of ingredients *'Ohhh, fancy some cocoa and some flour?'* they sell the fact you can have some fun baking, and it's super simple and easy.

When you share testimonials or more details about the course, remember that you are selling the transformation and what it means for someone – you are not just selling the *'nuts and bolts'* of the course.

For example, when I share client success stories in my emails, I'll show what the transformations represent:

☞ Security and an additional income stream at a time when there is so much going on in the world right now.

☞ Hard-working entrepreneurs are finally getting off the hamster wheel and feeling like they can create their dreams and get the freedom they have long sought, and no longer trade time for money.

☞ Seeing business owners create new possibilities and hope in the most challenging of times.

☞ The ability for all these supremely talented business owners to profit from their passion and wave goodbye to work that no longer serves them.

I know this is something I'm passionate about, but I'll stop because we all have our individual motivations for creating a course.

Whatever YOUR reason is for creating an online course, it is so within your reach.

Remember, you aren't sharing the mechanics of your course; you are selling the transformation. How will their lives change for the better? What are you teaching them?

Course details

On your sales page and in your emails, you also want to include what's included in the course.

Here's a sample of the details for my signature course, My Course Academy, and again, you want to focus on the impact and significance of your training rather than the nuts and bolts of the module itself. For example:

Inside the programme, you'll have access to:

☞ *Eight training modules showing you EVERYTHING you need to do to turn your expertise into a hugely successful AND profitable digital course.*

☞ *Workbooks to help you stay on track.*

☞ *Weekly Q&A calls over eight weeks where you get to talk directly with me in a small, supportive community to suit your timezone.*

☞ *Weekly tech Q&A calls with my tech whizz to help and support you.*

☞ *Access to a private Facebook group for personalised attention, accountability and support.*

☞ *Facebook live challenge to help with video confidence.*

Your course will be different from mine, and you may decide you don't want to have a live element (many of my courses do not have a live teaching component).

Also include the bonuses in your emails. These are additional courses or trainings that you can offer as extras to tempt your students to buy the course. It might be extra training or a workshop or going 'behind the scenes' in your business.

For example, if you're a health coach, perhaps a 21-day journal to help students stay on track. Or if you're selling a cheese-making course, think about some accompanying chutney recipes that your audience may be interested in.

All of the bonuses are designed to help your ideal client to overcome their objections. Continuing with the health coach theme, your client may have objections, including: 'Do I have time to do this?', 'Is it too expensive?', 'Will it work?'

So if you create bonuses that overcome some of these objections, such as a bonus workout with the kids or 'lunchtime session power hour', then you are overcoming the 'lack of time'.

Then share testimonials about how students are doing this instead of going to the gym, and share their success stories.

What next in the $10K launch?

Your sales launch period – when you're selling the course – will last for about five days. If your cart opens on a Thursday, it will close at midnight on a Tuesday. Or you could have a webinar on a Sunday evening and cart close on Thursday evening.

Think of your ideal client. Are they more likely to tune in at the weekend or during the working week? If you're selling a course focused on productivity in the workplace, the focus is more likely to be Monday to Friday. Still, if you're targeting mums, then perhaps a Sunday evening is an excellent time to have a masterclass. It's your rules; you get to decide what works for you and your audience.

During the launch period when you are selling, you want to send an email a day.

These emails will tell various stories and ensure that these are reflective of the pain points and objections that we talked about earlier.

What to include in your emails:

⇒ Include testimonials and success stories.
⇒ Drop-in additional bonuses.
⇒ You could add in an additional payment plan.
⇒ You also want to share images and graphic mock-ups of your course.
⇒ Overcome your clients' objections with your stories and bonuses.
⇒ On the penultimate day, say, '24 *Hours until this disappears into my digital vault.*'
⇒ On the final day, cart close, send four emails.

Go to makemoneywhileyousleepbook.com/bonus for help with your $10K launch.

To keep the momentum going during the launch, I add in additional bonuses. So I'll have an 'early-bird' bonus for people buying within the first 48 hours and I'll have a cart-close bonus for those people who are thinking about it but still undecided. I write about these bonuses in the emails that I send out each day to sprinkle something new throughout the content.

If you are selling a high-value course (over £1000), you may want to give people the option to book a call with you to discuss further in detail. Include details about this in the sales emails.

48 hours before the cart closes, I will introduce a payment plan for people who can't afford to pay in full. Then it means that people are paying with an instalment plan for six or twelve (or whatever you choose) months.

On the day of cart closing, I would send four emails with the timings I've mentioned below. However, if you have a global audience, consider time zones in your primary markets, such as the US, UK and Europe, Asia or Australia, so you may need to tweak these timings.

You could follow this format:

- 7am – email reminding them that this is the day the cart closes.
- 12 noon-ish – send a very detailed email about why your course is so transformational. It is similar to the email that you sent immediately after the course launched, and includes testimonials, bonuses, course details and transformation and also mention a payment plan.
- 8pm – remind them that the cart will close in a couple of hours.
- 11pm (or whenever you decide) – send a super-short email to say 'tick-tock, cart closing in the next hour.'

ADDITIONAL TRAININGS AND OPPORTUNITIES TO CONNECT

You could also offer additional Q&A sessions on Instagram or in a Facebook group. These are opportunities for you to discuss your course and break down any objections that may cause people to hesitate to buy.

Invite former students to come and share their success stories live on video.

Ahhhh! Things will go wrong

During my launches, I try to have fun as much as possible. For me, that means silly hats, and we try to make the sessions light-hearted and fun.

Launching is intense! It's stressful. There will be screw-ups, and things will go wrong. Do whatever works for you, and try to enjoy the process. I've launched to sales pages with the wrong pricing. I've had crazy Facebook lives that have failed and shown up in funny places. Sometimes your Facebook ads will be rejected.

Allow for screw-ups and tech woes – and don't worry, we ALL have them! It's all part of the learning experience! There will be failed launches or launches that didn't go as planned. The bots will reject your Facebook ads, people won't buy, and you'll have a roller-coaster of emotions.

Your energy is precious because how you show up will determine the success of the launch. If you're not having fun, then it shows up in the sales. Make sure you schedule in time for you. That means having a reiki session or massage, or going to a yoga class or going for a run. Do things that get you out of your head and your panic midway through a launch.

I always book in reiki sessions to help me get my energy back on track and help me to manage the stress of it all. Remember, just like

having a baby; you are birthing a new launch of your course . . .
How do you handle all those emotions? During your launch, your
mindset matters.

If you'd like my *Abundance* guided mediation audio, go to:
makemoneywhileyousleepbook.com/bonus

Emily Williams shares her tips for launching and talking about
money:

*Be crystal clear in your goals. How much money do you want to
be making in your sleep? What are the tangibles that you can
focus on and visualise before it even happens?*

*Don't be afraid to be bold and talk about money when it
comes to selling. I had a period in business where I had 54 no's
in a row! I think this was because when people wanted to work
with me, but they didn't have the money I believed them. And it's
absolutely not true that people don't have the money. People
find money for the things that they want all the time. But when
someone says they want to work with you but then the next
breath they tell you they don't have the money – be willing to
have the conversation and say 'I actually believe that you are
resourceful and you can find the money, let's talk about the ways
in which that may be possible'.*

*Know that the money is always there to fulfil your desires.
You just have to find it. So, for every problem there is an equal or
greater solution and that applies to money as well. So just be
willing to have the conversation and not be worried about talking money.*

*Keep your mission in the forefront of your mind and keep
moving forward no matter what.*

Know your numbers

There will be political and global events and upheavals that impact your sales. Know this is part of the curveball of being an entrepreneur, and that's why it's essential to guard your energy AND understand what happened in your launch from a financial perspective.

Sometimes launches screw up; know that this happens to everyone.

It's essential to be a data detective and use your metrics and data to understand how successful your launch has been.

Now, I'll be honest here. I hate looking at the numbers. It's the part that involves adding up things and maths, and it makes me get scared.

But the reality is when you know your numbers, you understand where your business is and if it was a success, as opposed to your perceived version of success (or failure).

Many course creators are not looking at the data and just use emotional decisions about their perceived success or failure of a launch. When you understand the following, it will help you make better-informed decisions.

I see many course creators coming to me and saying, *'My Facebook ads don't work, so I switched them off,'* or *'Selling courses doesn't work in my industry.'* Still, the reality is that unless you understand the data, then you are making emotionally based judgements rather than decisions based on fact.

- How much traffic did you send to the challenge sign-up page?
- Look at the number of visitors to your sales page.
- How many people signed up for the challenge?
- How many people watched your webinar? So, for example, 100 people watched your webinar and seven people signed up, then you have a seven per cent conversion rate from the webinar.
- How many people bought it?

Business growth strategist, Christina Jandali shares the three components to consider when launching:

First, a runway so that you warm people up to what you're offering. and build people up to the product. Creating conversation, and demand conversation around your topic versus just slapping it out, putting it out there for sale. It's list-building, connecting with your people in that period of time and building that runway to address objections and training your potential buyers to come back and view your content. It is more about building that launch runway and delivering them what it is that they are looking for.

Second, stay in the step that you are in. There are the three phases of your launch. There is the promotion of your launch, where you are promoting people to come to your launch sequence. There's the selling period where you are actually opening the cart and you're selling and then there's the delivery when you are actually delivering what you have promised, delivering on your programme however you have promised it.

And the final third point is know your numbers. Working back on knowing how many leads that you have to drive in. My simplified version for this is you can simply know the average conversion rate of 2%. So if you just say 2% is the average conversion rate then, if that's the case, just taking how many spots that you want to sell for your programme times 50, gives you the number of leads that you need to generate into your launch sequence. You need to know your numbers because if you don't you are not going to hit the target.

Debrief detective!

When you have a launch debrief, you will understand what's worked and what hasn't worked for your forthcoming launches.

Regardless of your perceived success or failure in the launch, understanding the launch will help you in the future.

You can also download a PDF version of this document from: makemoneywhileyousleepbook.com/bonus

---

Your Launch Debrief

Total launch list [challenge sign-ups for your free gift/signed up for the challenge]

Challenge sign-ups: [the people that signed up for the Facebook challenge and went through the experience with you] _____

Total buyers: [total number of buyers] _____

Total sales: _____

Total Conversion Rate: _____%
[number = total number of buyers/number of challengers. The ideal conversion from a Facebook challenge is 2%]

Earnings per Lead (EPL): £ _____
[number = total sales in £/number of challengers]

Total launch expenses: £ _____ [cost of virtual assistants, graphics, Facebook ads etc.]

Total launch profit: £ _____ [what's left after expenses]

Total cash collected: [total amount from pay in full buyers]:
£ _____

Total cash projected: [cash expected from people who bought on a payment plan]: £ _____

Study Your Sales Page:

Sales page Unique Views: _____ [number of people who visited your page]

Sales page conversion: _____%
[number = number of buyers/number of unique views on sales page]

Masterclass Metrics:

Number of sign-ups [total number of people that signed up to challenge]: _____

Number of attendees (total number that actually showed up:

_____

Show up rate: _____% [number of sign-ups/number of attendees – ideal is 30%]

Conversion rate: _____% [number of offers sold/attendees. Ideal is 10%]

Number that stayed for the pitch: _____% [number of people that lasted for the pitch]

Conversion rate attendees at pitch: _____
[number of buyers/number of attendees staying for the pitch]

How are your emails converting?

Day 1 sales: _____ Percentage of total sales _____

Day 2 sales: _____	Percentage of total sales _____
Day 3 sales: _____	Percentage of total sales _____
Day 4 sales: _____	Percentage of total sales _____
Day 5 sales: _____	Percentage of total sales _____

It's normal to sell one-third of your courses in the first few days, one-third in the middle and one-third at the end. For me, however, I always have a quieter period on day three.

Remember that it is industry standard in the online world to convert at 2 per cent. Two per cent of 100 people is two, and 2 per cent of 100,000 sign-ups is 2,000. It's just a question of the audience.

So, remember to analyse the data to understand what it is telling you about your launch and your business. If you have had a successful launch, why is that? What went well and how can you leverage that to improve even more? If you find things that are not working, deep dive to understand why that is. Were you able to have a full pre-launch, did you get your key messages across in the Facebook challenge or webinar? Did you properly explain the core premise and transformation your course will deliver? Did you properly SELL the course and talk clearly about your offering and pricing?

And finally, I just want to mention that the sky is the limit; hugely successful marketeers are spending thousands every month on Facebook ads and other forms of marketing. I love this blog post from online marketeer Jenna Kutcher from 2018, where she talked about adding 5,000 subscribers to her email list every day. Sounds incredible, huh? She also says that she spent $500,000 a month on Facebook ads and turned over $3,000,000 in revenue.

I love this because it's so inspiring and makes me see this is possible for us too, but as you can see, the glossy and glamorous numbers online are because someone has spent a great deal on ads.

So, the good news is that you don't have to stay limited just because you are starting in the online world or don't have an audience. You, too, can harness the power of online ads. However, not everyone has the budget for ads when they first start out, so you can use organic methods such as building an audience through Facebook, Clubhouse or YouTube that we talked through in Chapter 7.

But one word of caution about ads. There will be bumps in the road as the demand for digital ads rises and there are changes to the algorithm or technology, so remember to watch the data, stay agile and correct course as you need to.

I know that this can be intimidating, and I've struggled with making offers and selling, but the more that you sell, the easier it gets.

Survey your people

You know the phrase: 'Don't assume, ask!' Well, it's very accurate. You won't know what has worked and what hasn't unless you ask. Knowing who your audience is will help you to improve your launch next time around.

QUESTIONS TO ASK YOUR BUYERS:
- ☞ Why you said YES to the course!
- ☞ Consider asking demographic questions to understand more about your buyers.
- ☞ Current problem your course is addressing for them

You can ask your people in your Facebook group, WhatsApp group, on email or use survey software such as SurveyMonkey or Typeform. . However consider whether you want to keep responses private.

QUESTIONS TO ASK YOUR NON-BUYERS

You can send out a survey by email to your non-buyers using SurveyMonkey or Typeform, or similar software.

This data is gold dust because it will give you an idea of who your audience is and if they are right for you. Also, you will understand what was holding them back – time, money or not the right offer.

If you want, just ask them: 'Why didn't you buy?' Ask too many questions, and you might not get as many results back. And if you really want people to complete the questionnaire, offer a £10 Amazon gift voucher as a reward.

Use these results to address any issues for the next launch next time around. Remember, you are setting up systems to repeat over and over again.

Do the down-sell

A 'down-sell' offer is when your customer declines the course you were trying to sell, so you then sell a similar lower-priced course or digital product. The down-sell can help to increase the overall profitability of the launch and bring more cash into the business.

The down-sell course could be something that is more beginner or entry level so that they can get started with this course before buying your other course. Alternatively, you could offer a live training or workshop as a down-sell.

I will talk more about down-sells in the next chapter, with regards to mini-courses.

Reuse and repeat!

When you create your launch process, you build your blueprint for success and create a system to launch again and again or create an automated system to sell on repeat using the evergreen approach, that I will look at in the next chapter. There's no point automating your system until tested through a launch process.

You are establishing your system for creating wealth in your business. Each time you launch, use the same strategies and modify and tweak as few elements as possible each launch, so you will know from your data if it's worked or not.

Using your system, you will reuse and repeat your social media posts, sales page, emails and webinar. Using the data, you will understand if your webinar has converted or if the sales page needs tweaking. By making small incremental changes to your launch, you can identify what needs to change to increase your conversion rate.

When you improve your conversion rate by 1 per cent you change your opportunities to create wealth significantly.

Celebrate your successes!

As course creators and small business owners, I know how easy it is to finish off one launch and then be straight on to the next launch, project or 'thing'. But there are a lot of reasons to enjoy the celebrations too!

Regardless of the launch outcome, it's imperative to mark the occasion and celebrate your effort and successes. Even when you've not had the result you were hoping for, celebrate your achievements. Enjoy the fact that you gained fresh insights; you've improved your processes and created valuable learnings for next time.

Launching is tricky, and there will be highs and lows. Some

launches will work well, and others will flop. Failure is not a reason to give up; it's the momentum and motivation to propel you forward.

When you celebrate success, the brain releases happy hormones, including dopamine and endorphins. Dopamine is a reward chemical, and it is triggered when you experience pleasure or anticipate it. So that means when you celebrate your launch success, you'll be more likely to enjoy the journey next time around, and this can impact your performance in future launches.

Endorphins are the body's natural pain relief and help us to do difficult things. If you celebrate the small wins, you train your brain to repeat this behaviour for each of your successes.

On the other hand, when you don't celebrate your wins, you are training your brain to see the successes as not necessary, and when we regard things as unimportant, that can lead to a lack of motivation.

Author of *Lucky Bitch* and eight-figure online entrepreneur Denise Duffield-Thomas says it's essential to consider self-care:

I think it's really important – especially when you're launching – to book in self-care treatments after your launch, and people often forget to. You have to book in the massage or something like that because launching is really full-on energy-wise. So, I do everything; I'll see my reiki lady, my kinesiologist, I'll take my vitamins, and I'll book in a massage. In those early days, when you're launching, and you're dealing with all the money blocks, you can feel guilty about spending money, but it's really important to maintain your energy for the launch.

So, plan in that celebratory lunch out or spa treatment. I will have a reiki session to help me with my energy levels, which are depleted and drained after a big launch. I'll also have an acupuncture session for the same reason. And then I'll head out to lunch with my husband, Tim, who is very involved in the launch process, too.

Once I've recouped my energy, I'm then in a better space to consider:

⇒ What went well?
⇒ What would I change next time?
⇒ What have I learned about myself and my team?

Well done! You've nailed Chapter 10. Now is your chance to go and have your first $10K launch! It will be scrappy, it won't be perfect, but you have all you need to do it. My positive thoughts are bouncing off the page to you and cheering you on all the way. Please let me know how you get on; I would love to hear. You've got this!

CHAPTER 11

Selling Your Course on Repeat

Why are you reading this book? Although I'd love to say you're here for my elegant writing and wit, I'm going to assume it's because you want to make money while you sleep.

So, take note, if you want to create recurring revenue, day in and day out, then this chapter is the jet fuel for your rocket that really, really makes the difference.

When you have created a course, you've produced a digital product from your knowledge and expertise. And when you can sell your course over and over again, that's what gives you the financial security and stability to get the freedom and lifestyle that you crave. That's the fuel that enables you to travel, spend time with your family and pursue your passions.

The sell on repeat, or 'evergreen', sales model is about having automated sales processes that sell your digital products 24/7. That, my dear friend is Passive Income! The golden ticket to selling while you sleep!

You can build a sales machine and harness the power of YouTube videos or Facebook ads or TikTok to sell your low-cost products, and also run webinars to market your higher-ticket products and services every day.

The evergreen approach works really well selling mini-courses, but can also work selling signature products (but you do need to have a webinar in place to sell the course).

We will be talking in more depth about the evergreen model in this chapter, but let's first look back at your launch.

After you've launched for the first time, it's crucial to refine and tweak your marketing plan ahead of the next launch.

As we talked through in the previous chapter, you can launch and then launch again with the same marketing strategy several months later. Or you could adopt a hybrid system where you're launching a couple of times a year and selling your course on evergreen, or you could just sell on evergreen and never launch again! You get to decide what works best for you.

Remember, sometimes we make emotional judgements that our launch has been a perceived success or failure without really looking at the numbers, so it's essential to do the launch debrief that I talked through in Chapter 10.

Yep, I know that looking at the numbers can be tedious and not 'fun', but the fun part is knowing that your business is more profitable than you first thought and how you are two steps closer to financial freedom. So, focus on your dream, and nail those numbers!

It's easy to compare your launch to some of the more prominent influencers in the online world and wonder why you do not have the million-pound launch.

Remember that most entrepreneurs successfully sell their course to just 2 per cent of their audience. And just because they have created significant sums with their launch revenue, they will also likely have pretty big outgoings. So, while people love to talk about their launch revenue on social media and how much money they have made, they will often have to invest in Facebook and Instagram ads or affiliate revenue to help them successfully reach their audience. And remember . . . they would have started small back in the day . . .

Repeat the launch again and again

We talked through the launch process in Chapter 10, and once you've created your launch blueprint, you can use this same method to relaunch in the following few months.

You could decide to launch three or four times a year. Relaunching particularly works if you are an extrovert and you enjoy the buzz of launching. It's fun, and you get to have a big party. You may love the adrenaline rush of the live Facebook challenge or webinar and you enjoy selling to an audience. And if this works for you, then you want to get planning with your next live launches!

The benefit of launching rather than just selling all the time is that it gives you a reason to talk about what you're selling. You may decide that you love marketing and want to launch several times a year. And as a general rule, people have a higher conversion rate when they launch, so your launches could well be a more profitable option.

Launching often means making a significant chunk of your revenue within a week a year or every few months. Live launches can make a big publicity splash in the online world, and coaches and course creators will often post about their six-figure or seven-figure launches. And while these are incredible, you also have to remember that people often spend a lot on paid Facebook ads to achieve their revenue goals, as well as tapping into their existing audience AKA organic traffic. Always remember the data behind the launch.

Launching is full-on, and it may be that you have gone through the launch for one round of your programme or course, and now you have to teach the live elements of the course and then start preparing for the upcoming launch. I have in the past launched my signature course four times a year, so I was launching in January, April, June and September.

As a parent, I realised that I wanted to have more time for my son, so I have recently moved away from the intensity of a launch. I'm also an introvert, and I find the live launch full-on, and it takes me a chunk of time to recover.

I decided to move my business to the 'hybrid' model where I sell my high-ticket courses on evergreen all year, but I also launch once a year (and sometimes twice).

Note: I sell my mini-courses 24–7 on autopilot and haven't launched them since my initial launch. We will cover mini-courses sales in more detail shortly.

You may come to the conclusion you just want to launch one or two times a year and run an evergreen funnel. But I do suggest that you go through the process of a live launch when you first sell your product.

Here's a sample of a calendar for the year using the hybrid model. You don't have to launch at the exact times – you just want to do it in a way that works for you, your family and your business!

YOUR LAUNCH CALENDAR	January	February	March	Ongoing webinar promotion
	Launch			Marketing your webinar
	April	May	June	sign-up sales page 24-7 with Facebook ads or YouTube ads
	July	August	September	Consistent and quality content marketing to your
		Launch		list about the value of courses so that they buy
	October	November	December	when they're ready.
		Black Friday promo		

Eight-figure entrepreneur and money mindset expert Denise Duffield-Thomas shares her story of launching on repeat and how she created wealth in her business.

So probably about three years ago, I decided just to simplify my business. I've been running my Money Boot camps since 2012, and we had done it in a variety of ways; and at the time, I was launching and doing live rounds of the programme.

When I had my first baby, that's when I was like, aaahhhh, I really can't commit to these live rounds anymore. And this is where I think passive income can come into play because I realised that people need this when they need it, not when I can have the energy to teach it. So that's when I made it into an evergreen programme.

And so I said that to my husband, who's also our marketing manager, let's just do it for a year and just see if it impacts our sales. And if it does, then we'll bring back the launches.

Otherwise, I just wanted to simplify our customer service; simplify our tech, you know, just streamline things. I don't think there's a right or wrong way to approach it.

We do a big launch in January. And that sets us up for the year because we have the money from the payment plans to come in.

I stopped doing the big launches every few months because the course goes on for eight weeks, with a week intro and a week of clean up. So even if that's just four times a year, and then you've got the launch cycle, so you've got the pre-launch stuff, and then you're in sales mode, and then you're in delivery, and then you're in clean-up mode.

So I felt like I was in every trimester of pregnancy, simultaneously for a year. Because I would be in delivery mode, and I'd be exhausted from the launch. And then my husband Mark would be like, I need you to create these videos for pre-launch because he was already moving into pre-launch for the next or the next round. I was like, hang on; I'm breastfeeding the newborn baby that I just delivered.

And so I was personally really burnt out by that four times a year cycle, it was horrible, and I was resenting people because I would get to deliver the content. I'd be like, 'Can you all just go away? Can everyone just leave me alone?', but no, you can't because you've just sold this amazing thing. And then you have to deliver it.

So, I made the decision that we weren't going to do that ever again. We just do a big launch in January, and I have very little to do now in terms of the actual delivery of the launch, and I am focused on what we do in the monthly calls.

I found, too, that people jump on the format of the programmes without actually questioning them. They say, 'Oh, it's a six-week programme that has to be live.'

I realised that's a very arbitrary timeline for someone to absorb your work. It's completely arbitrary. I found that people would come in, they would do one lesson, and they would need to implement it, absorb it and make it part of their new normal for a couple of months. And only then were they ready to move on to something else.

Before, I was trying to jam in three different lessons a week for six weeks. And people would feel like they will, like, be getting behind. They felt like they couldn't keep up. And I would say, but there's nothing to keep up with, but I'd created this artificial pace and therefore the idea of 'getting behind'.

Now people join every day. And I find that there is one key lesson that they take a while to absorb, and it's different for everybody.

So, I have now created the programme that they really can jump in at any time and get something out of it because it's just

> *one different facet of looking at their money mindset. And there doesn't have to be an order or a progression to it. So I stopped forcing that kind of arbitrary timeline. And it's worked really, really well.*

The myth of the course fairy

Most people create a course and then think that magically it's going to sell itself. Sadly, there isn't a course fairy, and people aren't going to buy your course just because you've created one. And just because it's on your website doesn't mean that you are going to get a daily gush of people giddily scrambling over themselves to check out your course.

I know it's boring, and I feel like a nagging mother trying to get a six-year-old to stop playing with Lego and to get his shoes on to go to school, but while passive income may appear 'passive', you really need to do the work.

Your job once you've created a course is to attract a steady flow of leads into your business so that you can sell over and over again. Now, those leads are people. They are just ordinary folks who are struggling with the pain point that your course is going to solve. You just want to make sure there is a steady flow of people buying your course.

And that, quite simply, is your audience.

The rest of this chapter is going to look at harnessing your audience to sell. And before you holler, *'but I don't have an audience . . .',* that's precisely what we're going to talk about.

Don't panic. When I first started selling my courses, I worked three mornings a week on my business and juggled a toddler tornado. I would race to nursery, drop him off and have three precious hours to work on the business. By the time I'd dealt with clients, I didn't have time to faff about on social media. I had a small audience and felt frazzled by those expectations to be 'on' social media all the time.

I hated all the time I was supposed to spend commenting and engaging on social media (I just kept thinking there were much better things to be doing with my time). And as an introvert, I found it so exhausting. I wasn't the popular kid at school, and social media just felt like a social popularity contest for the people who were wittier, smarter, prettier or just got in there first. I froze when thinking about what to say and dreaded sharing my life online.

But, you know what? I wanted to put food on the table at home and pay the mortgage, so I got over myself. It's time to put aside those fears about social media (yes, I still have them) and do this! You too can step out of your comfort zone and create copy that connects and converts.

When you've created a course, then having to talk about it ALL the time is hard, so it was this thing that lurked in the background that I 'should' talk about and failed at miserably.

One of the biggest mistakes that I see people make is creating a course, talking about it in an email and writing a couple of social media posts . . . And then it disappears; it sits on the digital shelf, getting dusty. And they don't talk about it again. They expect people to go and find it on their website and miraculously buy it.

We all know that people don't behave in that way, so it doesn't sell, and then people give up and go and get a job and go back to the old ways of doing things.

If that's you, please stop and take note: there is another way. You don't have to stay trapped on the endless hamster wheel of work. You can create a life that works for you. Your course isn't a disaster that no one wants to buy. It just needs a sales machine to sell it on repeat.

Methods to sell your course

If you want to make money while you sleep from online courses, whether it's by selling a high ticket signature course or low cost mini-course, building an audience is something you just have to embrace. But the good news is that there are many different ways to sell your course, and we're going to talk through a variety of them.

Irrespective of if you attract eyeballs on social media or pay for them via ads, you are simply gathering people to click through to look at your sales page and then ultimately buy from you.

BECOME THE NETFLIX OF YOUR NICHE AND
HARNESS THE POWER OF YOUTUBE

Before I could afford Facebook ads, I had to look for other ways to build my audience, so I focused on YouTube. As you know now, YouTube is owned by Google, and it's all about the power of search. You are just wanting to answer the questions that your ideal clients are putting into Google.

I'd seen the stellar success of others such as Gillian Perkins, so I knew that it was possible; I just had to commit to consistently posting YouTube videos.

Two years in, my baby channel is still tiny but growing consistently every month, but I'm also selling my courses on the back of YouTube.

How do I do this? I create content that is about my relevant areas of business. I use the power of Google to find the topics that my ideal client is interested in, and then I create a video on that topic using the relevant keywords. And in case you've got a crazy sieve for a brain like me, we have covered this in much more detail back in Chapter 7 with Gillian Perkins' case study.

While I'm making a video, I am sure to mention my freebies that are relevant to my video. (Note: no one will download a freebie that is not relevant to what you're talking about.) So people download my freebie, which is either a quiz or a PDF such as 'Nine Smart Passive Income Ideas' or my 'YouTube checklist', and then once they've added their name to the mailing list to get the details, the thank you page invites them to watch a webinar.

My webinar is then selling a course that is upwards of $297.

I'm not a big influencer on YouTube, I'm just a small business owner, but even still, I'm adding thousands of people to my email list and selling thousands of dollars' worth of courses. Go to make-moneywhileyousleepbook.com/bonus to see my quizzes and freebies in action.

All I've done is to create an automated process with the sales pages that we've talked through in this book and invited people to watch a webinar. It's not rocket science, it's not super techie, but it works. And it means that you too can sell while you sleep.

THE POWER OF PINTEREST!

Back in the early days, when I was juggling a toddler and trying to make my business work, I had no clue what I was doing, but I did love writing and blogging. So I started blogging on my website and sharing on Pinterest.

As an introvert, I was much more comfortable blogging than posting and commenting on social media. It was my online journal, and I used it as a way to share stories of what I was up to in business and build an audience.

I love blogging and consistently create two blog posts a week. The blog posts also have pins on them that are added to Pinterest. Blogging consistently and sharing on Pinterest enabled me to build an audience of 1.3 million views a month. People are then browsing on Pinterest, seeing my pretty pin, and click to add it to a board. They might click on the link to read the post, and this takes them to my website.

By driving traffic to my website, they're then greeted with a 'pop-up' on the website that invites them to get a freebie or take a quiz.

And it's this same quiz or freebie funnel that I use on my YouTube channel. It's sending people to watch webinars and buy my courses. Just from one pin that I've created on Pinterest. And the great thing about this method is that you can use software such as Tailwind to repin your pins repeatedly.

For more about my Pinterest secrets, go to www.makemoneywhileyousleepbook.com/bonus.

GET FOUND ON GOOGLE AND SELL COURSES!

Who do you ask when you have a question? Where do you go when you have a problem? Ninety-five per cent of the world uses Google.

Think about your user experience on Google. Do you click on the ads or head for the organic content that ranks? Yep, if you're anything like me, you skip the ads and go straight for the content.

So how on earth do you rank on Google's search engine? The good news is that you don't need to be an established brand; you don't need a massive budget; you just need to understand how to use Google's search engine.

You can harness the power of Google search to sell your courses for FREE. Search Engine Optimisation (SEO) means that you rank in Google's organic search engine, and this is something that many course creators are missing out on.

> SEO expert Marion Leadbetter from The SEO Upcycler explains how to get found on Google for FREE.
>
> *Here's the three-step process that we used to increase traffic by 200 per cent and sell out our SEO course for FREE.*
>
> *While we teach SEO, I wanted to share that this isn't a complicated SEO tactic that only works if you have in-depth SEO knowledge.*
>
> *These SEO steps will work for anyone. So yes, I'm an SEO strategist, but the steps we used to sell our course can work for you too!*

The three-step process

1. Find your 'give it to me' keywords.
2. Create the content that will help them realise your course is the answer.
3. Keep Google happy with an excellent user experience.

Our course was all about learning the basics of SEO and sharing strategies to grow website traffic and increase sales.

So, the first thing we had to do was decide on the 'give it to me' keywords that we could not only rank in the search engines, but that would relate to our course and drive sales. The keywords that would make our target customers want our course.

We needed keywords that near-guaranteed victory, so we used a keyword research tool and found keywords with a good-enough search volume that weren't too competitive to rank the content quickly.

We made sure the keywords related to the topics taught within the course, and those keywords would allow us to answer a pain point and leave them wanting more information.

Then we set about creating blog content for the site based on the keywords we found. We went with two blog posts a month. Each was targeting a specific keyword phrase like 'How to find keywords', and then we wrote a detailed blog post that answered some but not all pain points of that topic.

We wanted to tell them enough that it helped but left them also eager to learn more. The blog posts would give them a win but also let them know bigger wins were available.

We knew it could take the posts a few months to rank, so we created and published them months before we launched the course, and we then included regular calls to action to sign up for our course waitlist and download our free checklist.

That allowed us to use Google to grow our email list, and when the course launched, we then swapped out the call to action from a landing page saying 'join the waitlist' to a sales page, which was the first part of our sales funnel.

Doing this allowed us to add 4747 people to our waitlist and enabled us to get direct sales from the blog posts. It also increased traffic to our website by around 200 per cent in the run-up to our launch.

However, keywords and content were not the only things to focus on. To ensure Google ranked the blog posts well, we had to make sure that the blog pages met Google's ranking factors. This meant we had to make sure the user experience was everything Google wanted:

☞ The posts had to be well written and answer critical questions the searcher was looking for.

☞ It had to have internal links to navigate other posts and pages on the site quickly.

☞ They needed to have external links to other authoritative pages to show we were willing to share other industry sites if it helped the searcher.

☞ It needed headings and small paragraphs to ensure it was easy to read, and that images and videos benefited the searcher and added to the overall value the content provided.

We increased traffic to our website using these three steps, grew our mailing list and sold out our SEO course on its launch.

You can copy and paste this strategy and make it work for you. Find keywords and create optimised content to give the best user experience possible.

Then your website can be driving traffic to your sales page, growing your email list and making you money while you sleep!

FACEBOOK

When I first started out on Facebook, I didn't have the budget to build my audience with ads, so I grew my audience organically. I created my Confident on Camera course and featured as an expert in other entrepreneur groups and memberships.

There are many entrepreneurial business groups on Facebook (or whatever your niche is), so I would recommend going into these groups and offering value. If someone posted a question on my area of expertise, I would answer the question and start a conversation. During this conversation, I would give value and then ask if they would like further information. This is an opportunity to connect.

Perhaps you could send them a DM and further connect, or maybe you could leave a link to your freebie. Slowly but surely you can build your email list.

Some course creators use their Facebook personal page to sell. You are creating engaging content about your life, your course and your business.

By posting every day, you build an audience on your personal profile, but you don't want to 'sell'. Facebook will punish you for selling on your personal profile, so keep it light and fun.

Sometimes other membership creators would look for experts to give trainings, and I would offer my services. I would go and provide a training about being confident on camera to a group of 30+ pet-preneurs, nail technicians or accountants. I would share my secrets for video and confidence. I'd create a 30-minute training presentation that I would share and then offer my course at a special 'discounted' rate to members. I would also use these relationships to get people with a bigger audience than me to be my affiliates and sell my courses on my behalf (and we would split the profits, so we both win).

You can also build a Facebook group and use this to nurture your audience. I have a Facebook group of 5,000+ people, and I try to create a warm, engaging environment. I will post in the group two times daily. One post is an engagement post that generates discussion and boosts the algorithm so that people see my content on Facebook; the other is educational.

This is where you can actually SELL your course! This is an opportunity to share your insights, learning and knowledge. People ask questions, you answer them, and then you can leave a link to your freebie or course.

Nikki Owers, from Sensational Creations, had an art studio helping neurodiverse (and neurotypical) children to develop their reading and writing through art and creativity. When Covid struck, she had to close her art studio and create an online course marketing her services to a global audience.

Covid lockdowns had a devastating effect on my bricks and mortar business, so I had to close my studio and pivot. I joined Lucy's My Course Academy and learned about creating online courses.

Facebook was my place to hang out. So I used my Facebook business page to market research to establish exactly what my audience was looking for and how they wanted it presented. I used a free prize draw attached to a questionnaire to promote engagement, and then I analysed the results and built the course around it.

I initially used my business Facebook page to launch and promote the course. This meant I was selling the course without any marketing costs. I then reinvested some of the sales into marketing on other platforms and Facebook ads.

I also developed a network of brand ambassadors to promote the business and the course online.

INSTAGRAM

Instagram is no longer just a photo-sharing site, and the platform's focus has shifted to entertainment, video and shopping. So you can use Instagram to sell your courses!

Creating reels on a consistent basis has helped me to build my audience. Go with whatever is 'new' on Instagram and use this as a way to stand out.

Using a series of images on one Instagram post can mean that people click through a few slides, learn from you and then act on it! If you tell them to click on the link in the bio, they'll go there! Make sure your course is easy to find from your bio.

How to promote your course with PR

A powerful way to build your audience is to harness the power of publicity to get online publications, newspapers and TV to do the talking for you.

I've written for high-profile websites such as *Huff Post*, *Medium* or *Thrive Global* that garner millions of views. Writing a blog post will enable you to get thousands of eyeballs on your thoughts and ideas.

Very often, if you are writing a piece for an online publication, you can link to a website at the end of the article. This could be a link to your website – or a freebie or quiz and then sell your course.

Imagine you've created a course about finding a career you love. You pitch a variety of articles to *Huff Post*, *Forbes*, *Business Insider* and *Thrive Global* around the theme of new ways of working and how to find work you love. At the bottom of each article, you can link to your website, and you use a URL that sends people to a quiz.

The quiz is quite simply a landing page that you've created, leading to a quiz called: What career best suits you? Someone completes the quiz, submits their email address and then on the back of this, they go to a sales page inviting them to a 30-minute webinar. They watch the webinar and then buy the £297 course.

That lead came from a blog post on an online publication. You didn't pay for the lead. You didn't spend hours on social media. It was just about writing a punchy article that gets eyeballs.

Many people avoid writing for significant publications because they fear that it's out of their league, but the reality is that it is utterly possible.

Natalie Trice runs a PR School helping entrepreneurs get seen in the media. She shares how you can use publicity to sell courses.

Publicity or public relations (PR) can be an incredibly powerful way to help you to make money as you sleep and is something I would suggest you bring into your business.

Contrary to popular belief, PR isn't just for big brands and celebrities; if you want people to know who you are and what courses, memberships and offers you have, PR is the way to get the word out there.

You can, of course, use your website, blog and social media channels to communicate with clients – current and potential – but working with others and allowing them to tell your story and spread the word about how awesome you are will amplify your efforts.

Imagine if you were to approach a journalist, influencer or podcaster about your course and they like it, try it and love it? Imagine if they then go out there and talk about you and your course to their audience, who also try it, and then they tell their friends, so more people see it. And on it goes.

The ripple effect of PR can be huge, and it's something that you can do. I would say that you need to start by looking at your target audience and thinking about or researching what media they consume, because those outlets are where you want to be seen so they will find out about you.

If you have a course about baking, you may want to be in food magazines. If you are teaching yoga, it could be that influencers on Instagram will be where your people are at. For those of you working in the health field, wow, the game is open to a whole host of magazines, newspapers and websites.

I would suggest you make a vision board of those places, follow them on social media and then start approaching them about how you could work together; this is a pitch! It could be that you offer to do a live in their FB group, an interview in your local newspaper could kick-start your success, you might get the chance to comment in a magazine, or even appear on TV – and I would say, go for it!

All of this is PR and will help you reach clients who need you and your courses. I know this can feel scary, and I know that holding back keeps you safe, but just imagine what might happen if you were brave enough to go out there and be seen by more people than ever, in more places than ever?

Public speaking

Building relationships and trust in the online world takes time because you can't have that instant rapport that you can create in the real world. Public speaking and networking events are a powerful way to establish yourself as an expert and build that 'know, like and trust' factor.

Shola Kaye is a public speaking coach. She uses the stage as a way to get people to sign up to her email list and, ultimately, her products and services. When you are on stage, you can then talk about your audience's pain point and offer a solution. You can invite them to sign up for a freebie or do a quiz and from there sell to them. She explains:

Public speaking is a fantastic, and often cost-free, way to grow your audience. There's a multitude of speaking opportunities available worldwide – you just have to seek them out, from speaking on podcasts to virtual summits to networking meetings with guest speakers. You can also approach owners of large Facebook groups and suggest doing a live for their audience. And the opportunities I've mentioned here are just the tip of the iceberg.

First, pitch the organisers by sharing the value you'll provide for their audience. During the speaking opportunity, make sure you share a link to a landing page to collect email addresses and nurture your new connections with a series of emails. You may already have something to sell, or you might continue to nurture them until your next launch.

Selling to corporates

Some of my clients hate social media, and they despise being showy and building an audience. They're happy doing their thing, selling and training corporates, and are very successful at it.

However, the pandemic made many trainers and consultants realise that while training corporates is fabulous, it's challenging to clone yourself to scale the business. Sometimes they grow the team, but the corporate client often wants 'you' the star rather than the sidekick.

So how do you grow the business without duplicating yourself or doubling your workload? This is where a course comes in because you can sell 'you' without needing to be a Houdini contortionist and be in three places at once.

Rather than building audiences and a tribe of loyal buyers, you are crafting relationships with key stakeholders within HR departments and sales teams. You're selling 5,000 courses to one person within an organisation.

The organisations may want to host the course on the company intranet - so you don't even have to host the course.

Jessica Lorimer teaches small business owners how to sell to corporates.

Selling to employees of corporate organisations or selling to corporate companies is not the sexy option for many people.

Most people start their businesses because they hate a corporate job. And you know, they didn't like a boss, or they had an awful experience or whatever. However, the other pervasive thing I hear from small business owners is I want to help people; I want to make an impact; I want to help more people. And yet, they insist on helping one person at a time. And that baffles me because one person is helping one person and then potentially there's knock-on effect to their family or friends or whoever.

When you work with a corporate company, you impact about 25 to 50 people if you're delivering an introductory workshop, and then that extrapolates if all of those people have a family where they've got a spouse and child. Suddenly, you're looking at 150 people from one workshop. So, if we're talking about impact, that's why small business owners who are selling to corporates will have way more impact.

The other thing is that in the UK the average corporate sale for a small business owner selling to a corporate organisation is

SELLING YOUR COURSE ON REPEAT

worth £10,000. The average sale value for a small business owner selling to an individual is £1500.

When we're selling to corporates, they're looking at the result. They're not buying with their gut. They recognise a gap that needs to be filled and ask: What is the transformation that we want? Can this person provide that for our employees and us?

The corporate world has been shifting to an employee engagement and well-being perspective for the last 10 to 12 years. That means we're not only seeing people make sales in HR or selling sales or marketing services.

We're also seeing companies invest in things that are designed to make a better impact on their employees and their work–life balance, and their personal development. We're seeing nutritionists, practitioners working in female health, fertility, the menopause field and they're making six-figure deals selling to companies.

This method works if you're selling your services or selling courses to corporates, as long as you're solving the problem they want to solve. As the business owner, you will know what method of delivery (courses, memberships or webinars) will work best.

We've got people who are selling courses to organisations that operate in countries worldwide, and want their entire courses translated and paid for by the company that wants to make sure that it can be available to thousands of employees.

The difference is that you are not having a big launch where you're trying to find a bunch of people and hoping they'll buy. Instead, you're approaching stakeholders and saying, 'Here's a problem that it seems you have. The best way to solve this is through a course that's going to help 85–95 per cent of your employees make the shifts and make the implementation easier for them so that the company can get the result they want.'

Is email marketing dead?

I regularly hear the phrase: *'Email marketing is dead!'*

And while we live in an age where we're saturated with information and bombarded with emails, it is still one of the most effective ways to sell your wares.

Marketeers have been using email marketing for two decades, and while what you say and how you say it has evolved, email marketing is here to stay.

According to Campaign Monitor, there are 3 billion email users on the planet, and while some may dislike email, it's still an essential tool to communicate with our audience.

Reaching someone's inbox is a connection with them on a personal level. Talk to them in a way that works for them, and be careful not to bombard them with emails, or they will send you to spam. Instead, nurture your email audience, and they will respond. They want to see you as an expert, so share insight and value. Give them something to come back for more and regard you as a leader in your field.

But also be human and be honest. Share your joys and passions – and your struggles. When I emailed my audience telling them about my experience of getting Covid-19, a ton of people replied wishing me well; when I wrote about the difficulties of running an Airbnb business during a global pandemic, I had a sackful of responses.

I created a real and raw connection, and people cared. For people to buy from you, they want to see you as an expert, but they also want to connect with you emotionally. And writing engaging and heartfelt emails will help build those connections.

People make purchasing decisions because they like someone and 'want' what they have, not because they 'should' have it. I should re-read Shakespeare's *Twelfth Night,* but am I ever going to? Unlikely.

Focus on what people want.

Writing to your audience consistently is essential. I try to write once or twice a week, and more often during a launch. I'll share tips and strategies to build a business, but I'll also give them training and free guided meditations.

I regularly write about my son and his love of tractors (and the joys and challenges of running a business while raising a little one), and people will send me tractors and toys from all around the world for him.

If I'm struggling with something (homeschooling my son, piling on the pounds, or my attempts to avoid procrastination with writing this book), I talk about it. The more authentic you are, the more people will relate to you.

You don't have to be perfect. Just be you.

I cannot overestimate the power of well-crafted emails. When you're working in the online world, your copy counts (and converts). Anika Watkins from Moxie Copywriting runs an agency for copywriters and advises:

One of the most influential and cost-effective ways to maximise the profitability and success of any online course is having the right email sequences in place.

Think of email automation as a non-stop sales machine that sells your course on autopilot, from launch sequences and abandoned cart emails to welcome series and nurture sequences.

It's all about working smarter, not harder.

So, what does it take to write compelling, attention-grabbing emails that get readers to click, read and buy? While there's no perfect science to writing emails that convert, here are a few crucial ingredients for success:

---

1. Create click-worthy subject lines

We've all seen them in our inbox – emails with subject lines that you can't help but open, even though you know it's probably just another marketing email. Nevertheless, you click away. What's the secret? It's all about using interest-piquing tactics that leave readers wanting more.

Here are a few classic approaches and examples to try:

The Curious Approach

I'm never doing this again . . .
You won't believe this, [name of person]
Can I let you in on a little secret?

The Friendly Approach

Is everything okay?
How are you doing?
Checking in on things . . .

The Shock Approach

Do NOT open this email (this is one of my personal favourites)
That's it. I'm calling it quits.
Stop what you're doing and read this.

2. Create brand voice and authenticity

Nothing is worse than a generic-sounding email that was copied and pasted from a template. People buy from people they know, like and trust. Email writing is no different. If your copy feels disingenuous, it shows. And so will your lack of sales.

Determine your personality's 2–3 core traits, then make sure everything you write aligns with that tone. Are you quirky, witty and friendly? Keep your emails punchy and light. Perhaps you're more formal, professional and authoritative? Aim for straight-forward, informative copy that's also easy to read.

> ### 3. Have a game plan
> *You know what they say: fail to plan, then plan to fail. While you may be tempted to dive in and start writing, hold the breaks and map out a game plan. How many sequences will you need? How many emails will you need in each sequence? How many subject lines are you going to test? It's much easier to write effective emails when you have a clear route to your final destination.*

Promoting your course with affiliates

You can create an additional revenue stream for your course by getting other brands and businesses to sell it for you. This is known as 'affiliate marketing'. In an affiliate programme, the other influencer or brand is given a unique link to market your course to their community, and you'll get a percentage of revenue.

You agree to the amount of affiliate commission payment ahead of time, and this can be anything up to 30, 40 or 50 per cent. You also provide the graphics, promotional support and marketing plan to help the affiliates successfully launch.

By having affiliates in your business, you add to your bottom line because you can amplify your message and talk about your course. When someone else talks about your course it adds weight and credibility, and that increases the number of potential buyers of your course.

> Kelly Morrison from CreateYourAffiliateProgram.com works with online business owners to help them successfully launch their online courses and products.
>
> *In case you're new to affiliate programs, let me share what an affiliate program exactly is: an Affiliate Program is what you put in place to ensure that your affiliates are well cared for! It*

includes all of the tech setup, email communication and affiliate onboarding pieces that you will need to have in place to run a successful and profitable affiliate program.

To show you the power of working with affiliates, let me share the story of my client Lala. Twice a year, Lala launches her $347 course. For her first course launch working with affiliates, I reached out to a small group of women who had already taken Lala's online course in the past to see if they would like to be an affiliate. As a result, eight women agreed to be an affiliate (a small number, but as you'll see . . . small can be mighty!) and they would each receive 50 per cent commissions for any sales referred.

Once the affiliates agreed to participate, I sent them through the affiliate program onboarding process. This onboarding process includes giving them their unique affiliate link, their affiliate promo materials and ensuring they have everything they need to promote Lala's course successfully.

The results?

These eight affiliates referred a total of 17 new buyers to Lala's course within a seven-day time frame!

17 new sales = $5,899 in sales.

Lala made $2,949 in new course sales.

The affiliates in total received $2,949 (50 per cent in commission).

This affiliate program I put in place for Lala is a win/win for all involved:

A win for Lala, who made almost $3,000 extra in course sales just from this one launch with a handful of affiliates, a success for the affiliates who made nearly $3,000 total and a win for the women who get to experience the transformation the client's program provides.

What would an extra $3,000+ in course sales mean for your business?

Selling *other* people's courses with affiliate marketing

Let's imagine you loved this book so much you wanted to tell everyone about it on social media. Every time you talked about it, you could earn a few extra pennies if you created an affiliate link for it on Amazon. Every time someone clicked through using your link, you'd earn a small amount of money.

If you then decided to talk about your favourite equipment and other books using Amazon links, this pot of cash would increase over time.

Once you've built your audience in the online world, you can sell your digital courses and products AND sell other people's courses and products. This is a low-stress way to add additional revenue to your business by marketing other people's products and services through affiliate links. Online course creators will negotiate 30, 40 or 50 per cent commission, and this can mean you're making thousands of dollars for every time you talk about their launch.

For example, people talk about my courses and memberships and they earn a commission. When you're first starting in business, this can be a valuable way to make some extra income without actually having to do anything in the long term. When someone purchases through your affiliate link, you get a slice of the action simply for recommending the product/course/service.

Some examples include Canva.com for design templates or software to automate and organise your business, such as Asana or ClickUp. Companies such as Awin, ClickBank, CJ Affiliate or ShareASale just manage the affiliate partnerships. You can search through the hundreds of companies they have partnered with to find businesses you want to promote.

I do suggest talking about products that you use and love. It's more authentic, and if you're talking about something you love, you have a passion for it.

I participate in launches for a few key influencers in the online world that have helped me grow my business, and I've joined their high-ticket affiliate programme. One important thing to note is that I ONLY become an affiliate for products that have helped me and been transformational in my life or business and fit my business messaging, such as Tony Robbins, Jeff Walker or Stu McLaren. That way, I can write emails that come from the heart, and I'm passionate about the experience and how it's been life-changing. But, if it's not authentic, then it's not a fit for my business, and I would recommend that you apply the same rule.

That entrepreneur will have a team of people wanting to help you sell their courses and programmes, and they will provide you with marketing material such as email swipe files, social media copy and graphics. They'll even give you ad suggestions and templates.

Talking about digital products can add thousands of dollars to your business bottom line every month, and the beauty of this is that it's easy!

Here's Kelly Morrison, from Create Your Affiliate Program, sharing more tips about adding an additional revenue stream to your business.

As a business owner, having an affiliate income stream is a total win-win. You get to make some extra moo-lah by sharing your sign-up link and knowledge with them about the product program or service, and your community wins too by hearing about great products and services.

Adding an affiliate income stream to your business is a good idea for three reasons . . .

* *Your overhead costs for doing affiliate marketing is ZERO. It costs you nothing but your time to bring in affiliate income. (And honestly, it doesn't take a lot of time to do!)*

- *Sharing your affiliate links with your community is easy . . . and you can promote your affiliate links in a super authentic way without being sleazy or salesy.*
- *You get to decide precisely what companies you'd like to affiliate for and how you want to share about them with your community.*

(Note: affiliate marketing works even if you don't have a business! If you don't have an online business, you can still promote affiliate links for products you use and love . . .)

How to get started with affiliate marketing

1. Decide what products/services you will affiliate for.
To be successful with affiliate marketing, you don't need a huge following, an email list or hundreds of social media fans. You just need a few products/services you believe in and the desire to make extra money by sharing about them with the people in your community!
2. Start sharing your affiliate links!
Once you've decided on the affiliate programs you'd like to be a part of, you'll want to start sharing your links!

- *Share on social media – one of the ways I share my affiliate links is inside Facebook groups I am a part of. For example, when someone asks a question like 'What course platform do you recommend?' I can chime in and share, 'My favourite platform is MemberVault. I love it because [I insert the specific reasons I love MV as it relates to their post]. Here's my link to check it out . . .'*
- *Share in your company's newsletter – if you send out a weekly or monthly newsletter to your community, pop in affiliate links when you share about a particular resource.*

> • *Share on a resource page on your website. Are there are specific programs or services that your ideal client could benefit from? Or are there things you find yourself recommending over and over? Consider putting up a page on your website that anyone can see when they visit your site with these affiliate links.*
>
> *You can earn a small amount or a large amount of 'extra' money through affiliate marketing. I highly recommend only promoting products that you believe in or have experience with – it'll make your affiliate marketing more authentic.*

You've got your customer . . . now KEEP them!

Once your customer has bought from you, you want to make the customer journey as clean and easy as possible. When they are on the 'thank you' page, share a video so they know what to expect and how to sign in to your course quickly.

You want your students to log in, take action, do the course and actually complete it! The failure to complete a course is super high in the course-creation industry, and when people haven't done your course, they won't get your wisdom, they won't have that life-changing transformation, and they won't know how awesome you are.

You might think, *'Hmmm, I've got the money, I don't care they don't do the course, they've paid for it.'* But you are the one that loses because you've missed an opportunity to establish a strong bond with that person, for them to talk about what you do, and you've lost that possibility of selling them into other products and services.

So, look after your customers. Make the course easy to navigate. Think about the user experience and how they go through the course.

Ask for feedback from your audience in surveys, and if you receive feedback asking, 'where is the XXX?' then take note (and action) because your customer is struggling, and you need to sign-post where they can find the elements of your course.

When someone joins your course Facebook group, you could send them a personal DM message or voice note to welcome them to the group. Despite the automation and the business that runs on autopilot, give them the personal touch and they will remember you for it.

Send them emails to check how they're getting on with the course and inspire them to take action. Remind them of the life-changing results they will get when they take action. People buy things on a whim all the time and then don't follow through.

Be the person that gets through to them. Be their accountability coach to support them.

Study your completion rates of each module within the course and look at where people are getting stuck. What could you do to support them further?

☞ It could be you simplify the content.
☞ It could be you create accountability pods for them to move forward.
☞ It could be that you host a workshop to move your students forward in one area where they get stuck.

The longer the customer's lifetime value, the more profitable the back end of your business is, and that is where the real profit lies. The stickier your customer is, the more profit you can build into the business without having to market to a new set of customers.

How long is your customer going to stick around for?

My favourite cafe is the Greenberry Cafe in Primrose Hill in London. There is a 40-minute wait to get a table at the weekend, and people will happily stand and queue.

Why do the other cafes in the street not get the same action? Because The Greenberry has learned the magic of exceptional customer service. The staff treat my son, husband and me like long-lost friends and create the most buzzing atmosphere. They serve up fantastic chocolate brownies, brunches and great kids' food. They feed the dogs, play with the children, supply great toys, print out tractor drawings especially for my son and make everyone feel welcome.

When I gave birth, our first outing, just the two of us, was to the Greenberry. And it was a bright spot in my days while struggling with a newborn and incontinence. I've seen everyone from famous models and A-listers squeeze into the tiny tables and dig into the great grub.

As a course creator, you aspire to be the Greenberry Cafe. You want people raving about what you do, and you want them to have the same virtual warmth and fuzziness.

It's important to remember that the purchase of a course is not the end of the journey; it's just the beginning. This is the component to get people into your funnel so you can go on and nurture that relationship. Ultimately you want them coming back and buying more from you.

The customer's lifetime value is vital; the longer they stick around with you, the more profitable your business. That means encouraging them to buy memberships, group programmes, masterclasses and one-to-one services.

The course is the chocolate brownie that you waft in front of them to get them into your business. Then it's up to you to upsell them to other products and services so that you can build more profit into your business on the back end.

How to deal with little setbacks . . . refunds

I know this one is such a kick in the teeth when it first happens. I remember being distraught when someone asked for a refund, and I sobbed, and I thought everyone hated me.

But the reality is that in the online world, some people will buy courses and then ask for a refund. They'll get cold feet, or they'll do the work and then be sneaky and ask for their money back. It's not pleasant, but it's normal.

Look at your percentage of people asking for a refund. If it's around 3-5 per cent, that's industry standard. If it's higher than this, or you are finding your refund rate is increasing, ask people why they're asking for a refund.

Is there something that you can do to help them access the support or information they need? Sometimes just an email or a quick call can reassure them and keep them on track if they have suddenly had a moment of imposter syndrome come knocking. Or perhaps your content is so overwhelming that people feel guilty about not completing it?

When someone requests a refund from my courses, it's important to be polite, respectful (no matter how you're feeling) and sort out the refund. When I first started selling courses, I couldn't always afford to pay for the admin, but I wanted to avoid the emotion of me being involved in the refund process. I would paste in a pre-written response and sign off 'Team Lucy'.

Every time I get a refund request, it does jab a little, but I try to remember that perhaps we're just not a good fit. Process the request quickly, send them good wishes and get them out of your system so you can concentrate on showing up for the people who do want to work with you!

Today my team are the ones answering emails, but you can still automate and streamline your processes as much as possible.

Here's a sample refund email response:

Hi XXX

Thank you so much for your feedback, we're always looking to improve our services and processes in delivering the course.

I have refunded you XX amount. The money will be transferred to your bank within 3-5 working days.

Wishing you a great day.

Team Lucy x

Denise Duffield-Thomas shared these gold and sparkling nuggets of wisdom:

How much are we over-delivering? People put too much into their programmes; they try to give too much and solve everyone's problems. So there's a couple of things that I did to curb my over-delivering. I stripped a lot of content out of my programmes.

Our refund rate was doubling, and I didn't know why. And I was like . . ., so we did a little survey when people were asking for a refund. And people were saying, 'I don't have time to do this programme.' And I was thinking, 'But you can do it at your own pace, like what are people talking about?' But they would log in, and they would see all of the stuff because we let them see the whole programme.

I had three lessons each week, but they would see the supplementary materials, the books, the TED Talks, the links to Oprah videos because I was trying to be thorough and give people the context of where I was coming from, but they were just saying: 'Well, I can't, even I can't achieve in this programme. I can't win at this. I can't do this. I can't complete it.'

And we stripped all of those extra things out, so it's just my content, and refund rates halved. And the feedback from people was, 'Oh, my God, the programme is so rich and deep,' and I was like, 'What? I stripped it all out!'

And so I was feeling guilty that I stripped it out because I felt like I wasn't thorough enough, but it was such a big lesson in not overwhelming people with content.

Dusty on the digital shelf?

My DMs on Instagram are stuffed with messages from people telling me they've created a course and it's not selling. Many people make a course, attempt a launch, give Facebook ads a go and give up. It sits on the digital shelf, getting dusty.

As a course creator, the challenge for you is not only to know your course content but also to embrace multiple ways to sell it again and again.

For many of us, that's not our thing, and it's challenging to create a YouTube channel or embrace social media, talk to corporates or to set up ad campaigns on Facebook (more on this in the next chapter). But the success of your course is determined by your audience and a constant flow of new customers into your business.

Think about the customer, where they would hang out, and why they would be tempted to buy from you. Then market to them accordingly.

Test, tweak and modify.

Yes, there will be curveballs . . . social media platforms will change, Facebook ads fail, algorithms will alter, your account gets hacked

– stuff happens. And sometimes, it will suck! Remain resilient and know that if you have a great product, you can sell it multiple ways.

Become a data detective so that you know what's working and what's not. If people are clicking through from the ad but they're not buying, then perhaps they don't resonate with the copy on the sales page. Or maybe it's the wrong people being targeted by ads. Look at the data, understand your numbers and then decide where you need to modify and tweak.

It was changing my sales page from pink to white that increased my conversions by 2 per cent. That small incremental change resulted in thousands of dollars being added to the bottom line of my business.

If people are going through the order page to add their credit card details, but they're not pressing buy, what can you do differently? Could you email them to follow up, so they do purchase? You can easily automate this process using software.

Or perhaps the reason they're not buying is that they don't have their credit card to hand. Could you simplify this payment process with Apple Pay or PayPal?

When I added PayPal into my sales funnel, 40 per cent of people started using PayPal. It makes me wonder how many people dropped out of the funnel because I wasn't offering easy ways to pay. Make it so easy to buy your course that it's an irresistible next step for them.

Ensure your course is the chocolate brownie equivalent of the gooiest, tastiest, yummiest – and healthiest – chocolate brownie going, and they'll be biting your hand to join.

Do YOU!

As you can see, there are plenty of ways to sell your course. And remember, most successful course creators have also embraced Facebook or YouTube ads. More on that in the next chapter.

For you, you just want to decide what works best for you and your business. With everything, building an audience or developing relationships takes time. Very often, you will be an 'overnight success' a few years in the making.

The more consistent you are, the more the channel will reward you. You just have to start! You know that you've got this. Create that YouTube video, share that Instagram post and get going!

One final word . . . don't be another clone of everyone else. Your Instagram feed doesn't have to be pretty if that's not you. Talk about whatever lights you up. Being different in a sea of boring bland will help you to get noticed. As one of my dearest friends, Rae Earl, always says to me, 'LuLu Gnu – do YOU!'

And that's what I want you to take away from this chapter. When you are completely and utterly you, then people will adore you for that, and they'll gravitate to you.

THAT is the way to sell on social media and beyond.

CHAPTER 12

Paying to Play

When I started my business, Facebook was the place that I knew best and focused my energy.

I joined entrepreneurial Facebook groups and programmes and networked with other small-business owners, and gradually I built my community. At the time, Facebook was one of the most accessible places to build an audience and find people who like what you do and want to buy from you.

Facebook has given me incredible opportunities to get my little business that I set up in my spare room into the eyeballs of millions of people, while my son was napping. It has enabled me to build an audience and ensure that my courses and content gets seen. I've felt very blessed.

However, times are shifting.

New platforms and new opportunities

I hear many people say that Facebook isn't what it once was, and while the audience is growing on the platform, the number of people using the platform in the United States and Europe is shrinking. The platform is still popular with those of us who are 35+, but younger people are increasingly looking elsewhere.

Facebook has also come under heat politically. I've seen some entrepreneurial friends and colleagues have their business pages or personal pages removed because of something they've said: yep, censorship is real on all social media platforms. I now hear many people say that they don't like or use Facebook anymore for business.

And while I say that Facebook has been hugely instrumental in enabling me to build an audience and ensure that my courses get found, I've also given Facebook a chunk of change for the privilege.

You see, I've harnessed the machine of Facebook and paid to play.

In February 2018, the founder of Facebook, Mark Zuckerberg, announced significant changes on the platform. Facebook wanted to declutter the newsfeed and shift the focus away from information consumption to building relationships and engagement.

Facebook has had a lot of criticism for 'fake news' and the detrimental impact that social media has on people's mental health. Mark Zuckerberg released a statement and recognised that his company also has to consider people's 'well-being'. Facebook's focus was now on '*meaningful interactions*' and the ability to '*connect with each other*'.

Overnight the reach of a post on the platform dropped from getting a steady flow of likes and comments to a trickle of views. So as a small-business owner, I went from reaching new audiences for free to a big fat ZERO. The changes were significant: people stopped seeing my content. Regardless of whether you were a big media publishing house or a small business, it was increasingly difficult to get noticed on Facebook. And the result was only one way: you had to pay to get your content in front of eyeballs. The era of 'pay to play' had dawned.

This was the turning point for me. As a small-business owner and content creator, I realised my content wasn't going to be seen in the way it had been before. I had to find another way . . .

So, like many small business owners, I began using Facebook ads to get eyeballs on my freebies and grow my email list. The freebie was the cookie to waft under the noses of my audience and encourage them to sign up for my free workbook or training.

I attracted people into the business in the hope that they would then convert into customers. But as more people began using ads, the costs started rising, and the maths didn't add up. That was the catalyst for my decision to create a mini-course that people bought directly from a Facebook or Instagram ad.

The course sale offset the cost of the ad, and I made a profit to boot, and I could then upsell my audience into other courses and services.

When I started, I had a tiny audience. I wasn't established, and as you've possibly gathered by now, I didn't have a clue how to sell myself. Harnessing the power of ads has enabled me to reach millions of people and sell thousands of courses, something that simply would not have been possible if I didn't use ads.

While using ads is a leap of faith at the start, it is nerve-wracking. While you can set spend limits, there is no guarantee the revenues generated will exceed the cost of advertising. But when you look at many of the successful online entrepreneurs and course creators, they've all done one thing: they've all harnessed the power of ads to sell their digital products.

This selling system has helped me sell thousands of courses because the cost of the course offsets the cost of the ads. And it also took the selling away from me. The process was automated, and I could handle setting up the sales pages and the systems, and then it did the talking for me and removed my limiting beliefs and doubts from the process. In other words, by automating the system, I stopped self-sabotaging my sales and my business!

However, there is one word of caution. As I outlined, Mark Zuckerberg made sweeping changes to Facebook, and overnight companies were affected by the changes in the algorithm. A similar situation could occur on other platforms, and I know other businesses that have been significantly impacted by changes to Google search, changes to YouTube or privacy settings changes.

You can now pay for eyeballs on Facebook, Instagram, TikTok, Pinterest, Twitter, YouTube, Google, LinkedIn, and many other spaces. What was once the next best thing will become the next MySpace. Trends will come and go.

The reality is that we are renting space from social media sites. We don't own our data on the space, we're merely harnessing the platform's potential, so it's essential to have a launch strategy in place and remember to build your email list as you go.

So, the first step is to find ways to sell your courses organically to build your profit and THEN invest in ads to build your audience further.

You get to decide what works for you. If I can give you any take-aways from this book and building an audience, it would be:

1. Follow your gut and instincts about all social media platforms to decide what you like and go with it. It's your time, your energy, and it's got to feel right.
2. Look at the algorithm and what people are saying. It's easier to be an early adopter on a new platform.

How to build a sales machine with mini-courses so you can sell on repeat

Let me walk you through how I sell my mini courses on evergreen. As I mentioned earlier, following my initial launch a few years ago, I have since sold these courses on evergreen.

While I am talking about mini-courses – typical value around £20-30 – many of these principles apply also to higher ticket signature courses.

Here is a simple flowchart of the process:

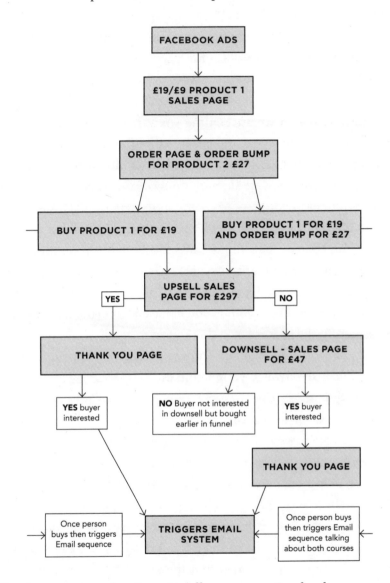

Here's my system that I use to sell courses on Facebook:

Facebook ad >> sales page for $19 course >> order bump for $37 >> upsell for $297 >> down-sell for $1.

With a mini-course, you are selling something at a 'no-brainer' price point that people don't need to think twice about buying. This isn't a course that sells for £997; it's something super affordable that hooks people in, whether that's for £9, £19 or £27.

And the purpose of the mini-course is to establish yourself in the marketplace, build your email list, and make some profit.

Using this model has enabled me to establish my business with a mini-course sold on repeat and has sold thousands of courses (40,000 and growing). I used Facebook ads to reach millions of eyeballs and sell my $19 Confident on Camera mini-course. This simple system takes me out of the process. My self-doubts, self-sabotage and screwups are kicked to the kerb. I can't mess up a sales call because I'm selling immediately. Creating a sales machine for my mini-courses has taken me off the hamster wheel of being an overwhelmed and underpaid small-business owner.

The beauty of this system is you can establish yourself as a credible expert in the process. You don't need to worry about freebies or hoping that someone will buy from you once you've paid for them to get your PDF or watch your webinar.

I created my mini-courses a few years ago now, and aside from tweaks, refreshes and updates, I don't touch it. It sells on repeat 24–7. However, I do work on building and establishing new audiences to buy my courses. Some of those methods are paid-for using ads, and some are organic that I touched on in Chapter 11.

However, the cost of Facebook ads can vary widely. In just five years, I've paid from 50 cents a lead to $19 a lead and everything in between. While you are paying for the lead at the front of the business, you also want to sure that you are driving profit. I'm going to use US dollars for this example because I pay for Facebook ads in US dollars, and my course sells in US dollars, but the same principle works in whatever currency.

> Note: I decided to take my business global and sell in US dollars, but you can be incredibly successful when you go all-in in one market regardless of currency.

I'm going to simplify my numbers so you can see how this is possible for you too. It's essential the mini-course is covering the cost of the Facebook ad (or wherever you are marketing) and gives you a little profit. For example, if my leads are costing me $15 and I'm selling the course for $19, I'm making $4 for every course I sell. Multiply that by 100 courses sold in a week, then I'm making $1,900, but paying out $1500 on Facebook ads and making $400 profit in a week.

But, if I then sold other courses and memberships at higher and lower prices within the funnel in what is known as upsells and down-sells, then I would increase the average order value. So immediately when someone is about to buy, they're offered an 'order bump' of another course for $37 called Sell on Camera, and then an upsell called Create and Scale for $297 and a down-sell of a membership for $1 (for the first week and then $29 per month).

So you can now see that:

- 100 people are buying the $19 Confident on Camera = $1,900
- 40 per cent of people are buying $37 Sell on Camera = 40 x 37 = $1,480
- 14 people are buying Create and Scale for $297 = $4,158
- 20 people per week are joining the membership at $1 for the first week and then $29 ongoing revenue = $20 plus recurring revenue (which we'll discuss in the next chapter).

TOTAL REVENUE: $7,658 per week
TOTAL REVENUE PER YEAR: $398,216

So then you can see that you're paying $1500 on Facebook ads, and this leaves you with $6158 gross profit.

Now imagine that you 2x, 5x, 10x or 100x your ad spend? Or you added other group coaching programmes, a masterclass or one-to-one sessions to your business. What impact would this have on your bottom line?

For example, I have two memberships that build consistent revenue into the business and have a higher-ticket signature course that I sell every day through an evergreen webinar (more on this shortly).

As you can see, just by increasing your ad spend, tweaking and refining your Facebook ad, your sales pages or your emails, you can increase the percentage of people buying your course. And when you do this, you can improve your profit margin by thousands every year.

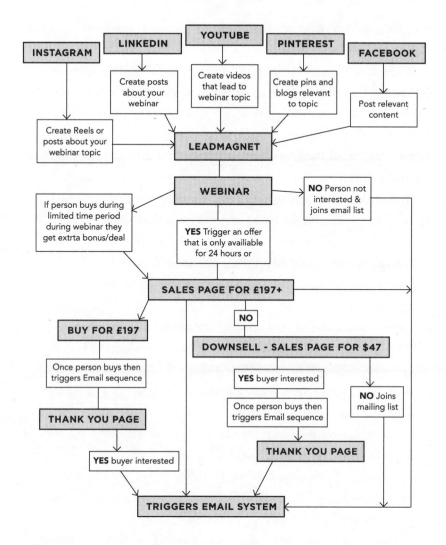

SIGNATURE COURSES ON EVERGREEN

Selling higher-priced signature courses on evergreen is a much harder experience to automate, but it can be done.

If the course is under £999 then you can sell the course via an automated experience that invites people via email or on social media to watch a webinar. After they've watched the automated masterclass they're offered the opportunity to join your course or programme. The webinar then links to a sales page where they can buy the course.

If the course is over £999, then people need a little more hand-holding to move them from interested to actually parting with their cash, so perhaps a sales call is needed. You can automate this process so that they book in a sales call with you (or your team) via call scheduling software such as Calendly or AcuityScheduling.

Note: I don't like selling, and I have in the past used a sales person to help me to sell and they take 10-15% in commission.

Using Facebook and Instagram ads to sell courses

Facebook ads strategist Lisa Stoops shares some tips for creating ads:

Facebook and Instagram ads are a powerful way to attract your perfect students. One quick and easy way to get started building up your audience for your course launch is to promote a blog post that is very relevant to your course topic. Set up this ad with the campaign objective: traffic.

If you are ready, I recommend getting started with list building ads 30–60 days before launching your course.

How much you spend on ads is different for every business. I recommend starting small – $10–30/day – and slowly increase your budget as you see ads converting.

Create a freebie offer that is in total alignment with your course topic and start testing audiences, ad copy and images/video. In the ad set section, be sure to pick one interest at a time so you can see what converts and what doesn't.

When setting up your ad, use the right objective for the goal of the campaign. For sign-ups and sales, you'll want to choose campaign objective: conversion.

Make sure the correct pixel code is on the landing page and

---

thank you page for conversion ads. Let ads run for at least 72 hours before making any changes. If you're getting conversions, let them run for one week. Facebook wants to see 50 results in one week to optimise the campaign entirely.

Don't forget about your existing audiences. You can target your email list, Instagram and Facebook page engagement, website visitors, video views and more! You can target them too.

What makes an ad convert? It's all about matching the market with your message. When you get it right, it's like magic, and the ad will convert beautifully.

So, three main things make ads convert: what you offer, how you explain what you offer (ad creative) and getting in front of the right people (audience).

Remember, mastering Facebook ads is a process. Don't feel bad when things don't go as planned, and don't give up too soon! The more data Facebook receives, the better your ads will be.

Using ads is an art and a science. You want to be creative and stand out, analyse data and dig deep to see what's truly going on.

Facebook isn't the only kid in town. You have to test to see what platform works well for you and your audience. Consumers on Facebook are used to making purchases from the platform and might not make the same buying decision on other platforms. You have to test and see what feels right and brings you a return on investment.

Start taking note of the ads that you like and the annoying ones. Deconstruct them to understand what makes them scroll-stopping (or skippable). Use this as a starting point to think about ads and where you'd like to show up.

Using YouTube ads to sell courses

Digital strategist Katrina Young shares how she uses YouTube to sell courses:

I love using YouTube ads, and I'm going to share some of the benefits of using the platform and the strategies that have worked for my clients and me.

Research long-tail keywords and use phrases and keywords that your customer is searching for. Think about their customer journey.

When you're setting up Google ads, you need to learn some of the basics of Google Manager and Google Analytics to understand how customers, prospects and people find you will help you optimise long-tail keywords and search terms.

What are the search phrases that your ideal client is searching for? You want to tag and target your videos so that you can target your demographic. When I first started with Google ads, I often watched cheesy ads on Google or YouTube, so my strategy was to create very natural, unedited, impromptu videos.

I treat the videos as if I'm having a conversation with a person, and I'm very low key and personable. I don't 'shout' and talk about limited offers and 'one space left'. You want to approach the ads as a reflection of your brand and business.

The language of the promo videos is critical, and it defines where my ads are shown, so it's important to study which groups you want to target. If you don't, then Google will offer to optimise ads for you, which could be less effective and more expensive for you. So begin to optimise ads, then build on best practices from previous campaigns. An example of this includes targeting particular niches or lifestyles where I want my ads to be shown and then refine the strategy.

When you run the ads, use a UTM such as Bitly so that you can track the success of the keywords and landing page

> *conversion (sometimes the Google ads systems aren't always accurate for each ad set). Review your end goal destination, such as a landing page.*
>
> *Review the end goal destination, i.e. landing page and the quality of the traffic you are trying to drive to a video, landing page, website or funnel.*
>
> *Data is essential for optimising campaigns and budgets. The success of your ads is down to micro tweaks to your ad campaigns, so play data detective! Ensure that you set up your Google Search Console and set up your Google Analytics with the relevant landing page, website code, and Google tags.*
>
> *The first couple of campaigns may not hit the mark, but as you continue to tweak and drive traffic, you will refine your strategy.*
>
> *Note: double-check that you have turned OFF the campaigns you don't want to keep running, it's easy to miss, and you don't want to waste money on ad campaigns that aren't working.*

Remember that stat that only 2 per cent of people will buy from you in the online world? This is why paying to play matters. This is how successful entrepreneurs from Tony Robbins to Russell Brunson scale their business and explode their impact. It's just a numbers game.

And this is the secret to making money while you sleep. Yes, admittedly, there are team costs and business expenses, but this gives you a consistent income while working on other business projects or spending time doing what you love.

I'm not special: I'm not good with maths, I'm terrible at selling, I used to work for free and yet I've created a business that turns over millions. This is possible for you too.

It's the Rule of Five:

1. Nail your offering

2. Create your course

3. Automate your processes

4. Sell on repeat . . .

5. Repeat steps 1–4

You are here reading this book because you want to make money while you sleep and get your freedom back.

This is the simple secret to doing so.

It's scary initially; your family may think you're nuts . . . (let them, or don't even tell them what you're up to). You can make your dreams a reality! The choice is yours.

Package up your magnificence and automate your systems.

Study the data; look at what's working and stop what's not.

It takes guts, grit and gumption and a willingness to make that leap. Side-step the snide comments; ignore the trolls. Don't do something because you 'should' do it; if a warning bell sounds or something in your gut starts waving a red flag at you. Take note. Put your ego on mute. Learn to trust your intuition. You know what feels right to you.

Remember that the weirdly wonderful stands out, so don't try to blend in with the flock.

Stand tall. Stand out.

Be unashamedly YOU!

CHAPTER 13

Memberships

When I was a teenager, I used to love going to Blockbuster and choosing movies to watch. I'd pick two titles and a big bag of caramel popcorn and settle into a rom-com at home with my besties. I think I watched *Four Weddings and a Funeral* about twenty times.

But fast-forward a decade or two, and it was Blockbuster's funeral we were commiserating. In September 2010, Blockbuster filed for Chapter 11 bankruptcy and was $900 million in debt. Having expanded to a global company worth millions, Blockbuster failed to move with the times and recognise that subscription businesses were the way to go.

I'm sitting writing this on the sofa as my son Ben is watching *Noddy* on Netflix, despite a struggling media landscape. In spite of the pandemic, companies such as Netflix, Amazon Prime and Disney+ are all flourishing. And would you like to know why they've succeeded while others have had to turn off the lights? Each month we are paying these subscription businesses for their services. These companies aren't selling; they are receiving payments month in and month out.

Amazon, Peloton and your gym membership aren't alone. They have recognised the benefit of a repeat subscription. And you can do the same thing for your business. You can create a repeat subscription, month in and month out, regardless of what's going on in your life.

Marketeers will tell you that it's much easier to resell to your customer than try to attract new customers, and this is precisely what you're doing.

If you've paid for Facebook or YouTube ads to attract your customer, and you've paid $15 for the lead, you as a small business owner owe it to yourself and your business to maximise that lead. You cannot afford to be leaving money on the table. You are eating crumbs while leaving diamonds sparkling in your backyard.

So how can you do this? Yep, it's just one magic word: membership. You can create a membership on the back of your course.

Memberships and courses go hand in hand, like burgers and fries. And talking of McDonald's, just think about when you're ordering your Big Mac, what happens next? The server asks you, *'Would you like fries with that?'* Your membership is the fries to your course. It's the place where your audience can access ongoing training and support each month consistently.

For me, I'm selling my membership daily. Every time someone buys my Confident on Camera course, I'm offering them the chance to join my Go Live and Thrive membership for $1 for a week's trial and then pay $29 a month after that. In joining my membership, the customer will get monthly tutorials, trainings, masterclasses, Q&A sessions with me and ongoing support in building an audience and going live on camera. And one week later, an automatic payment of $29 will go into my bank every month until the customer decides to cancel.

The membership is the financial cushion that provides my bottom line with a steady, recurring income every single month.

I love memberships so much that I've created two for different areas of my business. The Go Live and Thrive membership is for entry-level business owners just starting and wanting to grow their audience online. And I've created a membership for more established business owners called Make Money While You Sleep. This membership is for course creators to get ongoing support with course creation and building their own memberships. Here we have daily 'accountability' sessions to get stuff done, weekly Q&A sessions with me, weekly tech sessions with my tech whiz, and monthly sessions with Facebook ads experts, copywriters, SEO experts, and monthly workshops.

Now, you may remember that I said I loved memberships. It wasn't always that way. In fact, for a long time, I had a membership that felt like I was on a treadmill of content creation, and I wasn't very good at it. So, I had to streamline my processes and improve how I showed up.

Finding my feet with Facebook Paid Subscribers

Let me start at the beginning of my membership adventure . . . or perhaps I should call it my membership misadventure.

After signing up for some random Facebook survey, I seemed to be in Facebook's inner circle for small business owners. So I was invited to events and webinars to help grow my business. During one of these events, I was asked to beta-test (that means be the guinea pig) for a new Facebook product.

Facebook invited 25 entrepreneurs including me from around the world to test Facebook subscription groups. This meant that we created a membership within a Facebook group, and Facebook was responsible for the payment page to join the group and the payment methods.

As a relatively new business owner, this was such an opportunity for me, and it provided me with a great way of establishing a membership quickly. The downsides were that I didn't have control of the marketing strategy, the emails of people who joined my membership and also the payment systems.

One of the first hurdles that I encountered was that I wasn't ready when Facebook suddenly told me that the product was going live. So I found myself scrambling around to create content consistently every month.

The second issue was that I created lots of publicity to say that the membership was going live on Thursday at 8pm, but the reality was that the actual tech wasn't ready until 1am! That was hardly a great first impression for my big launch if the tech wasn't playing ball.

I had a waitlist of 300 people who had signed up to be on the list to know when my membership was launched. Within hours my excitement had dwindled because I thought I'd failed. I had 30 people in the membership. I remember sobbing to my husband and thinking that I was a failure. Little did I realise that a 10 per cent sign-up rate was pretty good going (remember that industry standard is 2 per cent).

At 1 am in the morning, Facebook finally turned on the lights to my membership, but most of my members were sleeping.

I recorded a video in a hot, sweaty mess in the wee hours of the morning to record my experience of Facebook Paid Subscriptions for a YouTube video. I'm not sure how coherent I was, but you can go to my YouTube channel, www.youtube.com/lucygriffithsdotcom, to check it out (and chuckle).

Being somewhat unprepared for the membership meant that I had planted myself slap bang on the content hamster wheel and forever felt like I was chasing my tail. Once I had created one month's content supply, it was up to me to make the next month ahead for the membership.

My biggest failure was that I tried to create a new course every month, which is rather ambitious when you don't have a team and you're just starting – and it was too much for my audience to consume. I had over-promised and created content on everything from publicity and PR to Instagram, Facebook groups and YouTube just to keep up.

I had created a monster of a membership, and I couldn't control the beast.

With the benefit of hindsight, I should have simplified my offering and switched to daily videos offering daily support in bite-sized chunks in the Facebook group offering live training. The membership was built around Facebook, so I should have leveraged this experience and promised a daily live that was inspiring, motivational and offered monthly or weekly training.

I soon learned that a thriving membership needs a consistent content plan and launch strategy. I didn't have either.

When I began selling my courses through a funnel, I wanted to include my membership in the funnel, but with the Facebook payment system it wasn't possible to integrate the system in the way that I wanted.

It was time to set up my own membership, on my terms, my payment systems and this time . . . with a plan!

Create a content plan

I can't stress enough how a plan for the year will help you map out what you're creating for the year and reduce overwhelm.

Decide on the key themes of the year. What do you want to teach or share every month? Perhaps you don't want to teach anything, and you'll just offer a template pack. Or maybe you want to invite experts into your membership each month to train the members on a particular theme.

It's your membership, your rules, so decide what works for you.

Now decide what content you want to make as the bedrock of the membership. What is a non-negotiable that you want to include each month? Remember that if you set a precedent with content, it's hard to un-promise what you've promised. It's much, much better to over-deliver and under-promise.

One of the issues I had in my original membership was that experts would promise to create content and trainings and then didn't show up. And then I'd have to scramble around to fill the gap in the membership schedule.

So, I've now got around this by paying my experts. It means they will show up consistently each month, and I avoid the overwhelm of having to do everything. I pay them for an hour of their time, and they also benefit from the exposure of being regarded as an 'expert' in the membership.

Map out your content for the year.

Your content plan!			
January	February	March	April
May	June	July	August
September	October	November	December

You don't have to create the content for the entire year – this can feel overwhelming. I recommend being at least three months ahead when it comes to content creation when you're first starting out.

(You can access this content plan by going to www.makemoneywhileyousleepbook.com/bonus.)

What to offer?

Each membership is different, and you can offer support in a variety of ways. In my Go Live and Thrive membership, I share audience building strategies for early-stage entrepreneurs, and I include training videos masterclasses. We have a live challenge component once a month.

Whereas in my other membership, Make Money While You Sleep, I'm aware that many entrepreneurs want a supportive community to get stuff done rather than learning all the time. As business owners, we're juggling 20 plates, and we can feel guilty if we don't have the time to 'learn' the systems we're paying for. So, the focus is on accountability sessions and actually 'doing'. Although I do bring along various copywriting, tech and other experts on a monthly basis, to help solve those burning issues members have.

Memberships don't have to be about business; I've had students create memberships for ballet, cheesemaking, yoga or for the parents of children diagnosed with autism.

Your course can be about anything you want it to be (providing there's a bunch of people prepared to pay for it). The membership can be a continuation of this. Consider the following:

- ☞ What would you like to include in your membership?
- ☞ What will be the content that is consistently there, month in, month out?
- ☞ And what content would you like to introduce as something 'new' every month or quarter?
- ☞ Will you invite experts to be part of the membership?

☞ Will you create a community so that members can support and engage with each other?

Create a community

One of the most essential factors in a membership for many is the community. It's a space where like-minded people can connect and support each other.

I'm part of a membership for small business owners called the Female Entrepreneur Association. One of the things that I love most about the space is the supportive community. It's a place to ask questions, support each other and ultimately grow your business. This could be in somewhere such as a Facebook group or on other platforms such as Slack or Circle.

Creating a community is a little like hosting a successful party; the food flows, the champagne and beer are chilled, good tunes are playing, and everyone's having fun. For the guest, it seems this seamless sense of fun.

For the host, it's been hours of preparation and a team of cooks, servers and bottle washers to ensure it all comes together.

Creating a community appears easy, but the reality is to keep getting consistent engagement in the group takes work. Ultimately, you get out what you put in. Sometimes, your community can feel like a ghost town. You can reinvigorate your community by spending time asking questions and building relationships.

So how do you do this?

☞ Ask engaging, open-ended questions.
☞ Encourage members to support other members in creating a safe space.
☞ Go live in the group regularly.

However, some memberships just aren't suited to a community space. If you are selling a subscription service of Pinterest templates, you may not need to create a 'community'. A Facebook group would probably be unused by your members and give you zero return on investment.

As an introvert, I know many other introverts who worry about running the community and managing their energy. It could be that you hired a social media manager for an hour or two a week to manage the community or ask some of the members to become administrators. It's your rules, your membership, and you get to decide how you want to run it.

I wanted to introduce some incredible memberships that hopefully will inspire you too.

Lucy Hall, founder of Digital Women.

In 2 years, we've been able to build an exciting online community of almost 30,000 Digital Women. Our mission is to empower over 1 million women through digital education by 2024.

Before the pandemic, all of our events were offline, and we had several events booked for 2020 with tickets that had already been paid for; we needed to find a way to retain this revenue, and so we pivoted our events online using the Heysummit events platform and also used other event tech such as Zoom and Facebook Events.

I soon realised that we had to change how we worked quickly to fund community growth and sustainability. In April 2020, we started a paid online membership club for women who wanted to gain extra training and support, especially during such a difficult time.

A year later, we have 700 paid members, which came about organically from our Facebook community and online events and have recruited new staff into our business to help with content and

---

growth. We've also seen national press coverage and have even been featured and interviewed on Facebook and Twitter blogs.

The availability and ease of use of today's technology mean that we've been able to run several online events, host online courses, networking and taking payments seamlessly.

Creating an online community is not only rewarding but is an incredible asset to our growing business. Anyone can start to form an online community that, over time, begins to look after itself and becomes a funnel for your paid initiatives such as events, training and memberships. But at first, you will need to put the work in; here are some tips for growing an online community without putting too much pressure on yourself:

- *Create a strong mission for your community that people can get behind; this will help people to promote and share your community.*
- *Delegate: find great moderators that you trust and assign tasks to them. When you have a team in place that's prepared to run things, it's easier to take a break so you can work on funding projects.*
- *Schedule or plan content for your community ahead of time so you don't have to spend time each day worrying about what to post or share. We use the Facebook groups post scheduler.*
- *Involve your members in the conversations by tagging them if you think they might love to answer a question from the community. I used to think I had to answer every question, but we have many very knowledgeable people in the community, and you get to see who they are, so now, when someone asks a question, members feel helped and also valuable.*
- *Put some boundaries in place for yourself. Ask yourself questions like: am I okay with community members messaging me all hours? If not, then it's okay to wait to respond.*

Where to host your membership?

Many of the tech platforms that we talked about to host your course can also host your membership, such as Kajabi, Teachable or MemberVault™.

One area that is worth consideration is your community. Many course-hosting platforms will host the videos and workbooks for a membership, but as yet there's no adequate 'all-in-one' solution for the community aspect.

You could use a Facebook group to offer live trainings and answer questions in a private space. Other options include Circle and Slack. Facebook is one of the most popular platforms to host a membership community. Now, remember my 'paid subscription' experience? The difference between hosting a Facebook community space and creating automation, payment options and community where you choose is wildly different to having Facebook control everything.

When you have your own sales pages, marketing strategy and email data hosted elsewhere, you are just inviting people to join a Facebook group, and you, the business owner, are in control of the space (unlike the previous experience where Facebook controlled the marketing, payments and data).

I host my membership communities on Facebook and have a membership area on Kajabi where I host my training videos.

The downside of Facebook is that there are many distractions and noise; it can be hard to find posts and see the content. And while Facebook is currently the most popular social media platform globally, with 2 billion unique users per month, its popularity is waning. Some people don't like Facebook and don't want to be on the platform.

So, where else do you look?

Some entrepreneurs use the communication tool Slack to provide easy to navigate ways to communicate and find content. And while it is less distracting and more efficient than Facebook, it isn't necessarily very warm and fuzzy.

The Circle Communities is a new solid contender in the marketplace and can integrate with Teachable and Kajabi. It provides the warmth and community of Facebook without distraction. Another option is to use the functionality of Facebook but pay for Facebook Workplace, which is less 'noisy'.

There are many different options that I have not mentioned; you have to decide what works for you, your membership model and your business. As with all these options, test them out while you're on the trial version and see what you think!

What to charge for your membership?

You want to think about your member. What will they be willing to pay? When is the point where the 'no-brainer, I'll join' slips into an 'investment'?

As you know, I love courses, but I think some courses work better as memberships. And for some courses, creating a membership makes the content more affordable and achievable for the students.

Think about it, if you're selling a course to consumers, very often they may think looooong and hard about investing in a high-ticket course. But a membership is more affordable and less intimidating. When you buy a course for £297, that's the cost of a mini-break away or the food bill for a couple of weeks or so. Whereas £9 or £19 a month feels manageable to the consumer.

On the other hand, business owners are willing to pay more for their memberships because they can write it off as a business expense. For example, I have two different marketing strategies for my memberships with varying price points. My entry-level membership price point is $29 a month for the Go Live and Thrive membership, and a higher price point for the Make Money While You Sleep Membership. You get to decide which price point works for you . . .

☞ What would you like to charge for the membership? What value are you sharing?

☞ What feels good to you?

☞ What do you think your customer would be willing to pay?

☞ What do you think your members can afford to pay?

What's your marketing launch strategy?

I don't sing and dance about my membership, it's hidden in my funnel as a 'downsell', so people buy one course, and then I sell them into the option to join the membership for $1 too. It is also on my website, but I'm not pushing people to see it on my website.

I don't have a webinar, and I don't post about it all over social media. It's the lazy person's way to launch a membership! This brings a steady flow of members into my membership without me actually launching or talking about the membership.

If you'd like to put a little more effort into your membership, you could think about launching . . .

This could involve offering a 3-Day Challenge or training (similar to the course launches we talked about in Chapter 10) involving a topic that you talk about within your membership. On the back of this training, then sell the membership via a webinar, in a similar manner to what we covered in Chapters 9 and 10.

This method is more intense, and you would perhaps be creating various trainings throughout the year, but it is a way to successfully scale your membership and FAST!

Ailish Lucas is the founder of The Glow Getter which is an online membership helping indie beauty brands learn marketing and social media skills so they can clarify their message, create raving fans and grow their revenue.

My background was in marketing but my passion was in beauty, so I started out on my entrepreneurial journey as a makeup artist then beauty therapist and created a blog focused around natural beauty blogging. I then started running free online events interviewing experts in health, wellness and natural beauty but saw that there were many amazing beauty brands that had incredible products but didn't know how to market themselves. So in 2019, I decided to pivot my blog to focus solely on my membership. I started off with no website and simply used Instagram to generate new members. I did this in a couple of simple ways.

The first was through creating content on Instagram which specifically focused on the indie beauty world and talking about problems which I knew they faced and how to overcome that issue.

The second was reaching out to my dream target audience and starting conversations in the DMs to get to know them. The focus was on building relationships, providing them with free value (for example a blog post, or video that I had created which was relevant to the conversation) and not asking for anything in return.

One of the key things that really made a difference was challenging myself to record a live video every day for 30 days. I let go of the idea of being 'Instagram perfect' and just showed up to provide value for whoever was watching. It was a mindset challenge to show up as myself and let the universe know that I was serious about the business which simultaneously brought in new members because they resonated with my message, my teaching and they regarded me as an expert in my niche.

Carrie Green from the Female Entrepreneur Association does this with her Member's Club so beautifully.

Carrie Green created the Female Entrepreneur Association and has created a lovely, nurturing business community. She's someone who really inspires me in the online world, and I have a dog-eared copy of her book, *She Means Business*, that I frequently turn to.

When I got started, it was just me, myself and I. I'd worked hard on building up my audience on social media; I had about 18,000 people on my email list. But this was the first time I was launching a paid product and I didn't know how it would convert, so I co-created the membership with my audience, which I think is important. I surveyed them, asked them what they most wanted help with, their biggest struggles and what their challenges were and asked questions such as: 'If I had a magic wand, what would you love me to help you do inside your business?' And then at the end of the survey, I said, 'I'm thinking about putting together a membership to help grow your business, would you be interested in joining: Yes or No? Would you want to pay for it monthly or annually?'

Over 81% of the people said they would join, so this was a good indication I was on to something.

As my initial launch got closer, I poured my heart and soul into telling them about the membership and getting them to connect to the feeling of it and the community. I wanted to create a place where you felt like you belonged. In order for people to think that they belong there, you need to paint a picture of what your membership means. What does it stand for?

I shared on social media and email, and within six weeks I had about 200 members joining. Each month, more people joined, and we got to about 1000 members in the first year. But the problem I'd found was because it was just me, myself and I, it was a lot to manage – creating the content, doing the customer support, and doing the marketing. So, a year after we launched, I closed enrolment to the membership and said this was the last time to join, and I don't know when we'll re-open membership. And that launch helped us go to 2000 members.

When I reopened enrolment with a launch, I shared a free three-part video series and opened enrolment for seven days for people to join the membership. And 1200 people joined the membership. I realised that I had more people sign up in seven days than had joined in an entire year, and it was so much easier. Launching with that scarcity factor created incredible growth that helped us to get to 5000+ members.

We've tended to do free challenges where we'll have a pop-up Facebook group; we'll be building a runway for a few months in the sense of just warming the audience up to that. So, if the theme is 'Visibility', we will start to create content around that topic. We'll share various content about getting visible, and then three or four weeks out, we will start running ads and sending emails inviting people to opt into the challenge. We will spend the majority of the money on Facebook ads and getting people to join the challenge.

As soon as they opt-in, they get an invite to join the Facebook group. In the few weeks leading up to the start date for the challenge we will warm up the audience with simple questions that are easy for them to answer as a way of introducing themselves. I'll go into the group; I'll do a welcome video for them and have a few bits of content that are scheduled to go out over those few weeks. I'll share my TEDx talk and other content so that people can get to know me.

We do the training over five days, and on the fourth day, I will *softly open up the membership, and on the fifth day, I sell the membership. And the following week, we include Q&As with members sharing their experiences. I'll send an email each day of the cart-open, and on the final day, I will send three emails saying that it's cart closing. Sometimes from a challenge, we'll do a downsell where they can do a trial for $1 if they've been teetering on the edge, but aren't ready to dive in. We're just taking the risk factor away.*

When you're launching, it's essential to speak to different people's buying decisions. Some people connect with the emotion of it all and the transformation that someone has achieved. Others are risk-averse, so we focus on giving them a taste of the membership, and we say: 'do this challenge, go all in, immerse yourself in content for 30 days and see where you can be in 30 days' time. If you just didn't have the time at the end of the 30 days, it wasn't the right fit. We will give you a refund, no questions asked. And we'll go our separate ways.' Many people just need you to help them to make a decision.

And finally, the scarcity factor helps them decide to go for it!

Keeping your members

One of the biggest challenges you face in running a membership is keeping your members. Memberships are an incredible way to bring consistent recurring income into the business and give you that financial security. If you keep your members, you can be even more effective, and you can nurture them to buy other products and services from you. The cost of attracting a new member is about ten times more expensive than retaining an existing member.

Many people stay in the membership on average for three months, so how do you keep them in your community?

Liz Beadon from Loyalty Growth Lab is a membership retention expert, and she helps entrepreneurs KEEP their members!

Memberships often enable entrepreneurs to provide group training and coaching in exchange for a monthly, quarterly or annual subscription from their members. An increasing number of business owners have launched their membership over the past few years.

To create a profitable membership, there are three levers at your disposal:

1. The volume of members in your membership

Membership growth is where most membership owners focus their time: on how they can grow their membership as much as possible, as fast as possible. While this intuitively feels like the sensible thing to do, you'll be setting yourself up for failure without focusing on the other two levers.

2. The retention rate of your members

When your business depends on members paying a recurring fee, it becomes more important than ever to ensure that your membership is sticky. When I say 'sticky', what I mean is that members join and don't want to leave. Too many memberships focus on bringing new members in the front door without considering their experience once inside. Ignoring membership retention is a costly mistake to make, especially if you're paying money to acquire new members!

3. The average spend of your members

This final lever is one that often gets ignored by membership owners. Your members are often your most loyal fans. As part of your membership, you should be considering opportunities to

> *upsell and cross-sell them where relevant (emphasis on the 'where relevant' part!).*
>
> *As a retention strategist, I specialise in those last two levers: increasing retention and average member spend.*
>
> *The best piece of advice I could offer a budding membership owner would be to listen to your members and put yourself in their shoes. Make sure you've baked quick wins into the experience so that new members can see the impact of your membership and hit the ground running.*

Your onboarding process is key to your success in keeping your member. Is it easy to navigate? Do they understand what they've signed up for and how to access the content, and do they feel 'excited' to be part of your community? If not, you're hosing cash.

When someone signs up, ensure that the thank you page has an introductory video from you sharing what to do and showing them how the site works. When members join up and feel happy – and heard – they are more likely to stick around longer.

You could also have an accountability session each week or once a month so that people feel loved and on track. Or provide them with a roadmap, so they know what they need to do next. Imagine you are creating a membership for your mum – keep it simple! And ensure you get someone else to test it.

Create trainings in different time zones. I attract people from across the world, from San Diego to Sydney and from Colorado to the Cotswolds, so I try to cover the globe with the training session hours.

Break down your content into micro-learning bite-sized chunks. People are busy, they're time-poor, and they don't want to be training for an hour. They want 5 or 10 minutes.

Automate your payment systems so that money is collected each month from your members without you having to think about it.

Ask people questions. It's so easy to assume what they want, so ask them and survey them often, because at the end of the day, happy members mean that they will refer you to others, and your biggest fans will become your biggest advocates!

So what are you waiting for? This is your time to create a membership!

I'm so excited for you! Your membership is the path to the financial freedom that you truly crave.

CHAPTER 14

Conclusion

And so here we are, fourteen chapters later, and we've covered all you need to build and sell your course on repeat.

While you may think that building a course is the end, actually, it's the beginning. It's the start of a lifetime journey of testing, tweaking and refining to improve your sales page and adapt what you do with feedback and updates.

When I first launched my business, I rewrote my website copy every night for one year, hoping to bring in extra clients . . . note to self: it didn't!

So, while I don't want you to throw the baby out with the bathwater and think your course needs to be re-filmed and rewritten, it is essential to test and tweak your sales page. Your sales page is THE thing that is doing the talking for you. So, if you are getting people landing on your page, but they are not buying, it's time to refine your copy and look at what works.

While I've built a million-dollar business, I've also spent thousands refining and tweaking the sales page and my offering so that it works on repeat. Passive income isn't about clicking your fingers and magically expecting your course to sell; it takes work and effort.

There are days when I work from early and finish late, but there is also lots of time to travel and be very present for my son. I'm there for the pick-ups and school trips and moments that matter.

The reality is that I've built a passive-income business, but I'm still working. I still work on the business, even if I take out chunks of time. You are automating your business, but you are not delegating responsibility for your business to the bots. You will still manage how your company operates, and what needs to run on autopilot and what needs the personal touch.

Back in 2007, I remember discovering *The 4-Hour Work Week* by Timothy Ferriss in a bookstore in Bangkok while working 16-hour days as a journalist. I wanted that life.

I've created my version of that life all these years later, but I can't say that I just work four hours a week.

I adore working on my passion projects, creating courses and I'm so thrilled that I'm able to write books and earn money as I write. I love that I get to choose what I work on and how I can delegate and automate the stuff that bores me, or hire someone who's better than me at doing that thing!

Creating a course-based business is utterly possible for you too. If I can do it, so can you! I'm not a natural salesperson, I'm not the most intelligent person in the room, I'm not good at the tech, and I didn't reinvent the lightbulb. It's just about consistently building an audience and then creating a course to sell on repeat through automation.

Creating a course has been so genuinely revolutionary for my family and me. As I write this, I'm listening to my husband on the phone to his uni friend who's worrying about being made redundant from his job of 20 years. He's not sure what to do next and scared to make the leap.

Stepping into the world of digital course creation is a massive leap out of our comfort zones. It's a steep learning curve of tech, marketing and resilience. But the reality is that you too can build a business where you wake up with a series of messages from PayPal and Stripe telling you how much money you've made.

You too can create that financial freedom for your family; my husband could leave a tedious job in banking that he hated and join me in the business.

We can take the summer off to travel around Europe and create adventures and memories.

Ironically, *Making Money While You Sleep* isn't about the money. Having a pot full of cash under your bed doesn't mean anything. You can't take it with you.

Making Money While You Sleep is about the financial and emotional freedom that comes from working less and living more. It's about being able to have the experiences that you dream of with the people you love.

I've given you the strategy for you to make money while you snooze. I'm handing you the digital blueprint right here on this page, and I'm willing you to do this.

Keep consistent. Keep building that audience. Stay resilient. Let me know how you get on!

I'm your number one cheerleader, and I'm willing you to succeed.

I believe in you.

I know this is possible for you too.

I know you can do this!

Much love,

Lucy x

Acknowledgements

When I was nine years old, my dad created a bookshelf for my 'books' in his woodwork class. It's just taken me 30+ years to actually write one: I wish you were around to read it.

And thank you to Mum and Dad, who packed up four kids and a trailer tent and trundled us off across Europe to live in West Berlin when I was just ten months old. You instilled a sense of adventure, independence and purpose from such a young age, and these life lessons have stayed with me whatever path I follow. Thank you for the many hours listening to my ideas for blogs and businesses. I got there in the end.

To my husband Tim, I love you and thank you for your reassuring pep talks when I doubt myself, for cajoling me when I wanted to throw my laptop out of the window, and for holding my hand when I wished I had the confidence to soar. I'm so lucky I have you in my life.

Thank you to Ben for being the motivation to embrace the world of entrepreneurship and being my "why": you are the reason I do what I do. Thank you for putting up with Mummy writing a book in lockdown.

Much love to Uncle Frank for showing me that you could get paid to tell stories and opening the door ajar to a career in journalism and writing. Thank you for all your whisky-fuelled debates that instilled in me a passion for politics, the conviction to challenge everything and the courage to fight for the underdog.

Thank you to my brother and sisters, Jo, Mark, and Emma, for inspiring me to seek an untrodden path of adventure, to leap into the unknown and pursue my dreams.

So much gratitude and love to my mother-in-law, Relda, for being my cheerleader and champion when I gingerly tiptoed into the world of business with baby Ben; your interest and enthusiasm meant so much.

Much love to Rae 'Raelet' Earl for your sage advice sprinkled with gibberish and for showing me that it's indeed possible to write a best-selling book and raise a small person.

To darling Rhian, who always encouraged and nurtured my ideas and helped me see what was possible.

Hugs to all my fabulous friends and family who've encouraged me along the way.

Thank you to my lovely team who put up with the whirlwind that is Lucy and help me make money while I sleep: Bianca, Louise, Rachel and Luke. Sheryl Jefferson, I am in much awe of you as a human juggling it all and in admiration of your magic with Facebook ads.

Thank you to Suzy Walker for all the friendship, love and for asking me why I'd not written a book, calling me out on my nonsense and giving me an extra springy springboard to leap.

Thank you to Carrie Green for smashing all my stereotypes about being successful in business and showing me what's possible.

Zoom hugs to Caroline Goyder; your wisdom and wit in helping me to write this book was sooooo helpful!

Thank you to all the bold and brilliant entrepreneurs who are part of this book and helped me craft and shape my idea: Denise Duffield-Thomas, Carrie Green, Lucy Hall, Katrina Young, Sheryl Jefferson, Lea Turner, Ruth Kudzi, Gemma Went, TerDawn DeBoe, Marion Leadbetter, Caroline Goyder, Christina Jandali, Sam Bearfoot, Anna Parker-Naples, Eloise Head aka "FitWaffle", Lisa Stoops, Erica Lee Strauss, Anika Watkins, Rachel Ngom, Gillian Perkins, Emily Williams, Vicky Etherington, Jessica Lorimer, Liz Beadon, Kelly Morrison and Maya Riaz; your incredible stories are so bloody awe-inspiring. And to all the course creators who have inspired me to write this book.

Thank you to Fiona Harrold for teaching me to 'Be Your Own Life Coach' in her book twenty years ago and being this constant presence in my backpack when I doubted myself, my abilities and lacked the courage to follow my dreams. Fast-forward to 2019, when she sprinkled some supercharged fertiliser over the germ of an idea to write a book.

And to Jo Bell, my agent who loved my idea for *Make Money While You Sleep* and gently coaxed me through homeschooling and lockdowns and helped me turn a nugget of an idea, formed in a hotel lobby just days before the world went into meltdown, into a proper book with pages and everything!

Thank you to my editor Briony Gowlett for getting "me", my pinkness and believing that I could somehow write a bunch of words in three months (despite lockdown and homeschooling) and magic it into a book. Thank you to Zakirah Alam, Huw Armstrong, Sahina Bibi, Kate Keehan and everyone in the team at Hodder & Stoughton for your patience and publishing prowess . . . and, of course, that fabulous cover: there are no words for my adoration – I am forever your cover lover.

To everyone who has supported me on my entrepreneurial journey, this is for you.

Index